the key to enterprise agility, innovation and sustainability

Design
Thinking

David West & Rebecca Rikner

Library of Congress Control Number: 2016962328

ISBN 978-0-9984770-0-8

Visit us on the web at: **designthinking.systems**

Table of contents

Acknowledgements

A book is never the sole effort of those listed as its authors.

In our case, the list of contributions and contributors is long indeed. We begin with the Patterns Community and particularly those that participated in the Writer's Workshops where this book was born. Special thanks go to those attending workshops at AsianPLoP in Tokyo and PLoP in Reno Nevada.

Next are our wonderful reviewers. Special mention must be made of Alistair Cockburn, who shared our enthusiasm for the subject matter and provided invaluable comments along with enthusiastic praise for our efforts.

This book would not have been nearly as polished and complete were it not for the selfless efforts and contributions made by: Dion Stewart, Michael Nygard, Miriam Langer, Christian Kohls, Dirk Riehle, Alan O'Callaghan, Hironori Washizaki, Pascal Costanza, Seung Chan Lim, Christian Köppe, Ademar Aguilar, Jean-Marie Brême and Joseph Thottungal.

Finally, but most importantly, deep personal thanks are due those who offered tireless support and encouragement.

For David these include his best friend, Mary Haley, and friends Dion Stewart and Jane Quillien.

First and foremost, Rebecca gives her warmest gratitude to David for a deep, rich and rewarding collaboration. This book would not have existed without David's relentless faith of its need. His strong belief of the value of the message in this book and the given tools is unquestionable. Thank you.

Secondly, Rebecca would like to thank Mathilde & Jonathan, her beloved children. May you always be protected from harm, in all its forms. May you be wise, safe and shielded from all those who wish you ill. May only goodness and kindness touch you for all your days. May goodness always prevail in your lives. And may my love for you, beyond measure, warm you on dark days.

We invite all who support the principles c

Many in the business community have come to believe that design principles can be used to enhance the workplace, improve business processes, increase sales, burnish image, and resolve a host of other enterprise issues.

We believe they are correct but naïve. We believe that business needs a more comprehensive understanding of what design is about and how to effectively use design approaches to accomplish their goals.

esign thinking to join us, and to find new ways to make this vision a reality.

Manifesto

We believe the purpose of design is to make the world a better, more humane, place to live and work.

We believe design is grounded in a way of thinking, an approach to problem solving, that complements and extends existing thinking and skills.

We believe design thinking is predicated upon an understanding of wholeness, complexity, essence, and simplicity.

We believe the role of the designer is to facilitate faithful expression of essence appropriate for a given context.

We believe enterprise design is systemic, concurrently applied to every aspect of the enterprise from image to IT.

We believe design matters!

Introduction

The challenges faced by business are qualitatively different from those faced a decade ago. Problems have thousands instead of tens of variables, with many of those variables being vague in nature and ambiguous in value. Every business operates in an increasingly global context.

Change is the only constant and the pace of change continues to accelerate. It is difficult to predict outcomes beyond the shortest of terms and impossible to predict disruptive change.

Rigid and static organizational structures impede innovation and response. Hierarchy coupled with command-and-control management are giving way to the need for cooperative collaboration among empowered peers. Optimization and risk aversion replace creative exploration and risk taking. Traditional ways of thinking about and solving problems are less and less effective.

We believe that, as difficult as these challenges may be, they can be met. Design thinking — a worldview, a set of perspectives, and a set of tools — provide the means. In the pages that follow we will show how this is possible and why your organization should make the commitment necessary to take full advantage of design thinking.

The Key Stone

In the rush to satisfy the demand for information about design thinking, much has been written: books, magazine articles, and websites focused on design and the application of design to business are numerous but many tend to be superficial and incomplete. When the response to genuine interest and excitement in a topic lacks sufficient depth, the result tends to be fad — quickly adopted and just as quickly abandoned.

Design thinking should be more than a momentary fad. Design is essential to the accomplishment of business objectives. Design thinking is appropriate, necessary, and valuable for application to every aspect of the business endeavor. The value of design thinking and its effective application to your enterprise requires more than memorizing a few practices. The benefit from design thinking is the enhancement of your ability to comprehend the philosophy, world view, and culture behind the ideas and practices used by professional designers. Providing this knowledge and understanding is our intent with this book.

Design and design thinking, should be seen as a key stone that complements other ways of thinking. Complex problems require multiple perspectives, multiple ways of thinking about and understanding both problem and solution. Design thinking is the keystone in an arch, where each stone represents another way of thinking. The keystone simultaneously supplies essential concepts and insights while assuring the integration necessary for the whole to accomplish what the parts alone cannot.

A keystone has a specific role, but most often its value comes from the way it connects to all the other parts of an arch. This connection requires a broad understanding and a comprehensive treatment. Too narrow a focus, e.g. the rounded corners of the iPhone instead of the design ecology

Construction of a fortification door made of stone, Masonry arch, vintage engraved illustration. Dictionary of words and things, Larive and Fleury, 1895.

behind Apple, perpetuates the notion that design is 'embellishment' instead of essential.

Similarly, ideas about design need to expand beyond traditional and familiar applications, e.g. marketing, branding, and product design. Non-design professionals benefit most when design language and concepts are translated and applied to domains of central concern, e.g. organizational design and software development. Others have shown why design thinking has worked in traditional areas like brand identity or customer experience. Managers will benefit most when design thinking is 'translated' and applied to domains like management and information systems where it is still unfamiliar.

Design thinking is far more than an easy 8-step program with lots of colored Post-It notes on the wall, mind maps on whiteboards, and paperboard models on the tables. Oversimplification of design thinking can result in its being trivialized and abandoned before its full potential is realized.

A corollary effect of oversimplification, of organizations attempting to apply design thinking by simple rote practice, are set up to fail. Design thinking requires a fundamental change, in worldview, in organizational culture, and in processes, policies, and practices if it is to be successful. After all, if it takes years of study and a decade or so of practice to become a master designer, why should organizations expect they will somehow acquire that same level of skill in a couple of weeks.

We are striving to ensure that our readers will truly understand design thinking. We want them to see the potential of design thinking in every aspect of the enterprise. Our readers must see exactly where and how design thinking requires a 'change of mind', or worldview. We want readers to understand the principles behind the practices, so that when it becomes necessary to adapt a practice, as it will, it can be done appropriately.

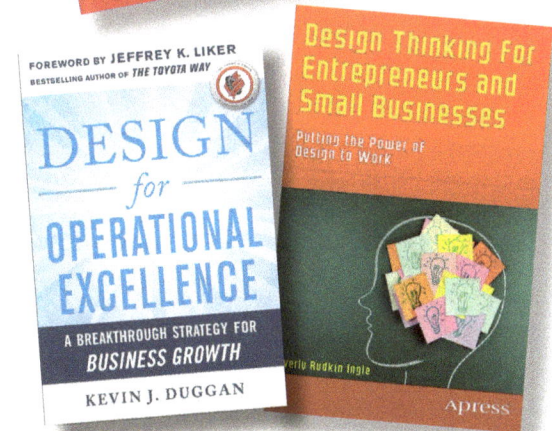

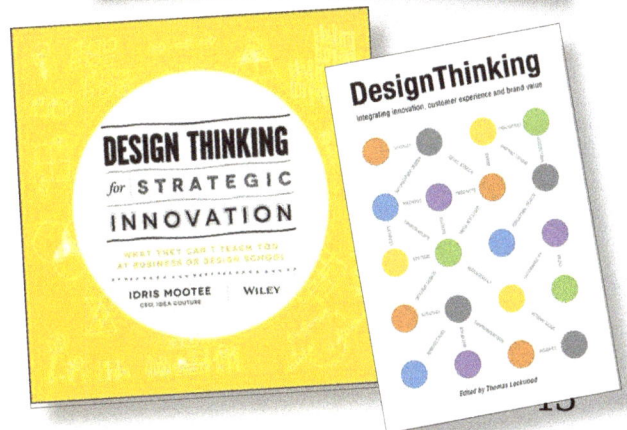

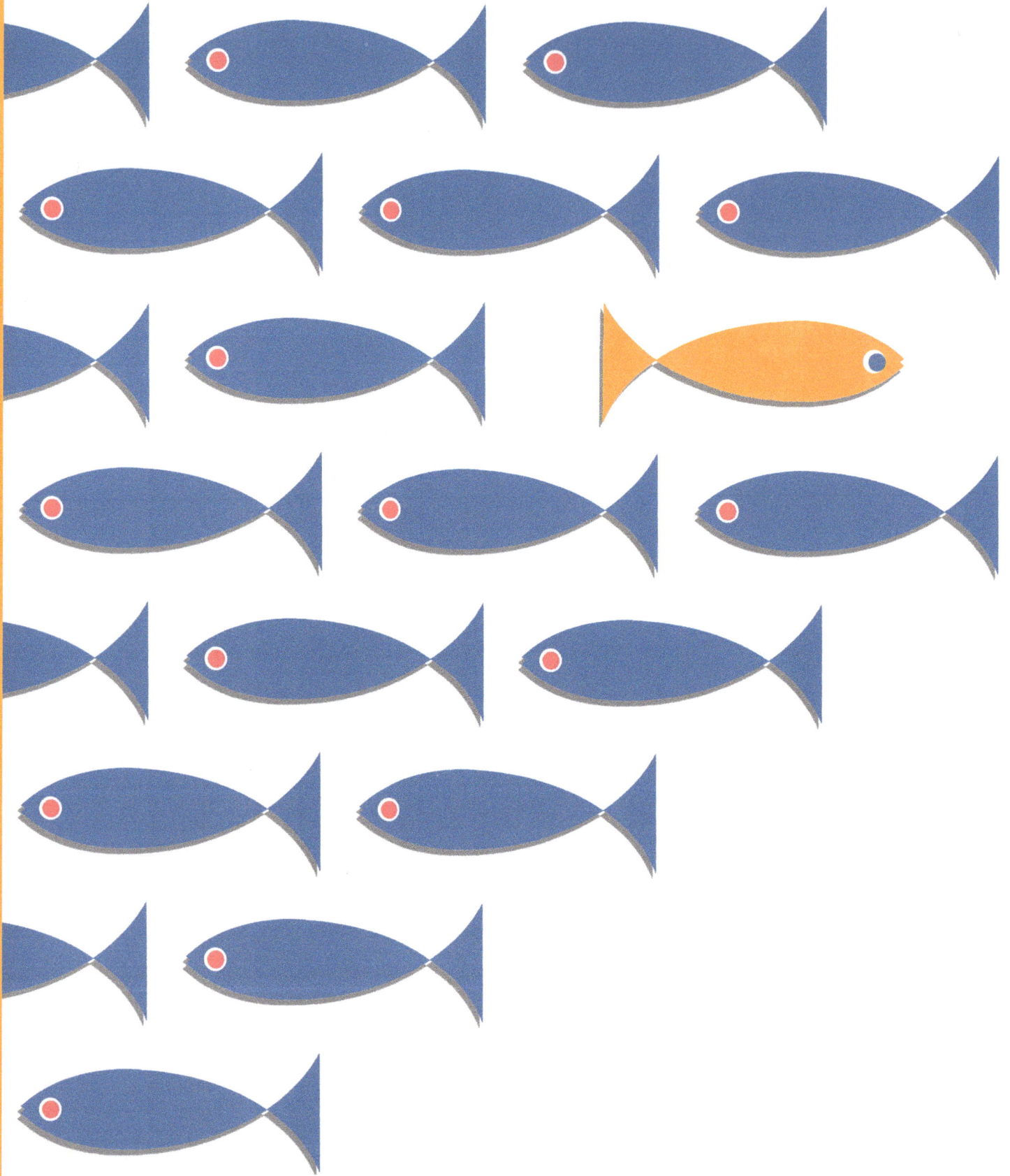

Design Thinking is Thinking Differently

The most difficult aspect of understanding design and design thinking is not the thinking, it is the mind you think with. More accurately, it is the worldview — the unquestioned assumptions you make about what is 'real', what can be 'known', what is valuable, and how things are done — that shapes what you think and how you think it.

Design and design thinking have deep roots. Centuries of thought and history have established a culture — shared worldview, values, customs, practices, and technology — of design. The design tradition parallels a similar, perhaps even as old, tradition of business.

Although design and business address basic human needs and therefore share some common points of concern, they are two very different traditions with different world views and are grounded in very different concepts.

Design, business, and IT thinking offer three labels for three professional cultures, each with its own worldview, language, and culture. All three are necessarily different from each other because they come from, and are embedded within, three separate traditions. Computing tradition is barely a century old while business and design have been around for millenia, but all three are distinct.

One obvious difference: design is considered an "art" while software and, until recently, business have been considered rational and "scientific." This distinction is artificial and fundamentally wrong but it can make it difficult for business, and especially IT, professionals to take design as seriously as they should.

Business became an academic discipline and area of research in the early 1900s when Physics was considered the exemplar of science and knowledge. Computer Science dates to the 1940s and Software Engineering to 1968. Both were shaped by an intellectual context dominated by philosophies of rationalism and the primacy of mathematics and logic as the basis for thought.

As powerful as science and rational thinking are, it must be recognized that they faciliate our understanding of only a small part of the world around us. As John von Neumann noted:

"Future computers will require but a dozen instruction types, a number known to be adequate for expressing all of mathematics. This number should not be surprising since 1,000 words are known to be adequate for most situations in real life, and mathematics is only a small part of life, and a very simple part at that. If people do

René Descartes. Portrait by Frans Hals, 1648.

not believe that mathematics is simple, it is only because they do not realize how complicated life is."

The philosophy, culture, and practice of design thinking is essential if we are to understand and enhance those complex systems that comprise "life."

Understanding your business and seeing how design can transform it, will increase in direct proportion to your ability to understand design in its 'native environment'. Business and IT professional must understand what design and design thinking means to designers in order to see what it can mean to them.

This understanding does require that you, like the cultural anthropologist, must suspend your own worldview, for a moment, lest it interfere with your acquiring an understanding of the culture you are studying. We will facilitate your gaining this understanding by, again like the cultural anthropologist, "making the strange familiar and the familiar strange."

We will help the reader see how to adopt, and adapt as appropriate, design thinking principles and practices to their own domains.

Focusing on the whole system, resolves one of the most persistent of business problems — Business-IT integration.

Sixty five years ago, the enterprise was whole: a single system with a few automated components integrated into business and manual processes. In the 1970s, automated elements of the business system were aggregated into a separate, centralized, and independent system.

These massive, centralized, and integrated systems came to dominate business — but were clearly separate and radically different in kind. Business was a complex adaptive system, IT was a complicated deterministic system. Although both IT and business recognized the problem, it remains, to date unresolved.

Design thinking principles and tools provide a means for re-establishing the natural integration that comes from seeing the whole, the single system.

Wholeness and Design

An essential aspect of design thinking is the focus on the whole. This focus is in direct contrast to "scientific thinking" that relies on the principles of decomposition and abstraction.

To see the differences consider what the scientist does when facing a large and complex problem. She immediately 'taking it apart'— decomposing it, dividing the whole into parts, each of which can be understood in its entirety. If sufficient care is taken in the definition of the part, the relationships among parts, and each part to the whole can, supposedly, be preserved. This is critical if you intend to put the parts back together, reconstructing the whole. It is further assumed that if you decomposed carefully and reconstructed correctly, your understanding of the parts yielded an understanding of the whole.

Almost everyone has heard the phrase, "the whole is other than the sum of its parts;" an observation that points to a problem with 'scientific thinking'. Our understanding of complex, living, systems has made it evident that the whole manifests properties and behaviors that are no understandable solely from a knowledge of its parts, even a perfect and complete knowledge of all parts.

Losing sight of the whole can lead to missing or misunderstanding key business challenges. For example how do you truly understand the "customer experience" if the only analysis at hand is that of discrete parts: an order-entry process, a billing process, an order fullfilment process, a shipping process, an inventory control process, etc. Typically different teams are engaged in understanding, modeling, and implementing each part and none of them see how the parts comprise a whole — the user experience that transcends each part.

The scientist believes, has been taught, that it is impossible to understand the whole, in all its complexity, as a whole. The designer does not share this belief. The manager expends all of his time and attention on understanding the part of the enterprise for which he is responsible at the expense of any understanding of the business. The designer assumes it will be impossible to understand the particular, a specific product or service, outside of its context — context which includes not only the enterprise but the life experience of the client or consumer of that product or service.

The scientist decomposes and understands parts, the designer contextualizes and understands the whole.

Abstraction, for the scientist, complements decomposition. After taking apart the system; each part is examined to reveal details, most of which are then discarded, in order to provide the scientist a 'proper' focus on the 'essential'. For the computer scientist, this means anything that cannot be represented in binary code and manipulated with formal computational algorithms. Computers cannot handle ambiguity, nuance, or metaphor.

In contrast the designer seeks constantly to add detail, to expand context, and to leverage both ambiguity and metaphor to engender greater understanding of the whole system.

Design thinking provides a perspective and a set of principles and practices that keep attention on the whole, that ensure context is ever present. Design thinking avoids attempts to understand parts independent of context, of the whole. These perspectives can, and do, lead to problem solutions that would be difficult to realize using more traditional, decomposition grounded, thinking. The persistent, and vexing, problem of business-IT integration being a prime example.

Designers are able to work with and understand the whole, but not because they have supernormal brains that consciously juggle more variables. The key is a different approach to abstraction. Abstraction comes in two, closely related, forms. First, we look at a collection of things, ignore the individual differences among them, and then name the set of shared similarities. This is classification and it is very common.

We see a large number of four legged animals that vary wildly in form, size, shape, and color. We ignore the individual differences, focus on the commonalities, and create a class name, 'dog', where 'dog' is an abstraction.

The second form of abstraction (we will call it Identity Abstraction, or IA) begins the same way, finding the commonalities among a collection of things and creating an abstract name to the collection.

One, critical, additional step is taken — all of the individual differences are discarded, deemed irrelevant. This has the effect of eliminating, invalidating in a way, all of the variability in the original set. It is no longer possible to see or talk about a Llasa Apso, only dogs. This second form of abstraction is fundamental to science, business, and software — causing problems in each area.

In science, IA is a critical mechanism behind the 'paradigm shifts' discussed by Thomas Kuhn and others. IA deems certain observations as real and all the rest as anomolous — until the anomolous overwhelms the 'real' and forces a shift in viewpoint and explanation. In business, IA, leads to rigid and absolute policies and procedures that too often have detrimental affect on customers.

In software, particularly in data modeling, it leads to an explosive expansion in the number of classes, abstractions, because the only way to deal with an 'irrelevant' characteristic that suddenly becomes relevant, is by creating a new class, a new and additional abstraction. The designer's approach to abstraction is subtly different. They too need to look at a large and complicated, or complex, domains and find generalizations, abstractions, that can be used to think and communicate with. Designer's seek abstractions in commonalities among a varieagated set of things.

The difference is, the designer is looking for commonalities that will evoke, recall to mind, all of the differences among members of the set, instead of hiding, or discarding them. The designer calls such commonalities, essences. The contrast between design abstractions, essences, and scientific, business, and software abstractions is analogus

Design thinking, unlike scientific thinking, thrives on ambiguity. Ambiguity is the foundation for creativity. Design thinking emphasizes what might be, not what is and always has been.

to the way poets and scientists use words. The scientist insists on a precise, unambiguous, well defined, and absolute 'meaning' for each word. The poet might use the same word, but in a way to recall to the mind of the reader all of the nuances and variations and context altering 'meaning' of that word. The poet preserves the understanding of the whole while the scientist abandons the whole in order to focus on the part.

Design is Humane

People matter.

Designers are more sensitive to this fact than business and IT professionals imply because the success criteria for design is the degree to which it makes a connection to people.

Business and IT professionals are more often concerned with profit and satisfying requirements instead, and at the expense, of the human.

A major contribution of design thinking is a direct result of focusing on the human and the humane as a prime directive.

The world has changed dramatically since 1900 and again, perhaps even more dramatically, since 1950 when computers began their advance into every aspect of our lives. It would be impossible to overstate the impact of computing, in particular, on our lives but we would be remiss if we failed to note that much of that impact has been at the expense of our individual and common humanity.

The problem is not that business managers, technologists, or software developers dislike or wish to harm human beings. The problem is that the scientific worldview and mindset of professionals in those fields cannot accomodate something as imprecisely defined, variable, and dynamic as a human being. We cannot model an artificial system, like a computer program, unless we can model each of the components, modules, of that system in precise, and deterministic terms. If our target system contains humans, those humans must be stripped of all attributes and characteristics that are not explainable to a computer. Humans must be reduced to lowest common denominator machines.

Design thinking, unlike scientific thinking, thrives on ambiguity. Ambiguity is the foundation for creativity. Design thinking emphasizes what might be, not what is and always has been. Designers care about, and understand how to work with, emotion, sensation, and perception. Design is intentially idiosyncratic — the best solution for the particular situation at a specific time according to the abilities of the designer.

We believe that design thinking will lead, almost inevitably, to more humane solutions to our common problems. We believe that design thinking can leveragechuman capabilities, enhance them and expand them; instead of trying to replace them with artificial, and therefore limited, simulations. This is the moral imperative for adopting and applying design thinking.

20

Design Tradition

Reality Design might be a good name for this new discipline, for the same reasons that Reality Construction is a good name for software development. The software that animates computers — computers that are pervasive in every aspect of our lives — very literally constructs the Reality in which we work, live, play, and even think.

Design thinking offers the hope that the Reality being constructed will not only change an existing situation into a preferred one, but will also assure that the new situation will affirm and nurture humans and humanity.

The idea that systems and artifacts, e.g. businesses and computer programs, should be "designed" is traceable at least as far back as the work of the Scandinavian School of Design and the work of Pelle Ehn and his colleagues in Sweden. The idea that there could be a 'science of design' which could provide theoretical and practical foundations for "designing" can also be traced to the 1960s, in Ehn's work as well as that of Christopher Alexander, an architect working in England. Herbert Simon, with his book, *The Sciences of the Artificial*, and his definition of design as, "transforming existing conditions into preferred ones," is an important contributor.

A recurrent and popular theme in the business press for the past decade concerns the need to "apply design principles" to business in order to foster innovation and gain strategic advantage. Much of this interest is driven by the perception that the success of Apple, becoming the most valuable company in the world, derives from its commitment to "design".

As ubiquitous as the term, designing, is, it is imprecisely defined, if defined at all. Everyone uses the word as if we all had a common understanding of what is meant. But we do not share that common understanding and professionals in different fields use the same word but with nuanced and sometimes conflicting meanings.

Perhaps the most obvious example: professionals in the applied arts and architecture see design as a form of art, while the engineer — business or software — sees it as a means of systems optimization.

However the term is understood, the fact that design, design thinking, and design principles are seen as 'the answer' to a host of business problems is undeniable. Companies have adopted their own versions of design thinking and generated numerous anecdotal success stories. *(We relate several of these stories in Chapter 2.)*

We believe the time has come to establish a discipline of design thinking, or perhaps the 'science of design' that was the objective of Ehn, Alexander, and Simon. Our ambitions are actually somewhat less grandiose, we are interested in a subset of that discipline, specifically how design can and should be applied and used to understand and re-express the enterprise. Because all enterprises, today, are inextricably entwined with IT, our focus extends to software systems.

Our ideas about the discipline of design are based, in part, on recognizing how the problems faced by businesses have changed over time. Consider, for a moment, how factors of scale, predictability, speed and unknowns have changed the essential nature of the problems.

Think about how the sheer volume of electronic communications has affected our ability to cope with the information deluge. Or, a corollary problem, finding a critical bit of information that you know is somewhere out there among the billions of pages on the Internet.

Scale does matter.

Eric Toffler and others, as early as the nineteen-eighties spoke of a kind of future shock brought about by the increasingly rapid pace of change. Our experience and understanding of time was irrevocably altered by Internet time. Business that was comfortable with decade long periods of stability now must reinvent and restructure themselves in months. The need for constant innovation and adaptation to changing market forces and customer demands. Phenomena like Facebook and Twitter show up and mandate the invention of new market strategies. Unknowns come in many forms. Two of the most important: as our understanding of systems and global interconnectivity increase, the number of factors that must be taken into consideration multiplies beyond our awareness. And, although the Web makes it appear that everything is known, all we really know is that the answers we seek are buried somewhere in the 42,387 hits returned by the typical Google search.

Today we recognize that the world is not a machine. It is, in fact, a living ultra-large scale, complex adaptive system (CAS) — non-deterministic, self-organizing, and exhibiting emergent behavior. Our understanding of the 'economic system' has changed dramatically when we began modelling it as a complex community of connected but autonomous decision making agents — a CAS. Observed regularities are no longer formulaic rules or laws, but are emergent macro-behaviors. It is overly simplistic to continue believing we can make predictable changes by altering the values of variables in supply and demand equations.

CAS pose 'wicked problems'. A wicked problem not only involves large numbers of variables, many of which have unknown values, but also involves a kind of circular feedback where the solution to any given problem has the effect of changing the nature of the problem.

We need a very different way of thinking about this new world. This new way of thinking will require an ability to

Wicked problems are hard to untangle.

22

deal with uncertainty, with ambiguity. It will need to be based on holistic instead of reductionistic principles. It will rely on the ability to blend multiple perspectives. It will be based on emerging techniques of collaboration and communication — ways we are learning to think together. There is a community of professionals that confront and resolve problems with multiple interacting variables, ambiguity and unknowns, where solutions redefine the original problem, and solutions require a holistic viewpoint. This is the community of Designers. Designers have developed principles, concepts, practices and techniques that serve them well and are worthy of investigation and use by the rest of us.

The design community includes the various types of applied arts: industrial, interior, and graphical design; but also architects, engineers, and many others. Design is an increasingly important topic in business and software development with hundreds of books written on the topic of design thinking applied to almost every discipline. There has been a change in emphasis on what is meant by design thinking in the fields of business, engineering, and software. As our understanding of deterministic, machinelike, systems has increased our ability to engineer them, design has come to mean little more than the optimization of large and complicated but deterministic systems. Design, as we intend to use the term, reflects the perspective of those in the applied arts, not professional engineers.

Designers have developed a different mode of thinking. One involving a very different worldview, grounded in different presuppositions and concepts, and driven by different values. This mode of thinking is so intrinsic and so fundamental to the Design community that, like any other culture, it is largely non-conscious. What the rest of us see as a very different kind of problem is, to them, familiar. Facing this kind of problem they almost instinctively see the path to potential solutions.

But, we are told, designers are different. They are right-brained artists with esoteric knowledge of line, form, and color who somehow magically distill imagery, layouts, and form-factors from clouds of possibility. Or so the stereotype assures us. And, like all stereotypes, there is some truth in our belief about designers and what they do — design. But if they are really that different from the rest of us, how can we possibly learn what they do and benefit from that learning?

We can learn Design. The principles, concepts, practices, values and techniques required to be a professional designer can be learned — after all professional designers also had to learn them. While it is definitely true that some people are predisposed to become designers because of innate characteristics and talents, they still have to learn design thinking and design culture. And, critically important, they must practice, practice, practice.

We are not suggesting that design is the only answer or that everyone must become a professional designer. There is much to be gained by adopting concepts and perspectives that complement traditional modes of thought, traditional analytic practices, and accepted scientific solutions.

The intention of this book is to capture the insights and knowledge, developed by and shared among the design community, and then communicate that knowledge to the business, software, and design professionals. Our goal is to articulate, and translate when necessary, the fundamentals of Design Thinking and demonstrate how we can be better at what we do if we learn and apply those fundamentals.

As noted above, we are specifically targeting business, software, and design professionals; but we believe the ideas in this book can be effectively used by almost anyone interested in and concerned with making decisions to improve their environment, their tools, their communications, even their happiness with life and relationships. The main stream of presentation will address our primary audience but we will include asides and notes and variations on our themes that will be of use to those in our wider audience.

We choose to organize this book in a particular way — explanatory prose followed by a sequence of patterns.

The idea of patterns has been important in the software, and later the business, community for twenty years now. The idea of patterns is derived from the work of Christopher Alexander, an architect.

Our own interpretation of patterns and their importance is less on "capturing known solutions to problems in context," as it is with capturing and preserving deep knowledge of problems and the factors that need to be considered when attempting to solve them. The 'solutions' are simple examples, they are not prescriptive definitions of 'what to do' or 'how to solve'.

Our Readers

We have written this book to appeal to a wide range of readers, almost anyone with an interest in design and design thinking as an alternative, or additional, way of thinking about problems and their resolution.

Within this general intent we have a very specific scenario in mind, one that defines our focus audience. The scenario begins with the business executive who has seen and been intrigued by the abundance of material published about design, business, strategy, and innovation.

We make no assumption that all of this material has been mastered, only that it has aroused curiosity and motivated a desire to learn more.

Our executive convenes a working group. Included in this group are individuals representing all the different aspects of the enterprise, including those knowledgable about connections among the enterprise and entities — customers, regulators, suppliers, etc. — outside the organization. It is absolutely critical for IT to be involved in this working group. We do assume that our executive understands just how deeply IT is interwined with the business and is, all too often, the biggest obstacle for realizing business goals like innovation and agility.

We also assume that some professional designers, perhaps outside consultants, are included in this working group. This book, then, offers several things to this group. First, it provides a common foundation for understanding design and design thinking. The book provides insights into how design thinking

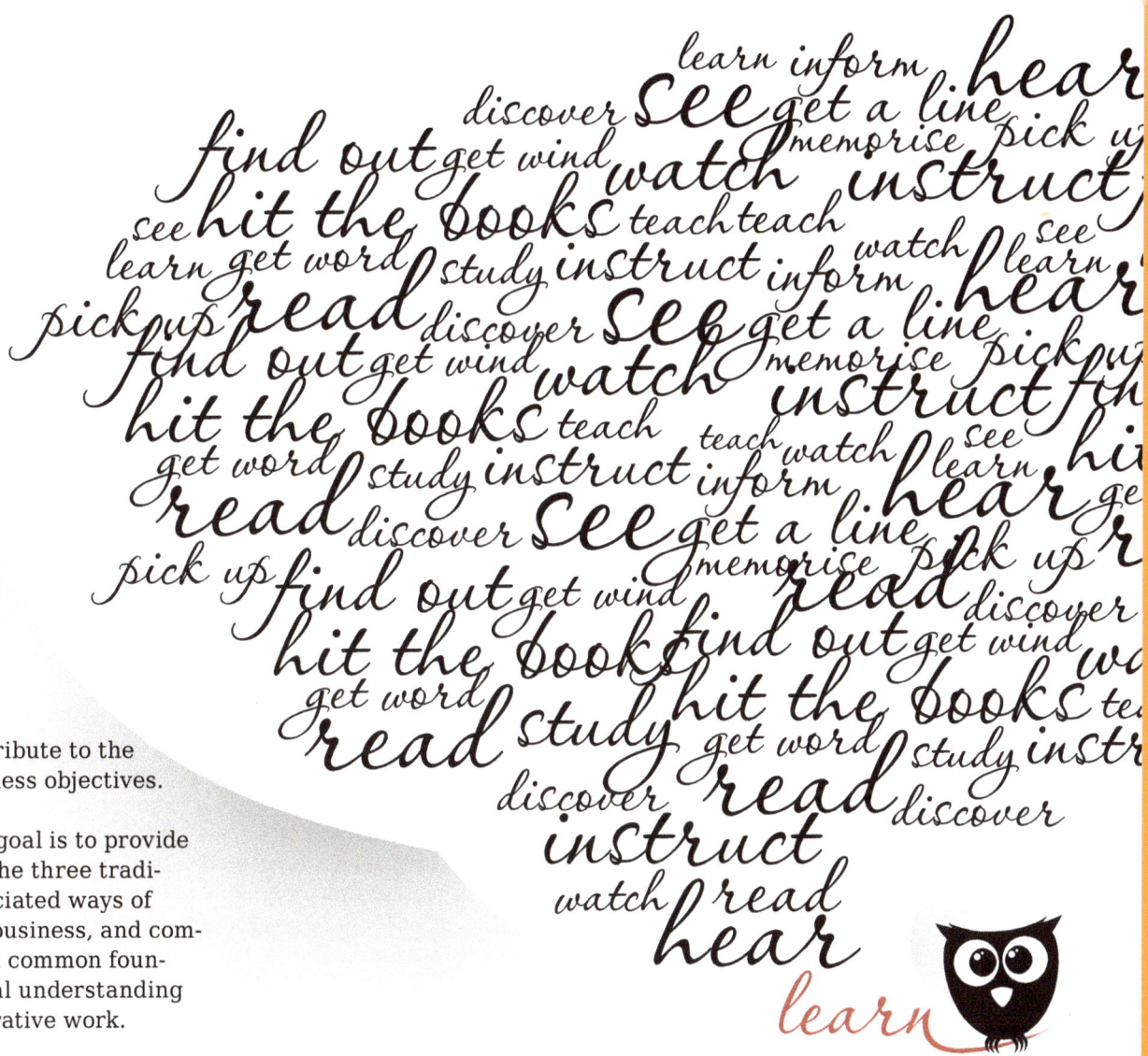

has, and might, contribute to the achievement of business objectives.

Our most important goal is to provide a bridge that spans the three traditions, and their associated ways of thinking, of design, business, and computing — providing a common foundation and the mutual understanding essential for collaborative work.

Finally we want to provide the conceptual tools necessary for the working group to apply design thinking to their own enterprise. We offer a four part toolkit: *One* — tools supporting a mind set, perspective, and world view that lead to unique insights and suggest fruitful avenues of exploration. *Two* — tools in the form of principles and foundational concepts. *Three* — tools of practice and technique that, sometimes with adaptation, are useful in almost any context where design thinking is being applied. *Fourth* — tools for evaluation, or progress towards solution and of alternative solutions.

We invite the reader to join us in this exploration of what design means and what a discipline of design might be — as we present the worldview, concepts, principles and practices that comprise Design Thinking.

" *We invite the reader to join us in this exploration of what design means and what a discipline of design might be — as we present the worldview, concepts, principles and practices that are central if design thinking is to be effectively applied to the world of business.*

25

Chapter 1
What Is Design?

Everyone Recognizes Design — but differently

Design is a very common word, used frequently and in many different contexts. The word 'design' is used as both noun and verb. Our goal with this book is to introduce design, more specifically design thinking, to those who are not professionals in traditional design disciplines, architecture and the applied arts. Further, we want to show how design thinking can be of great value to that audience.

Complicating matters, both business and information system professionals already use the word design and have developed theories and a practice of design that is different from that of professional designers. This can make it difficult for our readers to understand what we are saying. Our words being colored and interpreted through a lens of what the reader already "knows".

In this chapter we offer a functional definition of design and a preliminary definition of design thinking. The purpose is to provide a common foundation for introducing and explaining new concepts while simultaneously providing a means for comparing and contrasting those new ideas with existing assumptions and perceptions.

Herbert Simon said, "anyone concerned with changing existing circumstances to preferred ones is a designer". Most of life is a constant effort to change our circumstances for the better, so it can be said that anyone, and everyone, is a designer.

The first time our ancestors built a fire to keep warm and create a zone of security, they engaged in an act of environmental design. The first time someone gathered the clan around the fire and told stories that explained the world about them, they engaged in experience design. The first time a cave wall was painted in order to communicate and preserve knowledge, it was an act of design. When Confucious presented a body of rules for governance, he was engaged in social and organizational design. Design is ubiquitous in human history and, in many ways, a defining element of what it is to be human.

The profession of design is at least as old, in the Western World, as Vitruvius who is widely acknowledged as the first professional architect. Long before it referred to 'Danish Modern Furniture' or IKEA; the "Scandinavian School of Design" referred to the work of people like Kristen Nygaard and Pelle Ehn and their efforts to use design as a means of humanizing workplaces disrupted by the introduction of new technologies, especially computers. Hundreds of universities have established academic design programs and scores of specialized post secondary schools focus almost exclusively on the study of design. More recently a growing number of business schools have established specialized design degree programs.

The noun and the verb 'design' commonly used in English, comes to us from the latin, 'designare'. Readers and speakers have no difficulty understanding what is meant by phrases like: "just unveiled her design", "good design can help the reader", "with a lovely blue and white design", "changes were designed", "suspected of having designs", or "became a presenter by default rather than by design." Although easily understood, these various phrases reveal confusion about exactly what 'design' means. So common is the word, and so varied are the contexts in which it is used, it can be difficult to determine an exact and precise definition. There are dictionary definitions of course, but the quotes on the preceding page clearly illustrate just how much ambiguity and interpretation is associated with the term. This is especially evident in attempts to limn the core essence of design, either as a verb or a noun, and what makes design effective and appreciated. A common thread through the quotes exposes the idea that design is both ubiquitous and essential — unless, of course, you pay attention to paradoxical assertions that design is mere embellishment.

For at least a decade the businesspress has been full of effusive articles and books suggesting that design and design thinking are essential for business innovation and survival.

This body of work shares the same characteristics of the quotes at the beginning of this chapter — various interpretations, conflicting interpretations, and less than clear definitions. Although the interest in design and design thinking is certainly warranted, the lack of a clear definition of what design is and how design is done creates an immense risk — failure to realize all that design and design thinking have to offer.

Design is the activity which forms a major part of reality as we experience it.

Jonathan Pile

Design is a manifestation of the capacity of the human spirit to transcend its limitations.

George Nelson

Good design is intelligence made visible.

Le Corbusier

Design is everybody's business: we live in it, we eat in it, we pray and play in it. When I say that design is everybody's business, I don't mean that design is a do-it-yourself job. I mean that it affects everybody, at all times, in our lives. Unless we gain a better understanding of design, we shall witness our environment getting steadily worse, in spite of the constant improvement of our machines and tools.

P. J. Grillo

Most think of design in terms of putting lipstick on a gorilla.

Dieter Rams

Design plays a central, not merely ornamental, part in the creation of meaning.

Derick de Kerchhore

Design is transforming the invisible into the visible. It is also the operation of turning mental, social and spiritual entities into physical ones. Design is the process of the human creation of new realities. However, this assumes a thorough knowledge of the qualities and effects of the material world.

Kenji Ekuan

Design is not an art or a science, a socio-cultural phenomenon or a business tool. It is an innovative process which uses information and expertise from all these sectors. It uses creativity first to analyse and synthesise the interactions between them and, secondly to offer appropriate and innovative responses (forms) which, in application, should go beyond the sum of each sector's vision and capacity and yet remain recognisable and pertinent to them all.

A.M. Boutin & Liz Davis

A designer is an emerging synthesis of artist, inventor, mechanic, objective economist and evolutionary strategist.

Buckminster Fuller

The degree to which a televised broadcast signal is

def·i·ni·tion n.
The teacher gave of the new word of an image (pi TV set

The Need for Definition

The quotes at the beginning of this chapter suggest two things: first that there is no common understanding of exactly what design is; and two, that design is both ubiquitous and essential. The quotes also expose the various ways that people think about design: as fundamental, as something one does, a noun denoting a characteristic of a thing, as mere embellishment.

The past decade has seen a growing interest in "design" and "design thinking" but has not provided much in the way of clarity as to what, exactly, is meant by the word or the phrase. The interest itself, in part, stems from the perception that the success of Apple is attributable to design, but a larger part derives from very real business concerns — how to adapt and innovate in a world of exceedingly rapid change.

Although the interest in design and design thinking is certainly warranted, the lack of a clear definition of what design is and how design is done creates an immense risk of superficiality and faddishness.

If the potential of design and design thinking is to be realized, two things are necessary: first an understanding of what design means and how it is done in architecture and the applied arts (graphic, interior, and industrial design); and what concepts and practices are transferrable to new domains like business and information technology; and, a deeper understanding of the enterprise and the nature of the problems facing contemporary business.

Understanding the role of information technology (IT) as an integral part of the enterprise and as enabler or inhibitor of design thinking inspired solutions is equally important. We will argue that design thinking can narrow or eliminate the growing divide between business and IT. If both business and IT professionals incorporate design thinking with existing practice, the long sought goal of IT-Enterprise integration can be realized. Instead of being seen as a commodity, IT can be seen, once again, as a critical source of innovation and strategic advantage. The goal it for both IT and Business to recognize that the Enterprise is a single, unified, entity with mixed elements instead of parallel business and technology systems.

Any definition must reconcile and support both the 'artistic' and the 'scientific' aspects of design. Design is at least as old as architecture and proto engineering, meaning it has been around for more than two millenia. It is probable that design is as old as the first toolmakers, antedates writing, and, despite the claims of Boutin and Davis, for most of that time was considered as an art.

Like all other art, it was set aside from the mainstream and practiced only by those possessing an innate 'talent'. To this day, designers characterize their profession as the "applied arts." Even architects, who might lay claim to being applied scientists, aka engineers, are more likely to consider themselves artists first and engineers second.

More recently, circa 1950, there was a concerted effort to develop a 'science' of design — a set of formal operations that would resolve discrete forces to yield an optimal solution for any problem. Today it is generally recognized — with the exception of computing and software domains — that design encompasses more than that which can be captured in formula. Scientific thinking is important, but insufficient, for design thinking.

Any definition must support the idea of design as a skill that can be acquired without dismissing the fact that some individuals will exhibit more 'talent' than others and perhaps be more capable of great designs.

Finally, and perhaps most importantly, any definition must provide a path for transferring traditional and long standing design theory and practice to new domains of interest — business and information technology.

Design Matters

Design has too often been seen as a 'frill', as 'embellishment', or as 'making the functional pretty'. Design, like beauty, is seen as being 'skin deep'. This is evident in some of the preceding quotations.

Bang and Olufsen, B&O, makers of high quality and premium priced consumer electronics, made this mistake. They were on the brink of failure before they recognized their error.

In the 1990s, B&O was a highly successful, growing, company. Its products were considered exemplars of great design and were featured in museums like the Museum of Modern Art, Moma, in New York. At that time, B&O, had no designers on staff. All design work was contracted to outside design firms and followed the minimalist, "form follows function", design philosophy of the Bauhaus. This approach worked well when customers were happy to pay $20,000 USD for a work of art that just happened, almost by coincidence, to be a television set. Two examples illustrate the problem of misunderstanding the role of design.

First, the BeoSound 2, a music player released a few months after the first iPod. Bauhaus design ideals led to the omission of a screen on the BeoSound 2, making it very difficult to find and play a specific piece of music.

Second, was the Serene mobile phone. Really cool design, including a tiny electric motor that opened the "clam shell" phone for you, and a retro 'rotary dial' where the number buttons were arranged in a circle. Beautiful to look at, impossible to text with — at a time when texting among teenagers was the primary driver of the mobile phone market.

29

Defining Design

Design Matters

The phenomenal success of Apple's iPod, iPhone, and iPad is attributed to design. But it is essential to recognize that is was not the industrial design of the artifacts that mattered, it was the design of the system that incorporated those artifacts as elements that made Apple so successful.

Steve Jobs had a vision. It was not a vision of an artifact, or even a vision of a user experience. Mr. Job's vision was of the World, the complex adaptive system in which we live, and of how the World might be better. This new world would enhance human capabilities and human sensibilities.

People would interact with each other and with their environments in life affirming ways. Education and work would be transformed, replacing drudgery with joy.

A grand vision. No mere artifact could embody the entirety of that vision, but artifacts could advance or hinder its realization.

Hartmut Esslinger and Frog Design understood Jobs' vision and the system behind it. Frog created a design language, a tool that could be used by designers to communicate and with which to think as they collectively engaged in the task of understanding and modeling that system and the elements and relationships — including the artifacts that eventually appeared in the Apple Store — would exist and interact in that system.

If Jobs and his design teams — Esslinger and Frog and later Ivey and Tangerine — had merely designed beautiful artifacts, they would have been no more successful than Bang and Olufsen as cited earlier.

Apple designs worlds. Apple understands systems. Apple understands metaphor, e.g. Jobs' 'computers are the bicycles of the mind', and Apple is a prime example of why design thinking matters.

Design is the informed and deliberative modification of a system by adding, deleting or modifying one of its elements or adding, deleting, or modifying a relationship among elements; in order to establish the system in a more desirable state.

Our working definition of design has the virtues of being simple, direct, and abstract enough that it can be applied to any design endeavor. Our definition is pragmatic, eliminating both the inefffable aspects of "artistic" definitions and the artificially precision of "scientific" definitions. The definition also provides an action-oriented foundation for a discussion of design, design thinking, and designing.

The definition succinctly captures and synthesizes a large body of understanding — a good thing — but cannot be fully understood and appreciated without an awareness of that same understanding. A not so good thing. Specifically, the definitionhas limited utility until and unless the reader understands: why systems, what is meant by deliberative, what is meant by informed, and what constitutes a more desirable state?

Another, implicit and easy to miss, prerequisite understanding is the fact that design and design thinking exist within the context of culture. Culture might be ethnic, the broadest defintion of culture, or might be defined by narrower, more local, affinities like organizational culture or professional culture.

Our first task is to provide the reader with the background that prompted our definition of design and how and why we believe it will facilitate efforts to apply design and design thinking to the realms of business and information technology.

> " *Design is the informed and deliberative modification of a system by adding, deleting or modifying one of its elements, or, adding, deleting, or modifying a relationship among elements in order to establish the system in a more desirable state.*

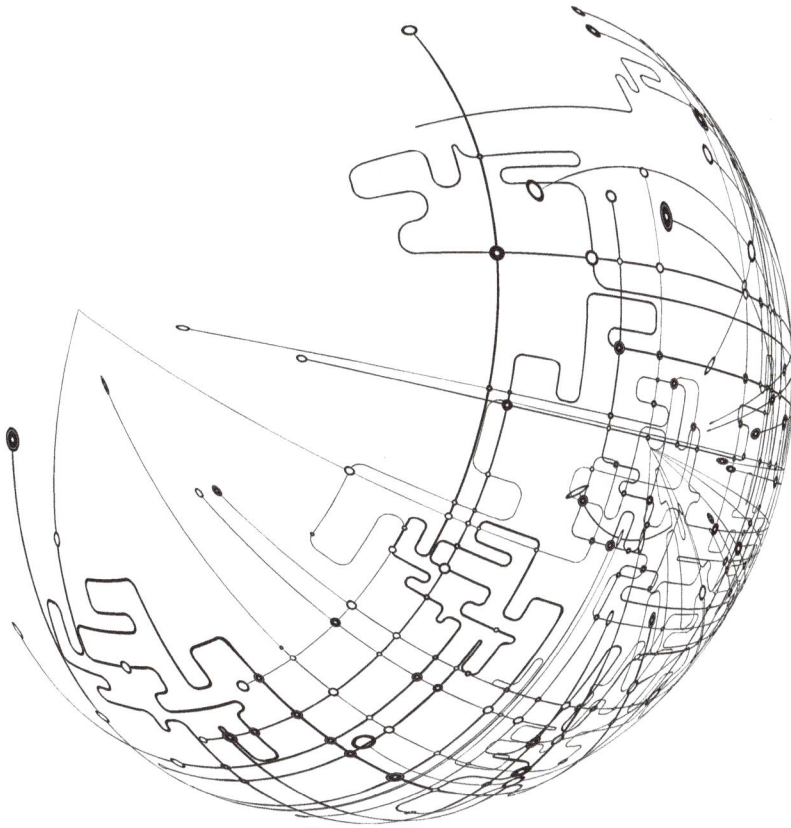

Design is Applied to Systems

The world is large and complex. It is difficult to understand without some kind of focus and absent some simplifying perspective.

Academic disciplines provide prime examples of how focus and perspective are provided. Physics, for example, focuses on the matter and the forces that arise from and are applied to matter, with the perspective of objectivity and method; while Anthropology focuses on people and their relationships and interactions with the perspective of subjectivity and comparative, "thick," description.

A common metaphor and model can be found behind the surface diversity of academic disciplines — the system. Astronomers see the Universe as a system, galaxies as systems, local aggregates of stars and planets as systems. Anthropologists rely on the concept of social and kinship systems. Graphic designers are familiar with color systems. Biologists with ecosystems. Ludwig von Bertalanffy, circa 1968, recognized the pervasiveness and commonality of systems and wrote a book proposing a *General Systems Theory* — a body of knowledge about systems as systems.

General Systems Theory provides a common idea and a common model that illuminates our understanding of the complexities of the world that is our particular domain of

31

interest. General Systems Theory asserts that "everything is a system", and that there is but one system, the Universe. Arbitrarily, for human convenience, the Universe is divided into subsystems. These subsystems remain embedded in the larger system and are connected to and influenced by the encompassing system. At each, nested, level of scale, a system is defined as a set of components and the relationships among them.

Each element and each relationship might, itself, be a system. For example, a business is a system with elements that include divisions, departments, employees, customers, policies, and vision statements. Each division is a system, with some unique and some common elements (e.g. employees). The Accounting Department is a subsystem with elements like CPA's, Auditors, Ledgers, and Reports. The Accounting Department has a relationship with all the other divisions and departments, including itself, and the enterprise as a whole. This relationship might have a label like, "records-or-documents-the-financials-of." The relationship link implies that the Accounting department documents the financials of the linked division or department. The relationship is itself a system consisting of accounts, charts of accounts, ledgers, and transaction documents and the relationships among them.

At any given point in time, the set of elements and the extant relationships among them is a 'state' of that system. Systems, because they are always dynamic are in a constantly changing state. A state change occurs whenever an element or relationship among elements changes its nature or value. Changes can also occur when elements or relationships are added or deleted.

Humans have the ability to alter systems simply by inducing a state change. There are limits of course; e.g. humans cannot change the solar system by adding or deleting planets or stars. Humans, individually and collectively, constantly and persistently exercise their ability to alter systems. Almost all human action modifies some kind of system because every action changes some aspect of our context, our relationships, or our physical or mental state of being.

Very few of these actions are deliberative — intentional or thought out in advance. Therefore, those actions can seldom be considered design. Before we move on to discuss deliberate and informed action it is necessary to make one more observation about systems.

Demoting Pluto from the status of planet did not alter the solar system, only our definition of it.

We recognize two fundamentally different kinds of system:

1. Those that we call deterministic which means that, in principle, all elements and relationships among elements can be known; and, transitions among states are governed by fixed, formulaic, rules. Given knowledge the current state of such a system you can, statistically, predict with accuracy any future state. These are the systems studied by physicists and computer scientists.

2. Those we call complex adaptive systems, CAS, characterized by their degree of dynamicism and the fact that both elements, relationships, and transition paths are often unknown and, in principle, unknowable. The whole system can exhibit "emergent" behavior unpredictable from perfect knowledge of the current state of the system. These are the systems studied by biologists, ecologists, anthropologists, and designers.

Computers and computer programs are deterministic systems. Herbert Simon, in his book *The Sciences of the Artificial*, presupposed the viewpoint of classical physics and essentially asserted that anything in the natural world could be replicated in the artificial world — by design. And the design required to do so was a formal, scientific, discipline. Once, business systems were deemed deterministic — a view that began changing in the 1980s when Tom Peters and others began exploring the problems of change, adaptation, and "chaos."

Pelle Ehn, working at the same time as Simon and equally concerned with design, recognized a different kind of system, the social, cultural, and political system in which computer artifacts were deployed. Ehn asserted that the systems of concern to him were qualitatively different from deterministic systems. Therefore the problems and concerns faced by designers like Ehn were not amenable to the "science of design" proposed by Simon.

As the reader proceeds through this book, it will become clear that the authors' understanding of design and design thinking echos that of Ehn rather than Simon. Design needs to be acknowledged as a discipline and a craft, not a science; one that provides the insights and reveals the actions essential to enhancing complex adaptive systems.

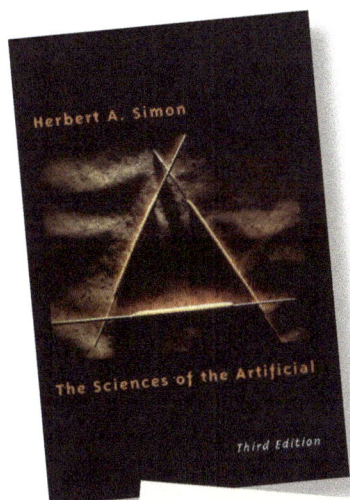

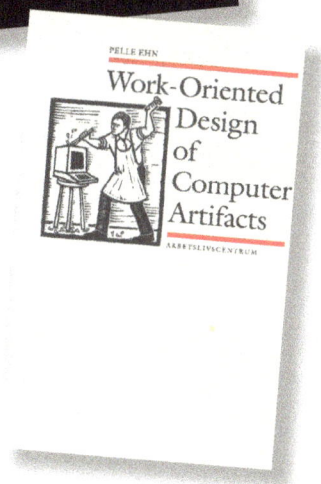

Design Is Intentional

Earlier in this chapter, we stated that humans are constantly changing systems, our environment, our relationships, our bodies, and even our minds. Often, perhaps most of the time, the actions that effect these changes are unthinking or merely reactive — e.g. we are cold so we turn up the thermostat, a simple, unthinking reflex. Even though these acts change the state of a system, we would seldom characterize them as acts of design.

An act resulting from a conscious decision does not necessarily elevate that act to the status of design. Turning up the thermostat might be a conscious decision on my part and might very well satisfy Herbert Simon's definition of design, "changing existing situations into preferred ones," but, for us, fails to satisfy the criteria of being a deliberative act. Mostly, because the act was based on an incomplete understanding of the system at issue and the consequences that arise from the act, as well as a lack of awareness of alternative acts that might result in the same desired situation.

It is possible for an act to be nonconscious and yet be considered design. We will not discuss this in detail, but instead refer to the work of Christopher Alexander, *Notes on the Synthesis of Form*, and his discussion of the "Non Self Consciouss Process" in that book.

Briefly, Alexander asserts that the design of a house, for example, and the actions required to effect that design are not explicit in the mind of the actor, but are distributed throughout the culture in the form of myth and ritual. The homebuilder designs and builds a house, only by following custom. The 'design' is actually a synthesis of generations of experience and trial and error maintained as culture.

There are times when designers, as we think of them, need to be aware of and to accomodate nonconscious design. But there are just as many occasions when the 'default' design provided by culture needs to be examined, modified, or overridden. The most important word in our definition of design is 'informed'. Comprehensive understanding and imaginative thinking necessarily preceed decision making and action — else it is not design.

Design is Informed

Designers are necessarily polymaths. Not in the literal meaning of the word — knowing all that there is to know — but in the sense of possessing and integrating knowledge from multiple domains.

Design is informed by a frame of mind, a guiding perspective, and at least three broad categories of knowledge: of design theory, practice, and experience; of the domain, the system, that is to be changed by design; and, of the concepts, tools, and techniques that support imagination and exploration. All of these will be explored and discussed in depth in the following chapters, but a summary is useful in this introductory chapter.

FRAME OF MIND. Design is predicated upon ambiguity, exploration, alternatives, and essence. Designers are challenged by illformed, ambiguous, and changing objectives — outcomes desired by clients who are unable to articulate exactly and precisely what is needed or desired. The problem space, is also the solution space. This space must be explored, potential 'solutions' must be discovered and evaluated, until a satisfactory design emerges. The desired outcome is discovered. An 'optimal' design is one that best expresses the essence of the problem/solution at a particular

time and in a particular context. There is no single "correct" answer. The process of design demands a designer who approaches the process without preconceptions, assumptions, or expectations. We will later use the metphor of Zen Mind, to convey our understanding of the frame of mind required or successful design.

DESIGN THEORY AND PRACTICE is the explicitly codified and implicitly communicated understanding that the design community has accumulated since designers first became aware of themselves and what they were doing. This will include the values, principles, practices, relationships, and means or modes of communication that all designers share and that can be found in textbooks. Practice is key here, as it is only by doing, and learning from experience, that you truly understand what is conveyed by texts. Community, culture, is just as essential. We explore this in the next section of this chapter.

DOMAIN KNOWLEDGE or understanding of the system that you intend to alter with your design. Designers tend to specialize, to focus on one domain — the design of systems with a particular set of components and relationships. For example, a graphic designer deals with systems that have elements like color, shape, boundaries, white space, and relationships that include arrangement, contrast, juxtaposition, opposition, etc. A landscape designer focuses on systems that contain plants, rocks, water and wood, but also uses some of the same elements as a graphic designer, e.g. color and texture, and arrangement, juxtaposition, contrast, and opposition. Shared understanding is part of the core discussed as theory and practice, above, but it is the latter knowledge that defines the speciality. It is possible to create a Venn diagram that illustrates what is shared and distinct among design specialities. [Figure 1.1]

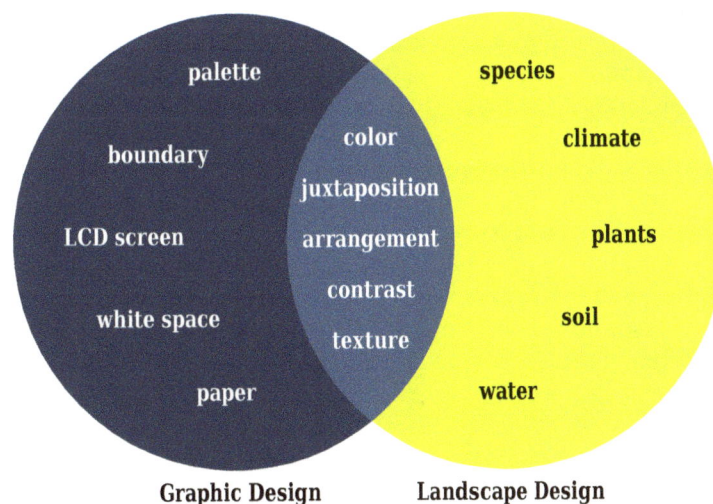

Figure 1.1
Design specialities and Common Core

Graphic Design   **Landscape Design**

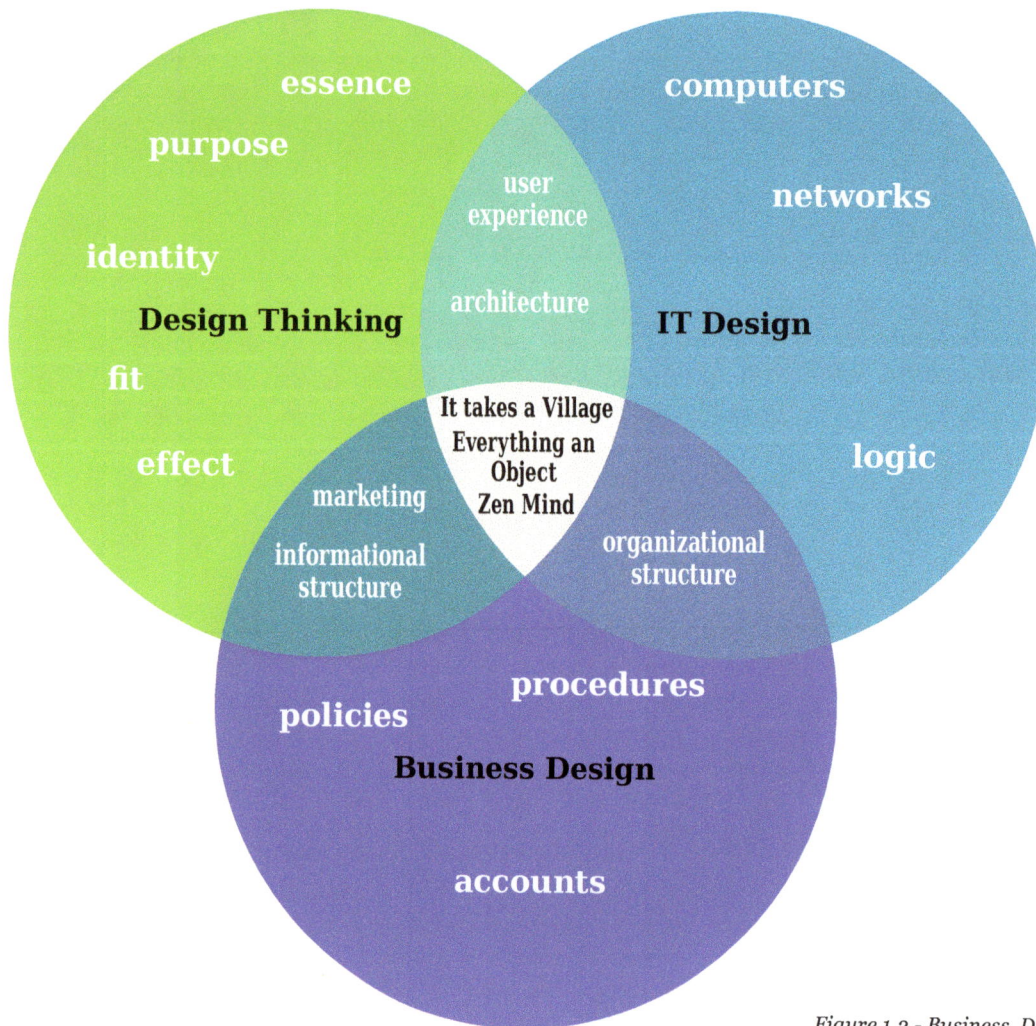

Figure 1.2 - Business, Design and IT

From this discussion it is evident that, if design and design thinking is to be applied in new domains, the effect is the creation of new design specialities. [Figure 1.2]

Traditional design disciplines have developed, over the years, a firm understanding of what are the elements and relationships that comprise their systems of interest. They also understand the ways they can make changes, and the consequences of making such changes, to an individual element or relationship. Professional designers understand their systems, its elements and relationships. If we wish to apply design thinking in other domains, specifically business and software, it follows that designers for those domains must have a similar understanding of the systems they will be working with. If a design professional in one of the applied arts wishes to apply their design knowledge in a new domain, an enterprise perhaps, they must acquire the same depth of understanding of that domain as they have of their existing speciality.

This is a non-trivial demand. Designers can have a tendency to discount the depth of their knowledge in their own speciality. For example, color. A graphic designer not only recognizes hundreds of different colors — while most of us are limited to the Crayola 16 we used as children — they also understand at least three different color specification systems.

Designers are very aware of how culture affects an individuals perception and naming of color and most importantly the emotions and reactions that people of different cultures have to the same color. They also understand how the medium in which the color is expressed, e.g. on paper or on a computer screen, affects the color's absolute and perceived values. Business systems designers and application software designers need to develop a similarly deep understanding of elements and relationships in those domains.

IMAGINATION is an intrinsic human capability — everyone can do it, everyone does it — at least, as children. Too often this ability is 'educated away', giving the impression that imagination is some kind of talent, unique to poets and artists. Designers have developed tools and techniques that enhance imagination, that support exploration as a critical tool for investigation and discovery. These tools and techniques constitute another body of knowledge that those wishing think like designers need to master.

For example — designers understand metaphor, its use and its limitations. Designers also understand how to recognize 'error' and, more importantly how to learn from it. Design uses techniques, like prototyping, that make true error very rare. The power of exploration, driven by both curiosity and imagination, is incorporated in the fundamental design practice of sketching and prototyping. Problems do not present themselves as clear and comprehensive requirements. Solutions do not spring to mind fully formed and ready for execution. Exploration, of problem or solution, is the asking of questions. Imagination reveals what questions are possible to ask. Feedback provides the guidance that focuses imagination and evaluates solutions.

Design is a Culture

Culture, like design, has no universally accepted definition, but, "a group of people with shared worldviews, values, customs, practices, and technology," is a commonly used description. Worldview is further understood as a combination of metaphysics, what is deemed real and the explanations of why it is as it is; and epistemology, what can be known and how it might be learned or understood.

Everyone is a member of a culture, and most people simultaneously identify with several. Our ethnic culture is the most obvious, but organizations, where we work, have identifiable and different cultures; and many of our affinity groups — motorcycle clubs, sports fans, sorororities, religions, professions, etc. — have distinguishing cultural aspects.

Most of us have little trouble juggling the multiple cultures of which we are part and moving flawlessly from culture to culture adapting our behavior and our mindset appropriately for the cultural context of the moment. Cultural conflict, however, is a very real problem and causes very real, and very practical, problems.

When groups of individuals from multiple cultures are working together, they leverage a shared environment and common objectives to develop a common worldview and even a common "creole" language. Successful teams are ones that resist forces (e.g. tacit assumptions, values and norms) that might lead to increasing disagreements, failure to see why X is the "obvious" course of action, escalating tensions, and even open conflict. In essence, each team creates its own, perhaps situational and temporary, powerful local culture; one that is largely invisible to those who share it.

Business, software development and design are three distinct professions and three distinct cultures. Business and software professionals, culturally speaking, have more in common with each other than either do with the design culture. And yet, the cultural differences between business and software professionals give rise to significant tension and too frequent conflict. When the design culture, really different from business and software, is added to the mix — as is necessary if the enterprise is to avail itself of the advantages that come from design thinking — the potential for misunderstanding, tension, and conflict increases.

Unless ...

Individuals from multiple cultures are able to articulate their own culture, listen to the articulations from the others, and collectively develop a respect and appreciation for the 'other' and use them to develop a common understanding, a foundation for communication and cooperation. Establishing this shared understanding is essential. Designers cannot contribute their expertise in any meaningful way unless they deeply understand the individuals, relationships and cultures intrinsic to those with whom they work. Business and software professionals cannot expect to obtain value from design or design thinking unless they understand the culture, the philosophy, and the worldview that generated the practices and techniques of design.

Articulating the culture of design and design thinking while pointing out areas of potential conflict and misunderstanding with business and software cultures will be a continuing thread throughout this book.

Design Thinking

Design Matters

A.G. Lafley, newly appointed CEO of a struggling Proctor and Gambel, P&G, believed that design thinking was key to saving the company. He set about establishing a "design organization" by changing the organizational culture. He appointed Claudia Kotchka to ensure that "design culture" became THE universal culture of P&G.

Infusing design thinking in the minds of tens of thousands of employees around the globe presented a supreme challenge.

Kotchka commissioned Roger Martin, Rotman School of Management, David Kelly of the Hasso Platner Institute of Design at Stanford, and Patrick Whitney of the Institute of Design at the Illinois Institute of Technology to create "Design Works" — an internal comprehensive program that allowed business teams to experience the use of design thinking on real, everyday, problems. The success of this effort is evident in P&G's assertion that "design thinking" is part of their organizational DNA."

The experience at P&G provides many lessons for those wanting to understand how and if design thinking can be transformative.

Culture changes slowly, and the larger the organization the slower the change. A third lesson is that this kind of change is unpredictable as to outcome. Perhaps the success of P&G should not be measured by dollars and cents but in the ways that the new culture had made the organization more sustainable, more adaptable, and more humane, for employees, customers, and communities.

As we define and discuss the concept of design we are simultaneously laying out the foundation for a definition of design thinking. Although it is a bit cumbersome, the working definition we will use going forward is:

Design Thinking is the utilization of a body of knowledge — sufficient in breadth and depth to comprehend and model complex systems — in accordance with a set of concepts and principles, while employing a proven set of practices; all within the context provided by a specific perspective, world view, and value system.

In the next few chapters, we will develop this definition focusing on those aspects that are emphasized by professional designers. It is important to remember that there is significant overlap in how any professional thinks about problems and solutions, but each 'thinking culture' emphasizes different aspects of the common while adding unique elements. As we proceed we will make every effort to clarify, contrasting as necessary, what aspects of the thinking we advocate arise from the design community and how they integrate with other approaches to thinking about problem solving.

BODY OF KNOWLEDGE Core to design thinking is the awareness that complex systems and wicked problems require extensive and interdisciplinary knowledge. The kind of specialization that is the hallmark of modern science is insufficient and the barriers to inter- and crossdisciplinary cooperation and collaboration are significant.

The design culture has long recognized the need for integrated knowledge that crosses traditional disciplinary boundaries. To address this need, two complementary approaches are followed. The first focuses on the individual and the need to become a kind of polymath. This approach dates to the founding of architecture and Vitruvius' definition of the ideal architect:

"The ideal architect should be a man of letters, a skillful draftsman, a mathematician, familiar with historical studies, a diligent student of philosophy, acquainted with music; not ignorant of medicine, learned in the responses of jurisconsults, familiar with astronomy, and astronomical calculations."
— Vitruvius 25 B.C.

The second approach focuses on establishing and nurturing a collaborative group, the members of which combine deep specialized expertise along with crossdisciplinary breadth. Providing the proper environment, tools, and practices that allow intense interactions among the group leading to common understanding is a significant contribution from the design culture.

CONCEPTS AND PRINCIPLES Part of the body of knowledge required for design thinking take the form of specific concepts or principles. Included would be concepts about systems and wholism or heuristic principles like treating every element and every relationship among elements as if they were one kind of thing — an object. Many of these concepts and principles have origins in areas of study outside of design. The design culture has, however, added important nuance and has evolved the ideas in ways that may make them somewhat strange to experts in the domain of origin. It is quite important to understand such concepts in their new context and not be deceived by thinking you understand an idea simply because you are familiar with its name.

PRACTICES Every profession develops its own set of standard practices — ways of doing things. Each practice, in turn, addresses the completion of a task or closely related family of tasks. Practices are honed for effectiveness in a particular context. Each design speciality will exhibit practices that are specific for that speciality. An "80-20 Composition Rule" might be a practice specific to graphic design. There is always some degree of commonality among practices across specializations and across disciplines. "White Space" might refer to a graphic design practice that is similar to, but not identical with, the use of lawns or gravel or bare earth, in landscape architecture. Visualization with abstract models is just as common among design specialities as it is in the domain of software development.

We are advocating the adoption of design practices, as a component of design thinking, in the domains of business and software. To support this advocacy we will show how specific practices, from design, must be understood, how they can be adopted, and to what extent they will need to be adapted in order to apply in business or software. A component of understanding a practice is making the connections to similar practices in the target domains and making it clear where and why similar practices are essentially different. The goal is to prevent a premature sense of understanding simply because of superficial familiarity.

PERSPECTIVE AND WORLD VIEW The primary and fundamental difference between design thinking and other forms of problem solving is precisely the difference in world view and perspective. This is fundamentally a cultural difference and therefore presents the greatest challenge for business and software professionals wishing to adopt design thinking.

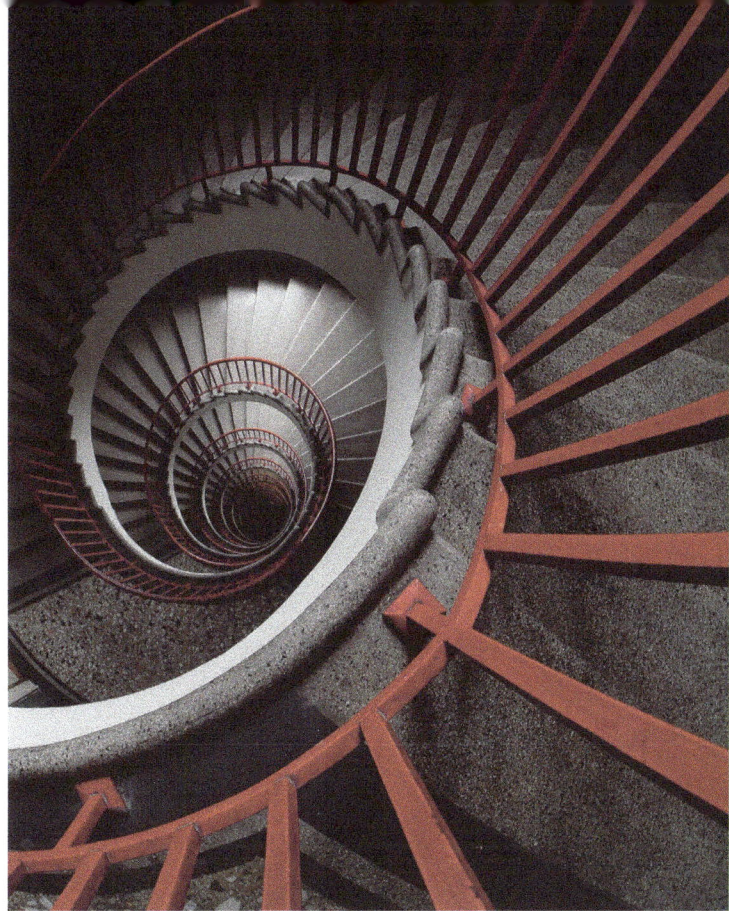

To the extent that design and design thinking are seen some kind of ineffable innate talent, potential design thinkers will be misled and will fail to understand how design is learned in the context of a culture; and how perspective, world view, values, and concepts create and are reciprocally supported by that culture.

Design is a Moral Imperative

Our working definition of design ends with the phrase, "more desirable state." Herbert Simon speaks of changing the state of a system to a "preferred one."

In both cases, questions arise: desirable for whom, preferred by ...? Also there are questions of what characteristics or properties make something desirable or preferred? These types of questions lead to questions about the responsibility of the designer and to whom?

Design has always been about making things better for someone — a client, a patron, an inhabitant of the world — being changed by design. Not in the narrow sense of providing a design that satisfies requirements, but in the deeper sense of ensuring a human being feels that her world is a better pla-ce to be because of what the designer delivered. Design has always been focused on the human element, with humans as an essential and integral part of the system being designed.

This does not make designers immune from moral failure. A graphic designer might serve the interests and enhance the world of a dictator with agitprop that demeans and denigrates the lives of the populace.

Designers do, however, have an edge over business and software professionals in the degree and the pervasiveness of being focused on the human and humane. This does NOT mean business and software professionals are bad or immoral: only that they have operated in a context that em-pasizes the abstract (e.g profit ratios, organizational struc-tures, data structures, and algorithms), instead of people.

Both business and computing became professions and academic disciplines at a time when the prevailing philo-sophical context was Rationalism and Determinism — the latter derived from classical Physics as already noted above. The enterprise was thought to be a 'machine' and the role of management was to take rational actions that were intended to make that machine more efficient and profitable. Computers are machines, and computer pro-grams are virtual machines. Computer Science and Soft-ware Engineering are all about making those machines better machines — efficient and error free.

In both cases, humans were seen as ambiguous, unpre-dictable, and the source of error. All that was human was reduced to statistical models, creating mock humans that could be treated as if they were machine parts. It should

> " *Design has always been about making things better for someone — a client, a patron, an inhabitant of the world — being changed by design. Not in the narrow sense of providing a design that satisfies requirements, but in the deeper sense of ensuring a human being feels that her world is a better place to be because of what the designer delivered.*

45

be noted that, in software, this applied to the professionals themselves — reduced to commodity skill sets and interchangeable parts.

Concern for the individual, the human, and the humane has become a priority concern of both business and software. Business is interested in the "customer experience" and how to enhance it; so to are application developers interested in the "user experience." It should be noted that both of these efforts are grounded in the ideas of design; e.g. Apple's focus on how a product is experienced, psychologically and physiologically, in day-to-day use.

The business community has recognized that their traditional approaches to managment and problem solving are not as helpful as they once were. This has prompted an investigation of design and design thinking as sources of problem solving approaches and collaborative/cooperative, self-managed, teams. Business has also recognized that creativity and innovation are intrinsically human and not replicable by machines. If managers and employees expand their abilities with design thinking, they will provide the means for realizing the innovation and adaptation needs of the enterprise.

As new design disciplines like Enterprise Design emerge, it would be a terrible loss if the concern for humans found in the Design community were replaced with the perspective of the traditional business and computing communities.

We recognize the immense power that designers will have as they apply their skills and knowledge sets to the domains of business and software. As Christopher Alexander noted, architects have had a direct influence on less than ten percent of the built world, but software developers affect 100%. A commitment to and acceptance of responsibility for, making the world a better place for all is a moral imperative. Emerging design professionals would be remiss to ignore it.

Chapter 2
Composite Systems
and Wicked Problems

Everything is a System

The concept of a system provides a powerful abstraction,
one that simplifies and clarifies our understanding of
design thinking; introduce a typology of systems, ways
of differentiating among systems based on critical differences; and most importantly, introduce nuances of design
thinking as they correlate with specific system types.

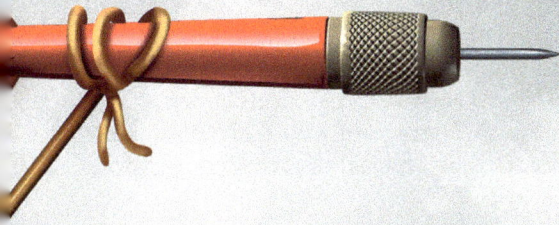

From the beginning, *General Systems Theory* (GST) was intended to be inter- and crossdisciplinary. In addition to Ludwig von Bertalanffy, a biologist, major contributors to, and advocates for, GST, included: Anatoly Rapoport, a mathematician; Kenneth E. Boulding, an economist; William Ross Ashby, a psychiatrist; Margaret Mead, an anthropologist; Gregory Bateson, an anthropologist and semiotician; and C. West Churchman, a philosopher. Gerald Weinberg introduced GST to computer science and software development as a way of thinking about systems that included computers, programs, and human beings interacting with them.

GST provided a single abstraction, the system, while identifying patterns, behaviors, and properties that were common across all systems. The definition of a system is simple: "an arbitrarily bounded collection of components and the relationships among them." Components and relationships may also be systems in their own right.

Systems can be differentiated on the basis of what components they contain and what relationships among those components that are recognized. An ecological system, for example, has components like flora and fauna, energy, and water; while a computer system has CPUs, busses, and programs. Disciplines can, in turn be defined on the basis of the systems they study: Ecology – ecological systems; Computer Science — computer or software systems.

In the following section, we will explore another way of categorizing systems — without modifying the fundamental definition — and show how that categorization correlates with different design professions, including the proposed new professions of enterprise design and software systems design.

49

Business professionals, especially CEOs, senior executives, and senior managers, have increasingly been concerned with a set of problems centered around adaptability, sustainability, and innovation. Disruptive technologies challenge traditional business models, policies and procedures.

Fundamental principles of management have been called into question as our understanding of the enterprise has shifted from its being a complicated but deterministic system to a complex, living, system. Formal models and algorithmic processes are found wanting.

The search for insights and new approaches has, for the past ten years at least, focused on the design profession and the belief that "design thinking" can address enterprise issues.

In this chapter, we will show why business professionals are turning to design thinking beginning with a discussion of systems and the intimate relationship between "type" of system and "type" of design thinking most appropriate for that system. This discussion follows from our definition of design from the last chapter:

An advantage of a common system definition is the bridge it provides: allowing things learned about one kind of system to be applied to another. For example, we look at biological systems and note that as they increase in size they devote an exponentially increasing amount of available resources to simple maintenance of the system. That lesson can be applied to governments, the larger they become the greater percentage of your tax dollars go to maintain the bureaucracy instead of providing services to constituencies.

The primary advantage aris-ing from systems theory is a common, very simple, abstraction that can be utilized to understand, model, and design almost anything — because everything is a system. A straightforward case in point: a book is a system with elements that consist of strings, characters, images, spaces, paper, and ink. Some books might also include components like pasteboard, thread, glue, and exotic covering materials like leather or wood. Intangible elements, like chapters, titles, or captions identify elements. Relationships can become elements, e.g. 'Table of Contents' or 'Index'.

A book, as a system, is also a potential element in systems of greater scope — like a library. Another such system might be called a "reading system" which would be composed of the book, the reader, the lighting, the environment — office, bedroom, easy chair, or beach, and constraint systems, e.g. "eating at the table," "reading in the hot tub," or "content-context mismatch." The last item would be something like reading a lurid murder mystery at church.

Identifying an appropriate system — e.g. a reading system — would be an essential first step for a designer of an ebook reader device. Once the system has been discerned, it is possible to use the definition of a system to guide the discover of elements and relationships and reveal what elements or relations might be altered and to what result; which is the actual act of designing.

Our example hints at another important point we need to develop — the correlation between different instances of design thinking and the systems for which they are best suited. Making this point begins with a discussion of system categorization.

Design is the informed and deliberative modification of a system by adding, deletingor modifying one of its elements or adding, deleting, or modifying a relationship among elements; in order to establish the system in a more desirable state.

Study of the flocking behavior of birds or the schooling behavior of fish — as systems — could lead to insights that could triple or quadruple the carrying capacity of our highway and road systems. Individual birds and fish act in accordance to a small set of simple rules. There is no master bird directing the actions of all. Birds can flock, in relatively confined spaces, in the thousands, without experience crashes or traffic jams.

If we could build air traffic control systems, for example, on this same basis we could dramatically increase the capacity of airports and airspaces while simultaneously reducing the massive complications inherent in building the kind of centralized hierarchical control of current software systems.

A somewhat sardonic observation: a secondary lesson to be learned is that flocking would notwork for a traffic system — at least as long as human drivers are in control of individual vehicles. Birds and fish follow the rules, humans are not so reliable.

Varieties of Systems

At a basic level, we can differentiate among systems simply by examining the elements and relationships that are noted within the system boundary. System A has elements like font, white space, glyphs, and images; and is called a graphic system. System B has elements like client, product, service, and price; and is called a business system. We can identify concepts and practices that designers would use in system A and B, while also identifying commonalities between system A and B.

We could then differentiate between 'graphic design thinking' and 'business design thinking' as well as creating a foundation for a nascent 'design thinking'. This kind of outcome was the original goal of General Systems Thinking. Our goal is a bit more ambitious and has a slightly different focus. To get to where we want to go, in developing design thinking, it is necessary to look at another way of categorizing systems.

We begin with a definition of a 'system space' — a two dimensional space [Figure 2.1] with a horizontal axis defined with the term "natural" to the left and "artificial" to the right and a vertical axis labeled "deterministic" at the top and "complex" at the bottom. By artificial we really mean that the state and nature of the system derives largely from human action. Scale, the relative size of the system, is shown with greater or smaller surface area. Using this space we will define some broad categories of system with typical examples of each. We can then associated different aspects of design thinking with each category of system.

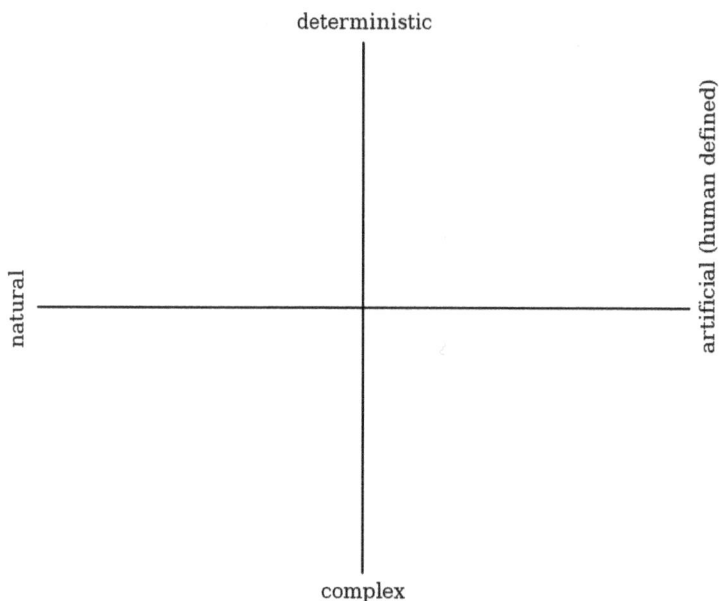

Figure 2.1
System space

Natural-Deterministic

A Science of Design

Herbert Simon, Christopher Alexander, and Horst Rittel are the three best known proponents of 'design science' — which is not the same as "scientific design." All three believed that a formal, mathe-matics-based, science of design was possible and urgently necessary for the solution of complex problems.

Alexander and Rittel, fairly quickly, changed their minds about both the feasibility and the desirability of a design science. Only Simon remained convinced. His book, The Sciences of the Artificial, remains the primary reference for advocates of a design science. Central to Simon's view is the conviction that all systems are deterministic, whether natural or artificial in origin, and therefore it is possible to build an artificial system that is the exact equivalent of any natural system. Simon's conviction domi-nates the world of software development and is evident in disciplines such as Artificial Intelligence and applied programming, aka Software Engineering.

These are the systems of classical physics, engineering, and mathematics. An easy example of a naturally occur-ring system in this category would be the solar system. Differing only in scale, another example would be a galaxy. Notice, in Figure 2.2 that we have placed the solar system further to the right than the galaxy. This indicates that there is a very small chance that humans can design and effect changes at the level of the solar system, but not at the level of the galaxy.

Humans have already, in minute ways, altered the state of the solar system simply by launching satellites. They have added new elements to the system. The degree to which they have changed the state of the solar system is negligi-ble — theoretically measurable in alteration to the orbit of the moon, but certainly not discernible. A subsystem of the solar system, near Earth space, has experienced an altered state; if to no other extent that the orbits of new satellites must include additional calculations to avoid collisions and even gravitational interference with each other.

Plans have been made to make other changes to the solar system. Terraforming Mars, for example would fit our definition of design, intentional alteration of an element of a system. Plans to move asteroids from existing orbits into near Earth orbits in order to facilitate mining is another example of system change where design would play a role. In both of these examples, the scale of the solar system would make it difficult to discern changes in the overall

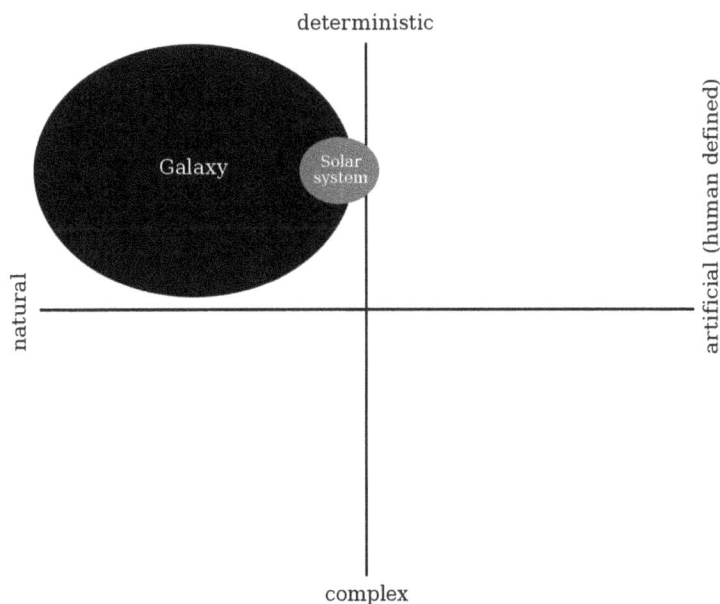

Figure 2.2
Natural-Deterministic system

state of the solar system. The state of local systems could be discernibly changed. One example that might have a discernible state effect at the level of the solar system would be the deflection of a meteor or asteroid that otherwise would have collided with the Earth, perhaps changing its orbit or destroying it altogether. For humans this designed change would be considered more desirable that the alternative state. Design in this arena, to the extent that it exists at all, would be characterized as 'scientific' design — see sidebar, *Scientific Design*.

Scientific Design arises from the conviction that the entire Universe, and everything in it, can be known along with all of the 'laws' that define state and possible state changes. We will not be concerned with this kind of design because, if it exists at all, it would apply only to those systems that are fully deterministic. If this were true, we could predict any and every future state of the system from a complete knowledge of its present state. Ernst Mach, a physicist, once made this very claim about the Universe.

Hybrid Natural-Artificial and Artificial-Deterministic

In Figure 2.3 three new systems appear: a watershed, a computer, and a computer program. The watershed is an example of a system that is part naturally occurring and part artificial, with some elements and relationships determined by human action. Both a computer and a computer program are artificial, completely human created.

The watershed is a deterministic system consisting of water, rain and snowfall, and channels carved through earth and rock. It is, at least statistcally, a deterministic system. A drop of water that falls to ground at coordinate X, will follow a defined path until it reaches the ocean at point Y. We say that this is statistically deterministic because some droplets will never complete the course, they evaporate instead, and some will be consumed by animals that move across watershed boundaries before excreting the droplet, altering it's course to the ocean. Watersheds are completely natural and arose long before the advent of human beings capable of altering them. Modern watersheds, with almost no exception, have been deliberately altered. Humans have built dams, deepened channels by dredging, established canals that move water hundreds of miles from its natural flowage, and even reversed the course of entire rivers.

Water sheds, because they have both natural and artificial elements and both na-tural and artificial relationships among those elements are considered as hybrid systems.

To the extent that hybrid systems are designed, the design in question is 'engineering' design — a subset of scientific design in the same way that engineering is the extension of pure science. Engineering design presumes the ability to define an accurate and complete, mathematical model of the system, the watershed in this instance.

Given this mathematical model new system elements, a dam for example, can be designed to withstand the forces created by water accumulation at a given point, where the dam is to built. Because the inflow of water to that point can be calculated — as both an average and a 20 year maximum — along with the depth of the channel and its myriad branches it is possible to calculate the maximum amount of water that can exist behind the dam and therefore exactly what dimensions the dam must have, and what components it must be made of, in order to resist the pressure of the accumulated water.

It is also possible, in principle, but not in practice, to calculate things like the ability of water to hold dissolved earth and the dissolvability of the earth along the water course and therefore determine exactly how much silt will accumulate on the floor of the channel at the dam. Silt will be deposited at the dam because moving water has a greater carrying capacity than standing water. In theory it would also be possible to determine how much water would be

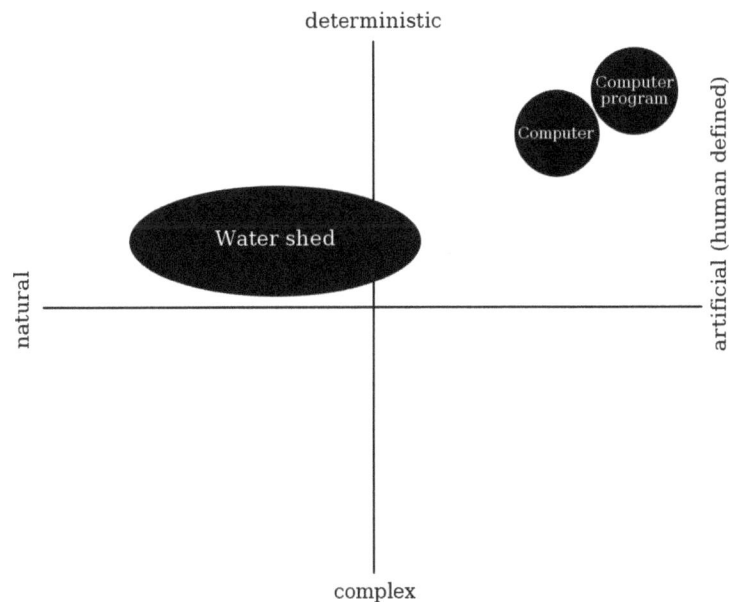

Figure 2.3
Hybrid Natural-Artificial and
Artificial-Deterministic

absorbed into the surrounding earth and rock and determine exactly when the lake formed behind any given dam will reach capacity.

No matter how many new variables are introduced into the overall system defining equations, engineering design can always find an answer. This is a statistically true assertion. It does not preclude, with absolute certainty, that there will never be a natural event, an unnatural snow depth coupled with an unnatural rate of thaw that would generate an inflow greater than that the dam's structural capacity.

In a hybrid system there will always be elements and relationships arising from the natural part of the system, that cannot be predicted with sufficient certainty to guarantee that no natural event will not cause a catastrophic failure. Engineering design can always be extended to accommodate more and more variables in equations of greater and greater complexity. But there will always be limits arising from the fact that, in a hybrid system, natural elements and relationships can be known only in a statistical, not absolute sense. Engineering design is more reliable when applied to systems, like computers and programs, which are paragons of artificial deterministic systems — as shown in Figure 2.3. Computers are deterministic machines. Their circuits and the movement of discrete, 1 or 0 , bits through those circuits can be modeled with complete mathematical accuracy. True, a computer is a physical device and therefore subject to disruptive outside influence — e.g. a magnetic field or a stray atomic particle.

Programs are virtual machines, even more deterministic than computers because they are isolated from external influences. Programs can be incredibly complicated and that complication is magnified by the fact that programs begin as statements in a context-free grammar and are translated into a finite set of discrete instructions that, in turn, are translated into current running through circuits. We cannot go into the how and why of error in programs except to note that: in principle it is possible to write error free, provable, programs. The outcome of a program, the resulting state of the computer running the program, is necessarily and deterministically exactly what was specified in the original source code as translated into current flows. Error — the state of the machine is not what was desired or what the programmer thought he specified — arises solely from the inability of the programmer to grasp all the complications and all the permutations of state changes and account for them.

Fred Brooks, author of the famous paper, *No Silver Bullet*, stated long ago that the lack of a mental model of the state changes resulting from the execution of a program was the essential problem facing programmers. Interestingly, his solu-

Fred Brooks

58

tion to the problem was "better designers." Brooks' notion of a designer is consistent with what we have been calling 'engineering design'.

Design thinking in this context would consist of identifying the formulae governing a given system, obtaining a precise, complete and unambiguous specification of a desired state, and then articulating the algorithm necessary to move the system from its current state to the desired one. All of this is deterministic, and therefore, given the necessary knowledge that governs the system and the specification of the desired state, the program could be articulated by a formal machine, e.g. computer generated, instead of a human being. We have already pointed out, that in hybrid systems, part natural — part artificial, there are limits imposed by the statistical nature of certain elements and relationships in the system. These limitations become even clearer as we consider additional types of systems and move closer to what we consider to be Design Thinking.

Programs can be incredibly complicated and that complication is magnified by the fact that programs begin as statements in a context-free grammar and are translated into a finite set of discrete instructions that, in turn, are translated into current running through circuits.

Natural-Complex Systems

Figure 2.4 (see next page) shows a type of system — an ecosystem — at various levels of scale and labeled: biosphere, ecology, micro-ecology, and aquarium/terrarium. As the levels of scale decrease, these ecosystems are located closer to the artificial side of the figure. Also included in the figure are systems labeled, animal, plant, and human being. These three systems are shown crossing the boundary between natural and artificial. Consideration of these systems will reveal some interesting insights into design thinking, especially our understanding, definition, and presentation of design.

The system we labeled 'biosphere' is essentially the zone reaching from some distance below the seafloor to the uppermost reaches of the atmosphere — the planetary zone where we have come to expect life. Living things are not the only elements of this system. Jet streams, water vapor, water, soil, sunlight, etc. are also elements. Relationships among those elements are complex and, to a great extent, still unknown.

We think of an ecology as a system at the scale of the Amazon watershed and jungle. A micro ecology as the scale of a farm, and an aquarium/terrarium being a tiny ecology existing within glass walls.

Clearly, all of these systems, regardless of scale, are subject to changes introduced by human beings. Every element

59

of an aquarium/terrarium was selected and placed with the intent of creating a system in a stable, self-supporting — excepting specific inputs like food, water, and sunlight — state. A farm has selected natural elements, e.g. naturally occurring grasslands and water supplies, animals and plants.

The Amazon basin is altered by human actions like logging. Even the entire biosphere has been altered with the introduction of extra methane, from all the cattle we raise to satisfy needs for milk and meat and hydrocarbons from factories and vehicles. Because we do not sufficiently understand all the relationships and elements that comprise large scale ecosystems, it is difficult to measure the actual impact of these human actions.

Those actions may very well be insignificant, lost in other, naturally occurring forces, or they might constitute a tipping point. The notion of a tipping point in biological systems dates back to Rene Thom and the notion of catastrophic change. A series of incremental changes can, at a tipping point, result in dramatic, catastrophic, change in the system as a whole — e.g. a massive die-off of species.

There is also a deliberate effort to alter the fundamental nature of systems like animals, plants and human beings. Medicine and the use of hormones to "improve" or increase natural occurring aspects, like milk production, or the ability to withstand the stresses of transport between distant points of production and consumption. Increasingly we are

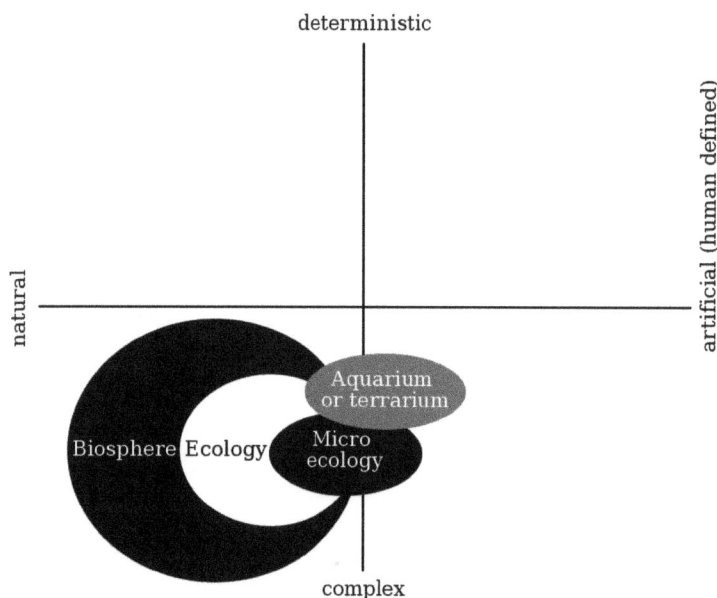

Figure 2.4
Natural-Complex

Informed by Design Thinking

Our definition of design thinking ...

"Design Thinking is the utilization of a body of knowledge — sufficient in breadth and depth to comprehend and model complex systems — in accordance with a set of concepts and principles, while employing a proven set of practices; all within the context provided by a specific perspective, world view, and value system."

... suggests that being 'informed' requires a breadth and depth of mastery that exceeds that expected of specialists. In fact, to be informed, as a designer, requires the designer to become a 'modern polymath', a topic we will discuss in far greater detail in a later chapter.

seeing examples of 'bioengineered' animals and plants, generated using techniques of recombinant DNA.

Three important points about design arise from our cursory examination of these systems; the first two, a consequence of our definition of design as "intentional and informed." The third arises from the nature of the system, complex adaptive systems (CAS).

First, consider intent. When we increase our cattle herds and drive thousands of extra miles in our cars, is it our intent to alter the biosphere, the climate? For most of us the answer would be no. Given that answer can we say that the change we introduced was, "by design." Further, our definition of design suggested that is was necessary to put the system in a more desirable state as a result of our action. Is Global Warming, more desirable? In a very narrow and technical sense, any change in system state resulting from an action can meet the definition of design. I did not drive my car by accident, and Global Warming will benefit some people and therefore be preferred — but this narrow sense of design is of little interest to us and will receive no further mention.

Second, and more interesting, are questions centered on the definitional requirement to be informed. How informed must we be to satisfy our definition? What if it is impossible to be fully informed about a system or about the effect of introducing a change into a system?

In the case of engineering design as discussed above, being informed means being fully informed only of the knowable elements and relationships — basically the machinery and software controlling that machinery. Engineering design would not take into account the examples cited in the sidebar, but Design Thinking as we define it, would.

Failing to incorporate knowledge — facts, awareness of elements or relationships— in a design means that the design is flawed — it is 'bad' design. When the engineers responsible for the Tacoma Narrows Bridge forgot about harmonic vibration and did not know all that they should

61

have known about wind patterns, the designed bridge collapsed, dramatically and spectacularly.

Perhaps the most constant and serious problem with software engineering arises from this exact point. For software engineers to design and implement a software system they must have complete and unambiguous requirements — perfect knowledge of the system. It is, effectively, impossible to obtain this kind of information, so all software designs are doomed to be flawed to some degree.

Third, Complex Adaptive Systems have elements and relationships that are unknowable. Emergent behavior, observed at the level of the whole and unpredictable even from perfect knowledge of the state of all the elements, is one example. Positive feedback loops indirectly threaded through complicated networks of relationships are context sensitive and unpredictable. This leads to solutions that fundamentally redefine problems—giving rise to what the design community calls, "Wicked Problems".

Ecosystems, humans, animals, and plants are CAS. Not only is there a lot we do not know about such systems, there are somethings that cannot be known. Does this mean that design of such systems is impossible? Short answer — Engineering design is indeed impossible for this type of system, but the Design Thinking we advocate in this book is well matched to the challenge; and does allow the designer to be sufficiently informed to generate good design.

Composite Systems

If you Google 'composite systems' today you will find lots of references to plastics and carbon fiber building materials.

In the 1990s the term was advanced in the Artificial Intelligence (AI) community to refer to systems that were primarily deterministic but also included human elements.

A prototypical example of such a system would be an elevator in a high rise office building and the problem of how to design the control panel.

The mechanical part of the system can be engineered and aspects of the control panel, e.g. buttons to open or close doors, can be included in the design. Then you add people to the system and you need to think about their behavior and how or when they might push the open or close buttons.

Should a person be able to push the open button in order to hold the elevator for a late arrival? For how long? How will that affect the others in the car and their need to move quickly to their destination? How might such an act affect the carefully optimized algorithms used to moving high volumes of traffic among floors?

Consider this case: the elevator has a button in the car to close the door and a button outside the car to call the elevator. If the doors are closing and the 'call' button is pressed on the outside, the door will stop closing and open. It is late at night and a single woman enters the elevator. A strange man approaches and the woman fears being "trapped" in the elevator with this man. Should she be able to press the door close button and have that action override the man pressing the call button to gain entrance?

A composite system is created when a relatively simple deterministic element, an elevator bank, is combined with a non-deterministic element, a human being.

Scientific Management

In the late 1800s, Frederick Winslow Taylor, established a school of thought called scientific management. It was focused on improving productivity and efficiency, particularly in manufacturing environments. Taylor had a very low opinion of workers, believing them to be of low intelligence, lazy, and less than honest — draft animals. (He did, however, believe that workers should be treated as if they had value, with breaks, reasonable working conditions, and pay.)

The essence of Taylorism was to rationalize and then optimize the work so that the role of the worker was reduced to the simplest and most repetitive rote tasks — commensurate with his estimate of their ability.

Between 1890 and 1930 this view dominated business management theory. It was elaborated by Gantt (famous for the Gantt chart used, still, for project management), the Gilbreths, and Henri Fayol. Officially, scientific management was discredited and disavowed by 1930. Nevertheless, the theory and practices it espoused still dominate management theory and education.

Taylorist theory is particularly evident in the world of software. Development is still seen as a production process; one that can, in theory, be done by a machine without human intervention. Programmers and developers are commodity components controlled and regulated by rigid methodology.

63

Living Systems

The only completely artificial system that might be considered complex is the Web. [Figure 2.5] The infrastructure, the Internet, of the Web is deterministic, as are the individual elements of the web, pages, images, animations, etc. But even a perfect knowledge of this formality is clearly insufficient to explain the Web, the complex system that emerged from the Internet.

We cannot learn much about design or design thinking by looking at the Web, except for noting that it is similar in many ways to naturally occurring complex systems like termite mounds, ant foraging, and bird flocking. These natural systems are studies as examples of 'agent-based models'. In an agent-based system, each element may behave in a statistically deterministic manner, the actions of each element obeying formal rules. The overall behavior of the system, e.g. the complicated architecture of the termite mound, is not predictable and the system as a whole is nondeterministic and complex.

We can also state that the Web is not designed and has no designer. Elements of the Web — from routers to individual pages, are, however, designed and have designers. Subsystems of the Web, a specific Website for example, are also designed. The design of something like Facebook, for example, yields, like the Web as a whole, macro-behaviors that were not designed and could not have been predicted.

It is important to note that the Web is not complex because designers are elements of the Web, they are not. Designers

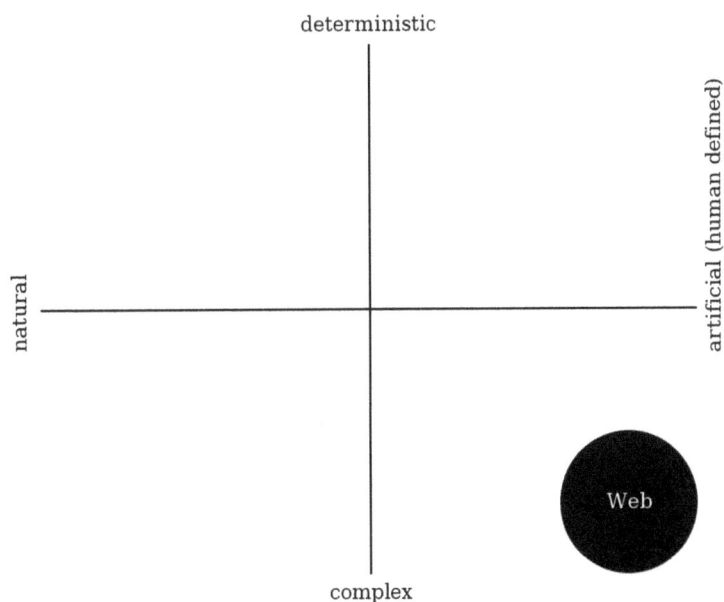

Figure 2.5
Complex-Artificial

65

are outside the Web but they introduce change into the Web system by adding servers, pages, and other elements, or by altering such elements by manipulating underlying formalisms like HTML, CSS, TCP/IP, HTTP, Javascript, etc. The Web is intrinsically complex because — like other naturally occurring, complex, agent-based systems — the Web is, as a whole, non-deterministic with emergent macro behavior.

Frank De Winne on treadmill at ISS.

Artificial systems, like the International Space Station (ISS) are incredibly complicated and deterministic. These systems become complex with the addition of non-deterministic, complex, elements; e.g. human beings. Any artificial system that contains complex elements, becomes complex. Not intrinsically, like the Web or an ecosystem, but by composition. Hence we call this type of system a "composite system." [See figure 2.6]

Composite systems are designed, as we define design.

Composite systems have been around a long time, and many systems, most notably the business enterprise, that once were thought to be artificial-deterministic in nature have come to be seen as composite systems. Composite systems present some significant challenges for designers! Figure 2.6 shows some examples of composite systems. Note that all examples straddle the boundary between deterministic and complex, reflecting the heterogenous nature of the elements comprising the system, and in some cases, like the business enterprise, they also cross the boundary between artificial and natural systems.

People have been designing composite systems for some time, often with notable success. The International Space Station (ISS) would be an example.

The engineering design of composite systems works if, and only if, you can somehow remove the ambiguity and unpredictability, from the non-deterministic elements — often, human beings.

You, must dehumanize the humans; turn them into machines.

In a system like the ISS, this is accomplished by establishing meticulously detailed procedures for every conceivable action that a human element might be required to take, and then forbidding any activity that is not covered by procedure. Further, you require that the humans, when taking action, follow a written checklist; eliminating the possibility of error from faulty human memory. Business enterprises have also been designed using this approach. The

Ultra Large Scale (ULS) systems versus Systems-of-Systems (SOS)

Business professionals have turned to design professionals instead of IT professionals for insight and inspiration needed to solve contemporary and future enterprise issues and wicked problems.

A 2006 report from the Software Engineering Institute at Carnegie Mellon University clearly illustrates why.

The report was titled, "Ultra- Large Scale Systems: The Software Challenge of the Future" and it states the need for "different perspectives", "breakthrough research in concepts, methods, and tools", "innovation, ranging from new conceptual models of the problem space to revolutionary solution approaches".

The 'Systems of Systems' approach is noted in the report. Not as an example of an innovative approach but as an engineering-based attempt to understand systems that are 'complex' and that have 'emergent' behavior. Despite the use of terms like "complex", "emergent" and "design" SoS is clearly an example of 'engineering design thinking' grounded in the 19th century conviction that the Universe is a deterministic system.

SoS is concerned with design, but it is the design of the circuit diagram, architectural blueprint, or the engineering drawing — not the 'artistic' design of architecture and the applied arts.

modern corporation exemplifies a system of policies, procedures, roles, and processes — not human beings or the skills and abilities unique to human beings. The ultimate example of this was the era of "scientific management."

As modern business adopted computing technologies, a shift occurred. Engineering design approaches were applied to the computer system that ostensibly supported and replicated the business system. Computers were first used to replicate processes, especially those that were intrinsically deterministic, like counting and sorting census data. As the era of 'data processing' was succeeded by 'management information systems', 'executive decision systems', ' knowledge systems', and even 'expert systems', the engineered systems diverged from the business systems. Severe problems resulted from the mismatch in systems understanding and design approaches.

While the information technology side of the enterprise was growing and pursuing Simon's dream, the business side of the enterprise was awakening to the realization that the enterprise is not a machine, that it does contain people, and that people are valuable with valuable and unique contributions to make. The term composite system was not used, but the notion of complex systems, the need for adaptability, and concerns about how to establishing a learning, living, organization came to the fore. More recently, concerns about how to establish a culture of innovation was added to the mix.

It also became common to deem a business system as "living;" attributing characteristics like adaptability and

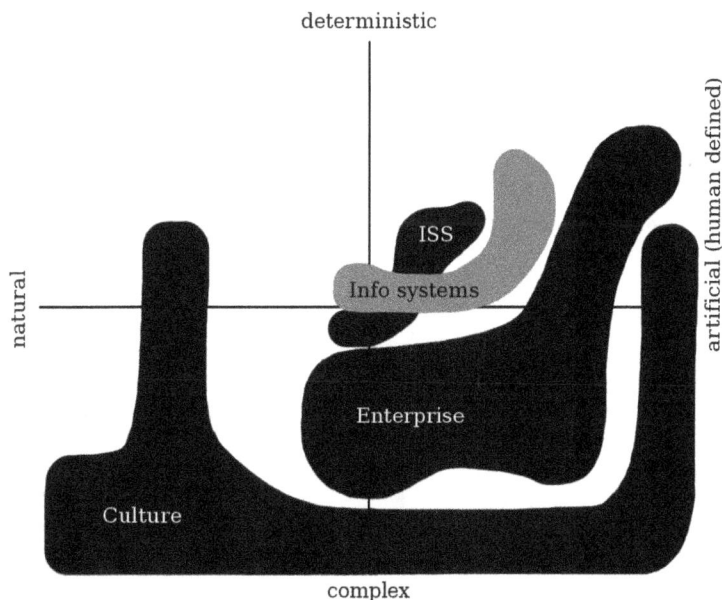

Figure 2.6
Composite Systems

67

A modern traffic system is composite — the roadways are deterministic but the traffic is natural and complex because of the human drivers.

capabilities like 'learning' to the system. This is an example of anthropomorphism — attributing human characteristics to non-human systems — treating both the organization and the human being as instances of living systems.

Business professionals, managers and executives, recognized the need for a design discipline that would address the challenges posed by living systems. It is very telling that business professionals did not turn to the information systems professionals for help in this endeavor. Instead they looked to designers.

Designers have had a role in business for a long time, but mostly in advertising or product development. Design was not considered a 'core competency' in most organizations. It might seem strange that design caught the eye of business professionals; until, you notice that designers deal with composite and living systems.

Figure 2.7 shows three system realms labeled by the type of design associated with them: architecture, graphic design, and industrial or product design. The first thing that we notice is that all of these system domains have substantial presence in the artificial and deterministic part of our diagram.

Graphic design delves into the natural and the complex area: reflecting the fact that graphic designers must concern themselves with human sensory perception, a natural system; culture, a complex natural and artificial system; and human cognition, another complex natural system. The result of graphic design is not an artifact, it is a system

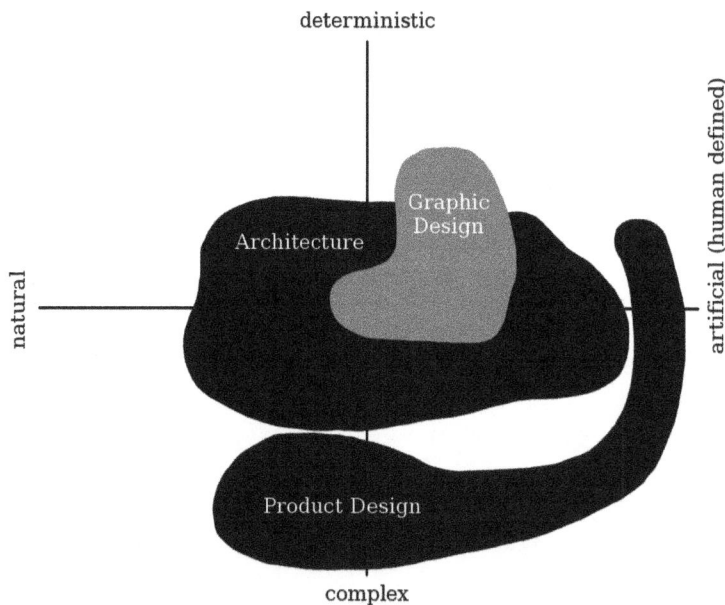

Figure 2.7
Design Systems Domains

70

that includes the artifact, the observer, and the historical-cultural context. Graphic design is concerned with composite systems.

Architecture is also concerned with composite systems including the landscape, the building, human beings, and roles and activities defined by culture and purpose. As architects increased the scope of their efforts beyond individual buildings to campuses, neighborhoods, and cities, their work became increasingly dependent on an understanding composite systems of increasing scale. As scale increases the systems of interest cross a threshold and their intrinsic nature shifts from composite to living.

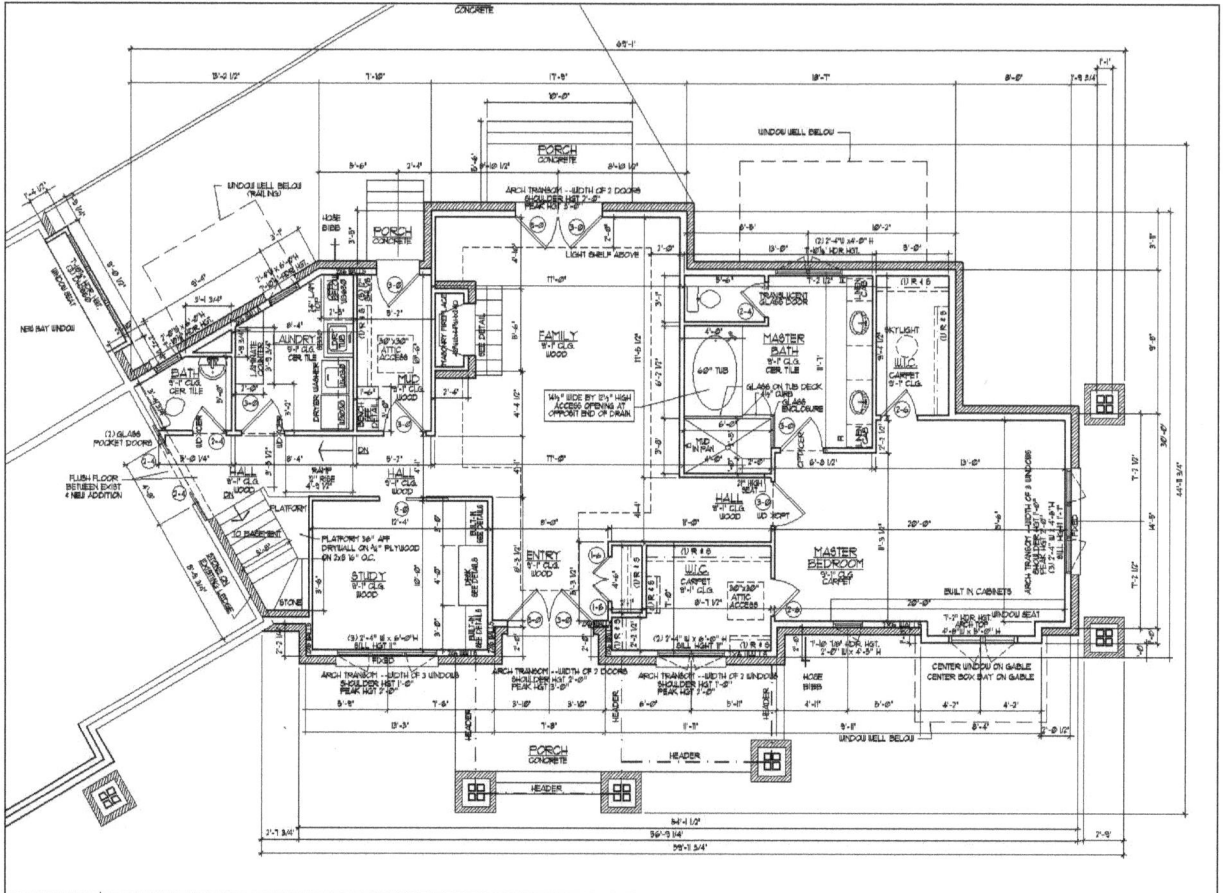

Architectural drawing of a whole first floor of a house.

Product designers have always been aware that they work with systems, not artifacts. Contemporary design firms, like Maya and IDEO, convinced their clients of this fact and significantly increased the role of design within client companies.

The phenomenal economic success of Apple, brought design to the attention of CEOs and managers everywhere. Business began to appreciate that design and design thinking were key for understanding the composite, and in fact the living, systems they now understood themselves to be.

Apple was not the first, but is certainly the most prominent, example of applying design thinking in non-traditional domains. Beginning with product design and the iPod artifact that was really part of a composite system including customers, along with the when, where, and why of their using the device, and, very importantly, the iTunes store and the entire context of music production, distribution, and consumption. The iPod is not a product or device, it is a composite system. An Apple store is also an example of composite system design, one of particular interest to busi-

72

Drawing by product designer Tony Ton.

ness professionals because retail and 'the customer experience' are pre-eminent concerns for many businesses.

Once business turned to IT for strategic advantage and innovation. No longer. Instead design as practiced by design professionals is seen as more promising. As long as IT persists in following Simon's notions of engineering and scientific design, it will lack the insights, the perspective, and the tools necessary to understand and design complex living systems.

"Artistic design"— i.e. the worldview, principles, and practices of architects and applied artists— complements the changes in perspective the business professionals have already adopted. It is important to note that design thinking, as we present it, does not entail wholesale replacement of engineering or scientific design. Instead we see design thinking as complementing, superseding and subsuming those other approaches.

Elements of composite systems, even living ones, can, be systems in and of themselves. They can be artificial and

73

CIRCOS – an information aesthetic for comparative genomics

M Krzywinski, J Schein, I Birol, S Jones, M Marra

Canada's Michael Smith Genome Sciences Centre // British Columbia Cancer Research Centre // *www.bcgsc.ca*

circos - round is the new square

We have created a visualization tool, called Circos, to facilitate exploring relationships between genomes and in general any kind of position *n*-tuples that relate genomic intervals. Structural variation data such as these, produced by sequence alignment and hybridization arrays, underpin comparative studies but are opaque to conventional visualization methods designed for 2D data sets. Compared to other tools [1,2], Circos is unique in its combination of **circular data domain layout**, support for a large number of **diverse data tracks**, global and local length scale control, extensive **customization and automation**, and maintaining a **high data-to-ink ratio** [3] without sacrificing clarity of presentation. Circos has been used within the genomics community [4-6] and its flexibility and aesthetic has garnered interest from mainstream periodicals and newspapers [7-9] and, recently, illustrate the dynamics of a US presidential debate [10].

DOWNLOAD CIRCOS AT http://mkweb.bcgsc.ca/circos

At present, laboratories are hard-pressed not only to store and analyze, but to visualize the reams of data produced by ultra-high-throughput technologies, such as massively parallel sequencing. Because analytically extracting informative patterns from these large data sets is very difficult, automated visualization tools that generate informative vignettes of the data are valuable in data mining and formulating hypotheses.

The design of Circos is based on the fact that a circularly composited ideogram layout can encode relationships between genomic regions more informatively than a linear layout. These relationships are visually encoded by links which can be either straight lines or Bezier curves whose control point location can be highly customizable. Other data types that are supported are **scatter plots, line plots, histograms, tile plots, heatmaps, text and glyph labels, highlights, ideograms**, and **labeled ticks**. The radial position of data tracks is controlled by the user and their angular extent is a function of the extent of the data domain. Data tracks such as the tile and text label have their individual elements automatically positioned to avoid overlap.

Circos uses **plain text files for both input data and configuration**. The latter controls the placement and format of each data track. The ability to generate both data and configuration files automatically makes Circos highly amenable to incorporation in web-based database mining and visualization.

A feature unique to Circos is not only the ability to adjust the length scale for each ideogram (e.g. display chr 17 at 3x normal size), but to **smoothly vary the length scale** locally, effectively zooming (or contracting) regions of interest while still displaying the entire data domain (Figures A1-A3, B1). This global and local scale adjustment is useful when illustrating genomic regions in which data density is highly variable. Furthermore, to help draw attention to important data, the ideograms can be divided into any number of disjoint regions, which in turn can be drawn in any order. The resulting **axis breaks** can be marked up in various styles on the final image to clearly mark the disruption.

Every aspect of the final image is customizable and output can be generated in either **bitmap or SVG** format. For example, the thickness, outline and color of the ideogram track is customizable, as are the corresponding features of the cytogenetic bands. The radial position for each ideogram can be independently set. Each data track, and individual primitives within a track, have an associated z-depth value, which controls how elements stack. Finally, every data type format characteristic, such as color, thickness, data value, label and visibility, can be adjusted by **dynamic formatting rules** based on data position and other format values at run-time (Figures C1-C3). These rule sets are stored in the configuration files and separate the definition and storage of formatting rules from the raw data.

1. Dobkin, S. & Sam-Swammar, P.L. Bioinformatics 20, 576-7 (2004).
2. Kozik, A., Michelmore, C. & Michelmore, R. Bioinformatics 18, 554-6 (2002).
3. Tufte, E. Visual Display of Quantitative Information (Graphics Press, 1992).
4. Ju Yon, O. et al. Nature 449, 463-7 (2007).
5. Avdy, J.M. et al. Nature 444, 171-8 (2006).
6. Campbell, P.J. et al. Nat Genet (2008).
7. Duncan, D.E. Conde Nast Portfolio (November 2007).
8. Ostrander, E.A. American Scientist 95, 406-413 (2007).
9. Corstantine, New York Times (23 January 2007).
10. Dorum, J. & Hossain, P. New York Times (19 December 2007).

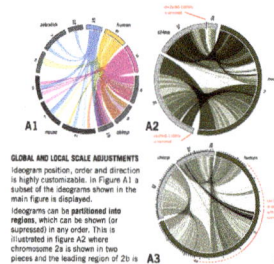

GLOBAL AND LOCAL SCALE ADJUSTMENTS

Ideogram position, order and direction is highly customizable. In Figure A1 a subset of the ideograms shown in the main figure is displayed.

Ideograms can be partitioned into regions, which can be shown (or supressed) in any order. This is illustrated in figure A2 where chromosome 2a is shown in two pieces and the leading region of 2b is removed.

The scale of any ideogram can be globally adjusted. In the main figure the ideograms are scaled by the corresponding species' genome size, in order for each genome to occupy the same fraction of the image.

In addition to global scale adjustment, the scale can be adjusted locally. Any number of regions of an ideogram can be expanded or contracted to create a continuously varying zoom factor along the length of the ideogram. In Figure A3 a region of ideogram 2 is exposed to reveal details in the link position. Length scale directives of overlapping regions combine automatically, with the consensus adjustment taken as the largest scale factor (zoom or constriction) in the region.

2D VIGNETTE: THE STACKED BAR PLOT

Figures D1-D4 show how stacked bar plots can be used to summarize syntenic relationships. The figures here show the total size of syntenic regions between a given window on the mouse genome and each human chromosome. Each stacked bar component is colored by the human chromosome.

Figure D1 shows the data in their original order, where bin components are ordered by chromosomes (1, 2, 3, ...). In Figure D2, components within a bin are reordered by their size. Thus, for any bin, the largest contributing stacked element is shown first.

Figures D3 and D4 show the same data set, but normalized by the sum of each bin's stacked elements.

Although Circos does not perform any data analysis, features such as variable stack order and stack normalization are implemented to help you determine the best way to show your data.

TILE TRACKS

Tiles are spans on ideograms that are drawn in layers to avoid overlap. Tiles are ideal for showing clones, genes, transcripts, and any regions which represent coverage, sampling or structure. Tile location is optimized automatically, based on the number of layers, padding and orientation of stacking.

The tiles in this figure represent the golden path (outer track) and end sequenced clones (inner track). Color is used to indicate source library (e.g. RP11 green, CTD black). Figure B1 also incorporates a local scale adjustment (see Figure A for more details about scale).

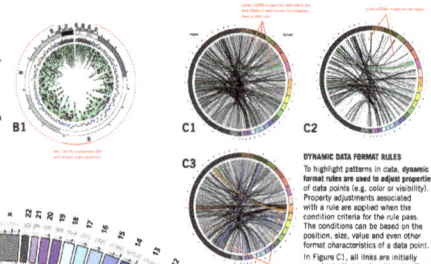

DYNAMIC DATA FORMAT RULES

To highlight patterns in data, dynamic format rules are used to adjust properties of data points (e.g. color or visibility). Property adjustments associated with a rule are applied when the condition criteria for the rule pass. The conditions can be based on the position, size, value and even other format characteristics of a data point.

In Figure C1, all links are initially grey. Links that begin within the first 20Mb of each human chromosome are dynamically (i.e., at run-time) colored green. In Figure C2, an additional rule suppresses the display of links whose extent is greater than 30Mb.

In Figure C3, links that begin on human chromosome 8 are orange, and those that end on mouse chromosome 2 are blue.

Rules can be chained and the chain can be evaluated multiple times. Thus, one rule can adjust a parameter which is then modified further by subsequent rules. Rules can adjust any property of a data point, including format (e.g. color, thickness, transparency) as well as the data point's value, position, or label.

FIGURE LEGEND

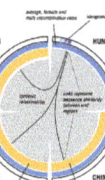

DRAWING 2D DATA

Drawing links is a core feature of Circos. However, it is usually not long before you will need to add other data types to your image, such as 2D sets best represented by scatter, line or histogram plots. Circos supports these, as shown in Figures E1 and E2.

Just like for links, every data point in a data track can be adjusted using dynamic rules. For example, glyphs in a scatter plot can have their size, color and/or visibility adjusted, among other properties.

Histograms can be drawn with an underfill and bins can be enlarged to fill the entire data domain.

All data plots can be drawn with axis divisions and a background color to provide context to the magnitude to the data points and to separate the track from other elements in the image.

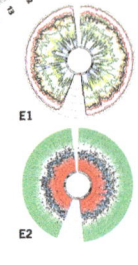

Work example of a graphic designer and the power of visualization of complex information.

deterministic systems. To the extent that such a subsystem/element is to be altered in order to affect the overarching living system, then engineering design principles and practices are likely the best approach to use to design that specific element.

CANADA'S MICHAEL SMITH GENOME SCIENCES CENTRE // BRITISH COLUMBIA CANCER RESEARCH CENTRE // 100-570 W 7TH AVENUE // VANCOUVER BC V5Z 4S6 // CANADA // WWW.BCGSC.CA

Ultra-Large Scale Systems

ULS are extremely large complex composite systems. Figure 2.8 shows some examples. ULS represent the challenge of the future and raise the question, "is design thinking appropriate for ULS?" Our answer to this question is, "Yes" — because the characteristics of remain consistent with composite and living systems as we have discussed them. We also look at the problems or issues that arise from ULS and discover they are the same kind of "Wicked Problems" that have motivated advocates of design thinking for the enterprise.

Characteristics of ULS begin with the fact that they are heterogenous: the elements are a mixture of complex, deterministic, natural, and artificial elements. All composite systems have this same mixture of elements. Does the relative proportion of the element types make a difference as to whether or not design thinking relevant? Does simple magnitude, the total number of elements, make a difference? We would argue, "no." Composite systems, whatever the scale, can be decomposed into composite systems of lesser scope and scale.

Eventually, at lower levels of scale, the elements exposed, even if still systems, might be of a different 'type', e.g. deterministic. When that occurs, it is perfectly appropriate to apply engineering design principles and practices to the designful alteration of those systems/elements.

Some characteristics of ULS are shared by all composite systems, but are more obvious at scale. Specifically, char-

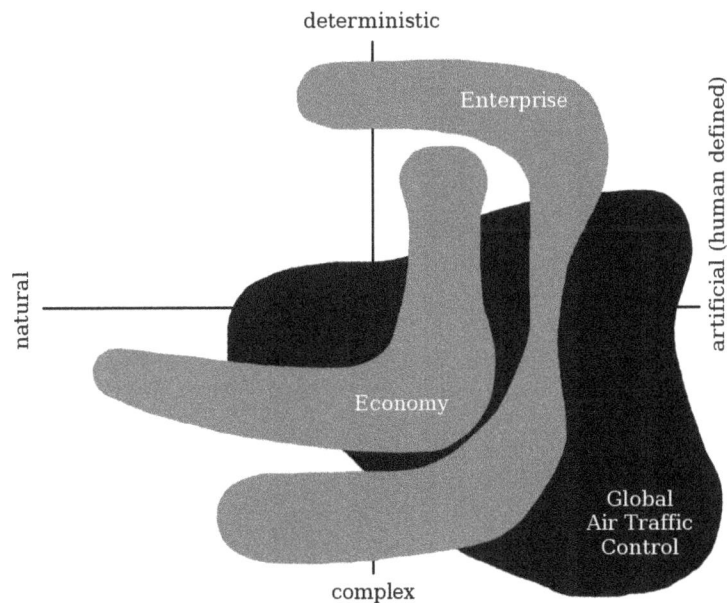

Figure 2.8
Ultra Large Scale Systems (ULS).

75

acteristics like the fact that all elements are autonomous, both in terms of operation and management. Operational autonomy has been recognized in the business world with responses like 'employee empowerment' and in the software world with the concept of object-oriented programming. Managerial independence was first recognized by Napoleon and his creation of a General Staff to run his army. Business has resisted, to some extent, this notion; choosing instead to focus on a single hierarchical 'chain of command'. Large multinational organizations forced the enterprise to acknowledge this kind of managerial independence and recognize that it applied within corporations at lesser levels of scale.

Perhaps the most interesting characteristic of ULS is the blurring of lines among and between elements — especially human beings and other elements. One of the most prominent examples, long known to the design professional, concerns the environment, the space, in which work is done and the human doing the work. Cognitive function is directly enhanced or impaired by the workspace.

Recognizing that the human being is more than a passive consumer of outputs from other system elements, and more than a provider of discrete, well defined inputs to other elements, is easier in ULS. This is a critical point for differentiating between 'engineering design' and 'design thinking' as presented in this book.

There are many other characteristics of ULS that are also characteristics of any composite system. Perhaps the most telling is the nature of the problems that arise — Wicked Problems as we will discuss next.

Wicked Problems

Look once again at our four quadrant categorization of systems and superimpose two additional, but intimately related, factors — breadth of knowledge and certainty of knowledge — as arrows beginning at the top of the diagram and proceeding downward. The arrow labeled certainty of knowledge is widest at the top of the diagram and narrowest at the bottom. The arrow, breadth of knowledge, is the exact opposite.

As we move from the deterministic to the complex any intentional design action requires an increasing amount, both breadth and depth, of knowledge. Knowledge of the system, what changes are possible, what the outcomes of

The internet is the largest example of a composite system — the complex Web, sitting on the deterministic infrastructure of the Internet.

76

the change might precipitate, and what the resulting state of the system might be.

Only with that knowledge can we be assured that the changes we introduce will result in a preferred state.

While the required knowledge increases in scope, the less certain we become as to whether or not we have all of the knowledge and have the right knowledge. There is also an issue as to how different bits of knowledge are prioritized or related. We are entering the realm of "wicked problems."

C. West Churchman introduced the concept of a wicked problem, based on the work of Horst Rittel, presented in a seminar that Churchman attended. A wicked problem, "is difficult or impossible to solve because of incomplete, contradictory, and changing requirements that are often difficult to recognize." The domain that prompted the first formulation of the characteristics shared by wicked problems was urban planning, city design.

Environmental change exemplifies the nature of wicked problems. Climate is intimately and intricately connected to economics, to public safety, to international politics, and culture-based human adaption to the environment — and more.

There is no "solution" to the problem, only various ways of ameliorating future effects. It is quite possible that whatever we do to 'correct' the situation today will cause worse effects in the future because "solutions" introduce positive feedback to a delicate system and can easily cause that system to deviate from any semblance of 'control' or regularity.

We mentioned earlier that Rittel, along with Christopher Alexander and Herbert Simon, once believed that design could be reduced to a science and engineering discipline.

Only Simon continues to hold to this notion. For Rittel, the characteristics of a wicked problem precluded the possibility of an engineering discipline because of the dependence of engineering on well formulated and highly specified initial and resulting conditions. If you cannot specify, completely and accurately, initial conditions and requirements, if there are no algorithmic paths to solutions, if there are unknown and even unknowable variables or values of variables, and if your solutions tend to create new and unexpected problems — you are confronting a wicked problem.

Some important characteristics of wicked problems include: the lack of a definitive formulation (it is difficult or impossible to state exactly what the problem is); solutions are relative and lack definitive tests (no right or wrong answers); every wicked problem is unique (there is no family of similar problems with similar solutions); each wicked problem is a symptom of some other wicked problem (there is no stopping point, a wicked problem with a definitive solution from which you can backtrace a solution set); finding a solution does not expand your understanding of the problem. In addition, in a composite or ULS system there is a huge potential for circularity, "solving" one problem leads to redefinition of the problem space and hence the problem.

Rittel also believed that "the social planner has no right to be wrong" which was really a statement about liability for the actions taken by the planner in attempting to solve the problem.

The most cited examples of wicked problems include global warming, economic systems, food production-distribution-consumption systems, urban planning, and healthcare. This kind of scale is not necessary for a problem to be wicked.

Many business problems, for example, are wicked problems, because they arise from dynamic complex composite systems, involve unknown variables, and require knowledge from domains, e.g. psychology and anthropology, not covered in a typical MBA education.

For example, consider a retail store with a goal of customer satisfaction. The problem: sometimes a customer is satisfied only if they can 'undo' a transaction. Therefore the store must design a 'return' policy and procedure. This is a wicked problem because there is no solution, no policy and procedure, that will not generate exceptions and/or create unintended consequences. An example of an unintended consequence would be the customer that makes a purchase, knowing in advance that it is for a one-time use, and then making a return — turning a "sale" into a "rental."

Wicked problems are common in the lower right quadrant of our diagram, human constructed and complex; and endemic, if not intrinsic, in the lower left, natural and complex. The largest domain for wicked problems are ultra-large scale and/or living systems. The challenge for contemporary business is that more and more of the problems faced and the solutions required occur in the realm of ultra-large scale, complex systems.

Wicked problems are dramatically different than merely hard problems, regardless of how hard the hard problems might be. Hard problems are solvable, in principle, with engineering design thinking. Wicked problems are not.

We can illustrate the difference by considering computer programming and information systems.

Programs and information systems are 'designed' — the programmer's actions are intentioned and informed and have the intent of transforming the state of a system to a preferred one. The knowledge required is precise definition of inputs and outputs and the syntax of a computer language. If we wish to optimize for efficiency and resource consumption, additional knowledge of algortithms and data structures, knowledge of how a compiler does its work, or even the operation codes embedded on the computer chip, can be useful.

Design thinking for computer programming is formulaic and certain — it is the subset of design thinking we have named, "engineering design." In principle it is even subject to formal proof of correctness. If we assume that inputs, outputs, and transforms are correct and complete, the program can, in fact, be created by another machine — another computer program — without human intervention at all. And it could, in principle, be written correct in one pass, no trial and error required.

If, in contrast, we look at information systems — on the surface, just a collection of programs — qualitative differences in the system at issue are encountered. For one thing all of the data becomes dependent on context and is highly variable. E.g., "salaried employees are not paid overtime, except ... and may take comp time calculated as ... instead." This has enormous impact with regard the ability to completely and correctly specify inputs and outputs to the system (collection of programs). This is part of the reason while Agile software development, as one example, attempted to replace specific requirements with a collection of aformal tools like user stories, on-site customer, test-driven development, and pair programming.

Engineering design sufficient for writing programs is not sufficient for designing information systems; nor business systems, as they are deemed living and not merely deterministic systems.

Additional thinking tools, embracing and leveraging ambiguity, support for design as a collective activity, integration of broad realms of knowledge — all of this is required for any discipline of design thinking sufficient to address wicked problems and enhance living systems.

Many of these tools, techniques, and practices have been developed in the traditional design community — architecture and the applied arts. Our task in this book is to bring those tools to the attention of the business and IT communities while showing professionals with design expertise how they can best use that expertise working with clients in non-traditional design domains.

Summary

Contemporary enterprises, from businesses to governments, need solutions for wicked problems arising from the fact that the enterprise is a complex composite system. The environment within which that enterprise operates is also a complex composite system, often a ultra-large scale system.

Traditional, science and engineering-based approaches were developed to facilitate solution of complicated problems arising from complicated, but deterministic, systems. Engineering design thinking is insufficient for the solution of wicked problems.

Design professionals deal with complex composite systems and wicked problems as a matter of course; and, they are aware that they do so. Designers have developed a perspective, discovered principles, and developed practices that facilitate their work and that body of knowledge and experience — which we call design thinking — can be applied to the enterprise and to domains like software systems design. The next chapters will show how.

Chapter 3
Designer's Mind

Designing is more than simply 'doing design'. Being a designer means being part of a culture — a community with shared world views, perspective, values, norms, practices, and technology. Those who have traditionally been recognized as designers are a part of this community and recognize in each other their common culture.

Extending design thinking to other disciplines like business and software requires more than simply copying some techniques and a conceptual vocabulary. It requires familiarity and understanding of the culture of design. We are not saying you have to be a designer to use design thinking, but you do need sufficient familiarity with the culture that you are comfortable and confident in your interactions with that culture.

Think of what you would need to do if you moved from your home country and culture to one quite different — what would you need to do in order to "fit in" and function smoothly in your new home? Business has long recognized the need to be culturally aware so as to avoid embarrassing situations that violate cultural norms. In the case of the design culture, the awareness and the sensitivity required prevents you from misunderstanding, 'taking things out of context', and failing to adopt and adapt practices in a beneficial manner.

Both business and IT have a long history of 'borrowing' ideas and practices from other disciplines — or innovative ideas arising from within business or IT — by rote, simple mimicry, or literal application. Absent any understanding of the culture behind the practices or the philosophy behind the ideas the inevitable result is disenchantment and abandonment. This history is rightfully mocked, e.g. in the popular Dilbert comic strips [Figure 3.1] (see next page), as a sequence of meaningless and valueless "fads."

Another term for rote adoption of practice without understanding is "Cargo Cult." [See sidebar next page] Whether or not design thinking will avoid being "just another fad"

Figure 3.1
Comic strip Dilbert by Scott Adams.

depends on the degree to which advocates are successful in communicating an understanding of the culture behind design thinking.

Meaning of Design

In Chapter One we offered a pragmatic definition of the concept of design but we did not look at the meaning of the word itself. A quick look at the dictionary definition, which is based on how the word is used, reveals divergent meanings.

Pervasive in all variations of definition is the notion of a "plan" and a model, e.g. drawings like blueprints. Even when the model is "in the mind" there is a presumption that it has formality and syntactic rigor. When computer scientists like Fred Brooks talk of 'design' it is precisely this definition of design that is in play.

Brooks is famous for a paper, *No Silver Bullet*, that discusses why programming is so hard. The most critical aspect of programming is the inability for the programmer to construct and hold a mental model, i.e. a design, of the program in operation. This model needs to be as formal and syntactically rigorous as the computer itself. In the paper Brooks said the only answer to the challenge of increasingly complex programs was "better designers."

Previously we have spoken of 'engineering design' by which we meant this dictionary definition of design — the construction of a formal model and a plan, a sequence of specific and equally formal steps, to be executed to change the system that the model ostensibly represents.

Those in architecture and the applied arts adhere to a quite different notion of design, one more closely aligned with the etymology of the word. Kostas Terzidis, an architect

Thus, from its Greek definition, design is about incompleteness, indefiniteness, or imperfection, yet it also is about likelihood, expectation, or anticipation. In its largest sense, design signifies not only the vague, intangible, or ambiguous, but also the strive to capture the elusive.

86

Cargo Cults

During World War II, the U.S. established military airfields on various Pacific islands inhabited by pre-industrial peoples. In addition to armaments, airplanes landing at those fields included 'cargo' of food, clothing and tools; some of which was shared with the native people.

When the war ended the airfields were abandoned and 'cargo' ceased to arrive. The natives began erecting primitive structures resembling airplanes and airport control towers and engaged in elaborate activities resembling the semaphore signals used by ground crew to direct the landing of airplanes. All with the intent of attracting planes and cargo.

The natives adopted, by rote and without understanding, practices that had worked for others. Their results were, of course, disappointing!

and professor at the Harvard Graduate School of Design, provides an excellent discussion in his book, Algorithmic Architecture.

> *"Etymologically, the verb 'design' is derived from the prefix 'de' and the Latin verb 'signare', which means to mark, mark out, or sign.*
>
> *The prefix 'de' is used not in the derogatory sense of opposition or reversal, but in the constructive sense of derivation, deduction, or inference. In that context, the word 'design' is about the derivation of something that suggests the presence or existence of a fact, condition, or quality. In Greek, the word 'design' is σχέδιο (pronounced schedio), which is derived from the root σχεδόν (pronounced schedon), which means "nearly, almost, about, or approximately." Thus, from its Greek definition, design is about incompleteness, indefiniteness, or imperfection, yet it also is about likelihood, expectation, or anticipation. In its largest sense, design signifies not only the vague, intangible, or ambiguous, but also the strive to capture the elusive."*

It is both interesting and important to note the relationship between the above etymology and a separate but related word 'sketch' (the Greek schedio/schedon in the quote above).

The sketch is central to the design process, often the very first step in articulating an idea. A sketch is clearly incomplete and imperfect but it also anticipates or expects, and it is intended to be almost and approximately the target, the outcome, of the design process.

Thinking about the sketch illustrates another inversion of meaning, in this instance the arrow of time, between contemporary and original meanings of the word, 'design'.

> *"Traveling further back into the origin of the Greek word schedon, one may find that it is derived from the word eschein, which is the past tense of the word eho, which in English means to have, hold, or possess. Translating the etymological context into English, it can be said that design is about something we once had, but have no longer."*

So, according to the Greeks, design is linked indirectly to a loss of possession and a search into an oblivious state of memory. This linguistic connection reveals an antithetical attitude towards design, one that, in the west ern culture at least, is about stepping into the future, as asearch for new entities, processes, and forms, frequently expressed by the terms "novelty" or "innovation".

Curled fern frond

With the addition of the time factor, a sketch is associated with memory. Sketching is an act that evokes memories, sometimes primordial memories, each line being the trigger for another aspect of memory, something we already know but have forgotten, until we reach the point that the sketch is sufficient to recall to memory the whole, and it is then that we can progress with our design efforts. Sketching merits elaboration and further discussion and we will provide this in the next chapter, Designing.

It is essential to put the definition, the etymology of design as a concept in its philosophical context — the world of Xenophanes, Parmenides and Zeno and a presupposition common to them all:

> "The assumption that nothing comes out of nothing and nothing disappears into nothing (i.e., nothing can just pop up or vanish without a trace). Such an assumption is very important to understand their reluctance to conceive, accept, or understand the concept of novelty in its modern sense. If everything is indestructible, then change is nothing but a transformation from one state to another; the appearance or disappearance of parts is only phenomenal; nothing is added or subtracted. Therefore, if something emerges, appears, or claims to be new, then it must be nothing but an illusion because, if it is not, it would contradict the initial premise of preservation. Such logic, while it may appear to be simplistic or absolute, it is also very powerful because it does not allow thoughts to be affected by sensory phenomena."

Design in this context is almost the opposite of the modern connotations associated with the word — e.g. novelty, creation, innovation — that imply design springs forth spontaneously in the mind of the designer, appearing from nowhere and grounded only in the genius of the designer.

Designers themselves know that the contemporary connotations are not correct. Authors frequently note that they are merely the instrument by which the characters express themselves and their story. Artists will say, "I paint what I see." Many architects, especially those in the participatory design school of thought, like Alexander, will note that the house is an expression of the people living in it and the site upon which it is built.

Central to design thinking is the notion that the 'form', the essence of the target of design, already exists and it is the designer's role to help that form take shape — an outward manifestation of form — a role more akin to midwife than mother. Christopher Alexander, in *Nature of Order*, speaks of a process of unfolding — a series of "essence preserving

transformations" that enable the form intrinsic to the seed to assume the shape of the flower. Alexander's ideas are completely compatible with the Greek philosophers and the understanding of design and the designer's role that we are expressing in this book.

This understanding is critical, because 'good' design, or design that exhibits QWAN (Quality Without A Name), arises only from a deep understanding of both artifact and context. You must understand the essence of the thing, the form, before you can see the transformatio necessary for proper expression. You must understand the context and the forces in that context that must be satisfied by the correct form assuming the optimal shape.

Terzidis offers a helpful perspective on what we are saying.

"The verb "to become" is used in English to denote the action of coming into existence, emerging, or appearing. In language, as opposed to formal logic, existence is a predicate rather than a quantifier, and the passage from copulative to existential can be misleading. The action of coming-to-be or becoming does not necessarily have to be associated with creation, beginning, or emergence, but rather may denote a process of derivation, transformation, or transition from one state to another. Indeed, transition is the act of becoming, except that its connotation is problematic because, as Evans points out, "… whatever is subject to the transformation must already be complete in all its parts".

Business and software designers confront a situation where much of their effort is actually focused on revisiting and updating previous ad hoc designs. As noted earlier, the past century has witnessed massive amounts of haphazard, unconscious design, with unwanted consequences. As we engage in design, in the present, it is necessary to acknowledge that our work is in a very real sense a continuation of the same effort. As we begin our design work, and seek to understand the system we are working with, we will see evidence of its history and evolution. We will see paths that have led to a perversion of the system's form as well as paths that affirm and preserve essence. We should seek to learn from these examples and conform current decisions to that history we understand to be affirming. Only then will we be in a position to design what we really want.

The importance of understanding 'what is', before undertaking an exploration of 'what might be', is familiar to software developers. From the first days of Structured Analysis, the first step of the process was the construction of a model of the existing system. Only when the current system, usually a manual business process or tangible

" *Design is a conceptual activity involving formulating an idea intended to be expressed in a visible form or carried into action. Design is about conceptualization, imagination, and interpretation.*

Design is a vague, ambiguous, and indefinite process of genesis, emergence, or formation of something to be executed, but whose starting point, origin, or process often are uncertain.

It is about the primordial stage of capturing, conceiving, and outlining the main features of a plan and, as such, it always precedes the planning stage.

artifact, was understood, it was claimed, was the software developer/designer in a position to identity what changes might be made and where they might be applied in order to transform the system to a desired state.

Similarly, the second step was to model the desired state of the system in a way that did not presuppose implementation. You were supposed to understand the elements of the existing system in their own terms before you force-fit them into whatever shape allowed by a particular programming language or development environment.

Additionally, it is useful to see design in contrast to terms with which it is frequently associated, or even used as if they were synonyms. Planning is such a word. Terzidis points out:
"Planning is the act of devising a scheme, program, or method worked out beforehand for the accomplishment of an objective. Planning is about realization, organization, and execution."

Design in contrast:
"Is a conceptual activity involving formulating an idea intended to be expressed in a visible form or carried into action. Design is about conceptualization, imagination, and interpretation. Design is a vague, ambiguous, and indefinite process of genesis, emergence, or formation of something to be executed, but whose starting point, origin, or process often are uncertain. Design provides the spark of an idea and the formation of a mental image. It is about the primordial stage of capturing, conceiving, and outlining the main features of a plan and, as such, it always precedes the planning stage."

Another association subject to misinterpretation is between design and innovation.

In contemporary times, we see innovation as an act of invention — "Invention is defined as the act of causing something to exist by the use of ingenuity or imagination. It is an artificial human creation." Innovation, in this understanding of the term does not exist. Instead innovation, if it is to be properly associated with design, must conform to our understanding, in etymological and metaphysical terms, of design.

This, in turn, leads to a different association — design is closely aligned with the idea of discovery, "Discovery is the act of encountering, for the first time, something that already existed;" and, a different definition of innovation as adding embellishment or of recombining elements and establishing alternative relationship among them, elements that are and always have been. Design is discovering the essence of what is, and always has been, and bringing it into contemporary awareness.

Implicit throughout this etymological discussion is a critical point concerning 'ego'. The point can best be illustrated with an analogy. Consider a farmer. A farmer might take great pride in facilitating the growth of a crop, of meticulously determining the needs of the crop and tirelessly working to create optimal conditions for the crop to grow, to express itself as mature and nutritious. The farmer responds appropriately to changing conditions — conditions over which he has no control, like the weather — affording the crop the best possible environment in which to express itself. The farmer does not, however, take credit for the the crop itself. The essence of the crop was always implicit in the seed — the initial state of the crop — and the farmer takes credit only for facilitating that seed to express itself.

The same can be true for the designer of artifacts, software, business processes, and systems.

Designer's take pride in their ability to discern pre-existing essence and in the facilitation of that essence to express itself in the manner most appropriate for the context of that expression. Designer's do not take credit for the essence itself.

Making a distinction between where the designer's ego is and is not appropriately manifest — as stated above, in the facilitation, not the essence — becomes a major issue when design is seen as subject of study in academia. Christopher Alexander's discussion of the "self-conscious process of design" illustrates what happens when a professional design practice — in his case architecture — becomes an academic discipline. We will explore in the following section; but the critical point is how academic forces shift the manifestation of 'ego' to focus on 'theory', and all abstract theories about that essence, instead of facilitation.

Art — Science — Discipline

A philosophy of design begins with the understanding of language and the meaning of terms, as we discussed in the preceding section. The practice of design evolved to being a profession and then an academic discipline — prompting the perceived need for a rigorous philosophical foundation that would support the education and training of new entrants to the profession. This philosophical foundation, as

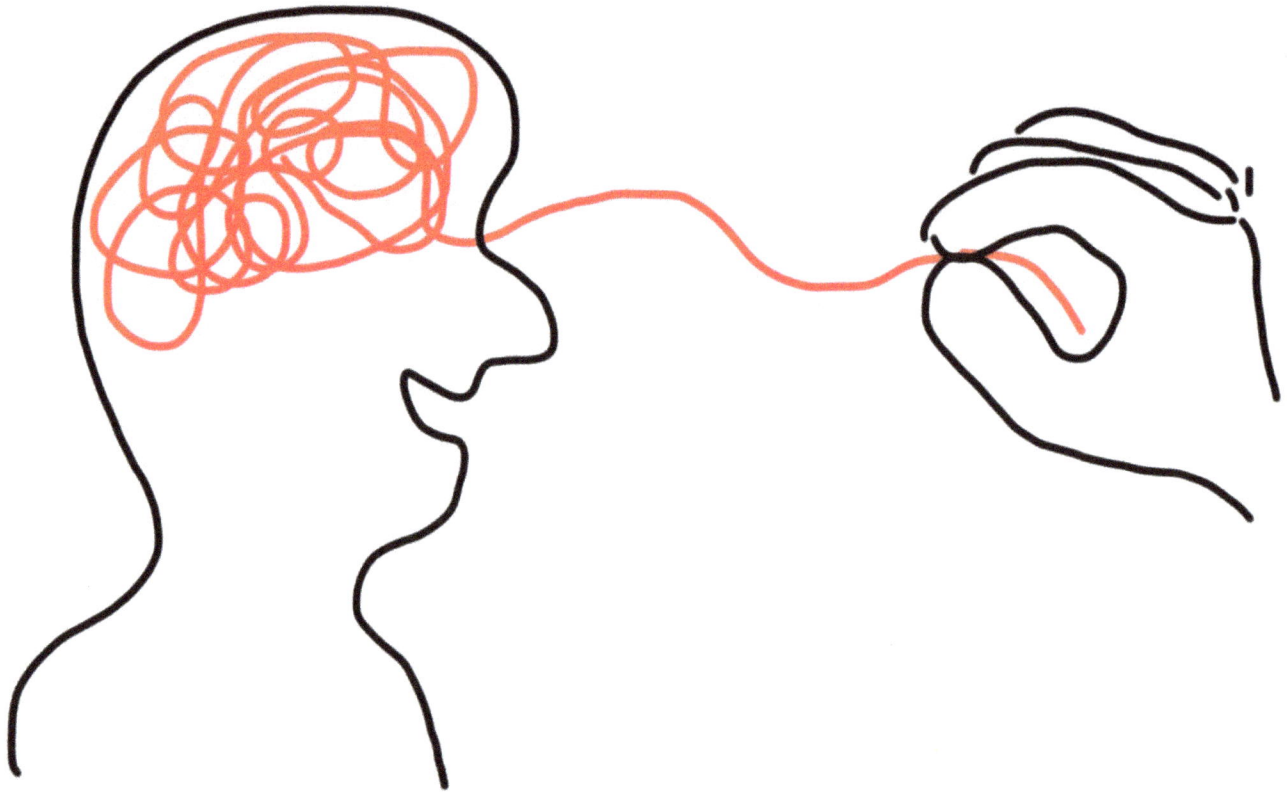

Alexander pointed out in "the self conscious process"
is focused, wrongly, on 'theory'.

Initial efforts in this direction came from designers who
engaged in retrospection as a means to discover and
articulate what it was that designer's did, what concepts
and ideas were fundamental to that doing, and what criteria could be used to determine the "goodness" of design
efforts. Initially, this effort focused on 'practice' and was
concerned with the knowledge that would help designers
be better practitioners.

When reading this material today, one is struck by the
implicit and explicit assumption that design was an "Art,"
acknowledging that some aspects of that art — particularly the discernment of essence — could not be captured in
formula or process.

In order for design to become a credible academic subject
it was necessary to go beyond teaching and explaining
"mere practice and technique" (trade schools could do that)
to the development and refinement of abstract theory that
"explained" the foundations of practice and technique. Of
special importance was the need to "explain" the ineffable
'essence' of any and every design. The result, as Alexander

94

pointed out with architecture, was an efflorescence of 'theory'.

A designer's merit or ability then shifted as well: away from facilitating the expression of innate essence in context, to rigid application of formula that assured a design outcome conformed to the dictates of the design theory being employed at the moment. [See sidebar on epicycles, page 99.]

In the late nineteenth and early twentieth centuries, the Western world was enthralled with the idea of "Science" as the ultimate good. In the University, academic legitimacy was dependent upon the degree to which a field of study was 'scientific' in nature and approach. Both existing, e.g. sociology and psychology, and emerging, e.g. business and computing, were determined to express themselves as formal, quan titative, and experimental — to be "just like Physics."

The field of Design was not immune to this impulse and in the mid-twentieth century there was a concerted effort to develop a "Science of Design." In an earlier chapter we mentioned four individuals who made significant contributions to our understanding of what a 'science of design' might be: Herbert Simon, Horst Rittel, Pelle Ehn, and Christopher Alexander.

Herbert Simon is the only member of that group who dogmatically insists that design should be a formal "science" — "intellectually tough, analytic, formalizable, and teachable." (See page 100) He constantly sees design as engineering and optimization. He describes the design process thusly:

"The 'inner environment' of the design problem is represented by a set of given alternatives of action. The alternatives may be given in extenso: more commonly they are specified in terms of command variables that have defined domains. The 'outer environment' is represented by a set of parameters, which may be known with certainty or only in terms of a probability distribution. The goals for adaptation of inner to outer environment are defined by a utility function; a function, usually scalar, of the command variables and environmental parameters perhaps supplemented by a number of constraints (inequalities, say, between functions of the command variables and environmental parameters). The optimization problem is to find an admissible set of values of the command variables, compatible with the constraints, that maximize the utility function for the given values of the environmental parameters."

"Sorry George. Teaching, however inspiring and brilliant, is NOT sufficient if you want to be a part of this team. You MUST publish."

In contrast, Christopher Alexander, the architect, also began a quest for a "science of design" in the 1960s. In his book, *Notes on the Synthesis of Form*, Alexander sought, and posited, a formal 'calculus of design' but quickly abandoned those ideas in favor of patterns and a search for the properties essential to 'Life'.

Horst Rittel, also an architect and designer, did not author a book that documents his ideas on the science of design; instead delivering those ideas in lectures that were documented and commented upon by others.

Pelle Ehn presents a more interesting case: proposing a 'science of design' that is in dramatic opposition to Simon's rationalistic design science. Ehn knows and understands Simon's program and this understanding enables him to point out where and why that program proves inadequate to the design tasks that dominate Ehn's own interest and experience.

Ehn was a central figure in what was called "The Scandinavian School of Design". He was committed to two design ideals: democratizing the workplace; and, the design of skill enhancing tools for the production of quality products and services. His goal was the 'Utopia' of a democratic, pleasurable and creative working life in the era of the computer.

Immediately apparent in Ehn's work is a different 'scoping' of the system that is being designed. Simon is interested only in the artificial system — the computer and the program(s) that the computer executes — while Ehn is interested in the contextual system, the enterprise, the artificial artifacts (computers and software), the people interacting with those artifacts, and the socio-political environment of the whole enterprise. Ehn is concerned with the kind of system that we described in Chapter Two as a 'composite system' — a complex system of interacting complex-natural and complicated-artificial elements.

The breadth of knowledge required to understand and design changes to such a system is far greater than that required to build a large scale but merely complicated artificial system. Ehn concludes that Simon's program is inadequate but does propose a curriculum, a program, for teaching design and grounding it upon an appropriate theoretical foundation.

Ehn draws from the work of a diverse group, including: philosophers like the Dreyfus brothers and Churchland; computer scientists and software engineers like Naur, Floyd, Winograd; designers like Rittel and Alexander; and, social theoreticians like Ackoff. Ehn eventually proposes

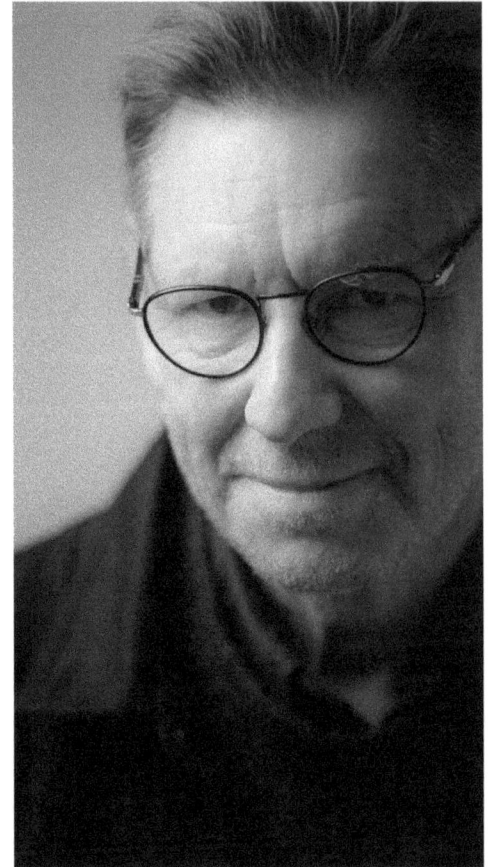

Pelle Ehn is Professor of Interaction Design at Malmö University's School of Arts and Communication in the south of Sweden.

a design curriculum and program, not a self-contained 'science', of design. His program emphasizes understanding social systems over engineering systems and practice over theory. Design is ultimately mastered through practice and the comparison of one's own practice with that of master designers. His curriculum and program parallel how Art is taught in the university, not how science is taught.

It is also worth noting that Ehn's focus on the interdependency of computing (designed artifacts) and the workplace (context in which they are deployed) along with his recognition of the need to design for the integrated whole, anticipates the impact that design thinking can have on the enterprise. Today, the business and its information technology are seen as two separate systems — interdependent to be sure, but still separate. Integration of these two systems has been a kind of 'holy grail' for decades but, despite efforts ranging from objects to service-oriented architecture (SOA) to Agile development, has yet to be achieved.

Active participation in design by non-designers, e.g. unions and workers, was another hallmark of Ehn's work. Design, according to the Scandinavian School, is not something done by an external group of designers and then imposed on others; instead it is a participatory activity where those affected by the design are co-designers. Christopher Alexander echo's Ehn's ideas and makes participatory design central to his theory of architecture and building.

Organizations should be aware that the effectiveness of design thinking increases with the breadth of participation. A business with a pervasive design culture will see better results than one with a design department.

The value of design, for Ehn and the Scandinavian School, was primarily moral — design was seen as the key to assure that computer artifacts and the system in which they were deployed enhanced work, enhanced the outcomes of work, and enhanced the work place and the enterprise. Enhancement was seen in terms of humanity and society: design is valuable to the extent it makes the world a better place.

Perhaps the key difference in the two approaches comes from the fact that Ehn was interested in 'designing the world, specifically the workplace, and Simon was concerned with designing artificial replicants of the world. When it came to computer artifacts, something central to both approaches, Ehn saw them as tools deployed in the world and interacting with people in that world, while Simon was concerned with how the computer artifact could accurately and faithfully mimic the world.

Alexander and Rittel essentially abandoned their initial interest in a Simon-like science of design to adopt perspectives and programs that paralleled Ehn's efforts. Both men were motivated, in part, by their work in urban planning and the design of large complex systems like cities. Alexander, in *A City is Not a Tree*, argued why a city could not be systematically and algorithmically designed as a hierarchical decision tree structure, the way that Simon claimed it could and should be. Rittel found the city to be the same kind of living system as Ehn's workplace: artificial artifacts deployed in a composite system with complex-natural (people, culture, communities, parks) and complex-artificial (economics, governments) components. Rittel refocuses his work on approaches to the solution of "wicked problems" as discussed in the previous chapter.

Alexander focused his efforts on unquantifiable qualities, like beauty, fit, QWAN (Qual-ity Without A Name), and eventually "liveness." Alexander's work also reflects a desire for a discipline of design, albeit without the kind of mathematical formality that he pursued in his earliest work.

All of this lead to the conclusion that a designer's mind is a disciplined mind. Like a master musician, the designer's insights and interpretations derive first from practice, then from understanding the work of prior masters, then from theory — theory that is descriptive, e.g. the mathematical ratios among notes of a scale — not prescriptive. A disciplined mind is applied to problems in context, just as the musician shapes her performance of the essence of the musical work, for this instrument, in this venue, for this audience, at this time — no two expressions of the music being identical because no two contexts are identical.

"As professional schools, including the independent engineering schools, were more and more absorbed into the general culture of the university, they hankered after academic respectability. In terms of the prevailing norms, academic respectability calls for subject matter that is intellectually tough, analytic, formalizable, and teachable.

In the past much, if not most, of what we knew about design and about the artificial sciences was intellectually soft, intuitive, informal, and cook-booky. Why would anyone in a university stoop to teach or learn about designing machines or planning market strategies when he could concern himself with solid-state physics? The answer has been clear: he usually wouldn't."

Herbert Simon

Epicycles

The astronomical theory of Ptolemy (et. al.), as popularly understood, was intended to scientifically and mathematically explain the orbits of the planets in our solar system. The theory presupposed that the Earth was the center of the system and that perfect circles and spheres structured that system. Observations, however, contradicted the theory, the planets did not move as they were supposed to. So the theory was elaborated with epicycles, and epicycles within epicycles, to better account for observations. Epicycles and "adding epicycles" became, unfairly, the epitome of "Bad Science." As a metaphor for how academic theory influences practice, however, epicycles are dead on. This was the point of Alexander's discussion of the "self conscious process."

Ptolemy and his work.

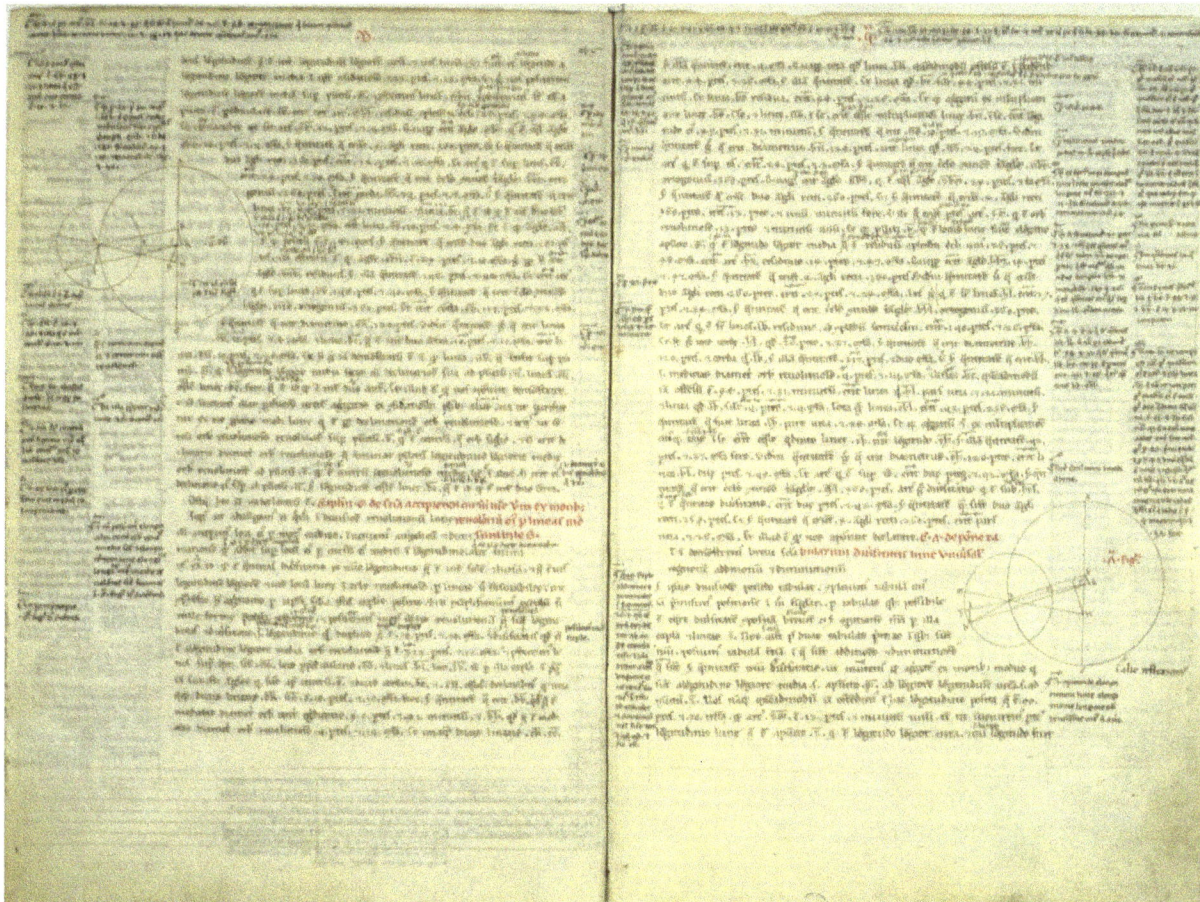

Empathy

Empathy is both a corollary and an elaboration of the ideas discussed as we explored the etymology of the word 'design'.

Design begins with the (re) discovery of something already present, already existing, and not the creation, from nothing, of a new thing. To be good at design is to excel at seeing and recognizing what is already there. Moreover, that which is 'already there' is an essence that may only be partially evident in the current expression of that essence. Discovery often requires seeing past mere shape (expression) in order to discern form (essence).

Recognition of essence or form is the beginning of design but the re-expression of essence is the outcome, the goal. This cannot be successfully accomplished without a deep understanding of the essence and an equally deep understanding of the context that simultaneously facilitates and constrains any expression. The understanding of essence reveals potential and possibility — an imaginative space of what might be. Understanding of context facilitates the decision as to which of the possible is the optimal, at this time and in this place.

A designer's understanding necessarily transcends the merely intellectual enumeration and comparison of characteristics and attributes. This is the reason we use the term 'empathy' as we discuss designer's mind. Empathy implies emotive aspects of understanding, like respect. Empathy transcends recognition and requires identification.

A craftsman respects both the material he works and the tools he works with. A sculptor is able to discern exactly which of the blocks of marble before him contains the statue that will emerge. Craftsmen have a multitude of tools because he respects the fact that each tool is capable of doing something special and he would not think of asking a tool to violate its integrity by using it in an inappropriate circumstance or for the wrong task. Respect is a manifestation of 'identification' — seeing yourself in the other and the other in yourself.

Identification and empathy are almost synonyms. We see this when we say we empathize with another human being — we identify with that person, seeing in them our own nature and their nature as our own. We have more difficulty in empathizing or identifying with things other than people and seldom assert empathy with a business or a piece of software. In part, this is because empathy is a continuum. At one extreme we have the mystical empathy / identifica-

The Breath of Empathy by Maja Vuckovic.

101

tion of self with the Universe and at the other the seemingly total lack of identification of ourselves with, for example, a machine.

The empathy required of a designer's mind is an appropriate balance between the two extremes. This balance can be found by addressing two forces that inhibit empathy: alienation and theory.

Alienation arises when we see, or believe, that there is no commonality between ourselves as human beings and the Other. For example, we believe we can have empathy for other people and have little trouble extending that belief to "charismatic mega-fauna" like dogs, cats, elephants and dolphins. Empathy is more problematic in the case of reptiles and insects; even more so in the case of viruses that share only the trait of being a living thing. Non-living things are completely alien — a galaxy, machine, or computer program.

Humans in general, and designers in particular have and will find great value in 'simulating' the circumstances that allow us to feel empathy with things that would otherwise be alien and from which we would otherwise be alienated. Personification and anthropomorphization — naming and ascribing human characteristics to non-human things are very common examples. We might name our car, for example, and talk as if it were human; cursing at it when it obstinately refuses to start on a cold winter's morning.

When the concept and metaphor of "object" was introduced to the software community, it was stated that an optimal approach to the design of a software object was to be found in anthropomorphization. Think about an object as if it were a tiny human being, a homunculus, with resources, abilities, responsibilities, and knowledge. Thinking this way created a kind of 'artificial empathy' which, in turn, led to very different designs for software modules; designs that maximized cohesion and minimized coupling — two essential criteria for optimal modularization of computer programs.

The other barrier to empathy we loosely labeled 'theory'. By this we mean, essentially, what Christopher Alexander described as the "self conscious process." Alexander noted that when architecture became a profession and an academic discipline, architects and teachers of architecture tended to focus their efforts on the creation of grand theories of what architecture should be. They evaluated architectural designs in terms of its conformance, or lack thereof, to a particular Theory. Any and all sense of an essence expressed appropriately in context — a building fitted to its

102

site, its use, and the nature of its inhabitants — was lost.

Examples of this kind of thinking abound in both business and software. A theory of management or employee motivation is developed in the academy and thousands of graduates try to force fit that theory on actual enterprises. Seldom with the desired results. Bright programmers will invent a programming language and argue that that language, and that language alone, is the solution to every conceivable computing problem.

A designer's mind is an empathic mind. Empathy is not mystical, it is entirely practical and nothing more than openness and sensitivity: refraining from projecting what 'should be' onto the systems, elements and relationships being designed; and deliberately seeking, via metaphor and observation, to understand the other as ourselves. A designer's mind is a curious mind, capable of making connections among and across diverse subjects and areas of interest. They are, or at least aspire to be, "polymaths."

Polymath

The following quote from Vitruvius — credited with founding the discipline of architecture — appeared earlier in our book. We repeat it here as an introduction to probably the most challenging aspect of Designer's Mind.

> *"The ideal architect should be a man of letters, a skillful draftsman, a mathematician, familiar with historical studies, a diligent student of philosophy, acquainted with music; not ignorant of medicine, learned in the responses of jurisconsults, familiar with astronomy, and astronomical calculations."*
>
> Vitruvius 25 B.C.

With the possible exception of statecraft and military strategy, Vitruvius states that an ideal architect should know everything there is to know. At minimum everything that would have been taught in his equivalent of a university.

Knowing all that there is to know is the classical definition of a polymath. More commonly, polymath refers to individuals who have mastered multiple disciplines, ala Rennaissance figures like Leonardo Da Vinci. Other historical figures that are known as polymaths include: Michaelangelo, Paolo Sarpi, Ibn Sina, Copernicus, and Francis Bacon. The last person considered to be a polymath in, more or less, the classical sense of knowing everything, was Wilhelm Leibniz.

The idea, and the ideal, of being a polymath has fallen out of favor in the modern world. As the amount of knowledge has exponentially expanded and the number of discrete fields of study at university have expanded from five or six to several hundred; the notion of knowing it all is considered impossible. We still hold to the ideal of a "well-rounded education" and the ideal of the liberal arts — the notion that you cannot be well and truly educated without some exposure to, and understanding of, fields of knowledge external to whatever specialty area you focus on. The typical university still expects one or more 'minors' to accompany your 'major' and require all students in all majors to complete a common core — the vestige of the classical liberal arts education.

Business and design literature discusses a less literal meaning for polymath.

In 1991, David Guest, coined the term "T-shaped skills" to describe the ideal business employee. [Figure 3.1] Such an employee would have an area of particular expertise represented by the vertical bar of the 'T' — and a breadth of shallower expertise — represented by the horizontal bar. The horizontal skill set was essential for communication and collaboration across specializations.

Figure 3.1

"T-shaped people" we call people who have a profound expertise in a certain area reflected by the vertical part of the letter "T". In addition, they possess numerous complementary skills and interests as well as broad general knowledge (the horizontal part of the "T"). In the HPI* D-School many "T-shaped people" come together and will be enabled to cross disciplinary boundaries, work collaboratively and apply their capabilities to new problem contexts in a creative way."

The Hasso-Platner Institute*

104

Figure 3.2

Generalist/Broad knowledge

Specialist

T-shaped

Generalist/Broad knowledge

Specialist   Specialist

Pi-shaped

Generalist/Broad knowledge

Specialist   Specialist   Specialist   Specialist

Comb-shaped

Figure 3.4

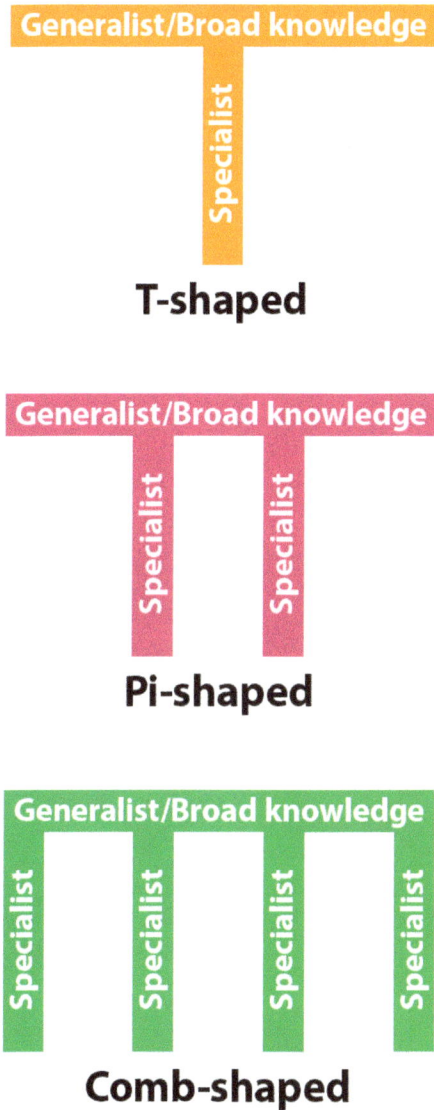

Tim Brown, CEO of the IDEO Design Consultancy, elaborated the idea of T-shaped skills as fundamental to the establishment and operation of the interdisciplinary teams, deemed essential for successful design efforts. It did not take long before "the T-Shaped Professional" became the number one recruitment goal for business and even software development organizations.

It also did not take long to recognize the limits of being merely 'T-shaped'. 'Pi-shaped' people [Figure 3.2] have two areas of specialization supporting general breadth. "Broken-comb" professionals [Figure 3.2] have multiple areas of specialization each to variable depth. In addition 'broken-comb' people have two anchor specializations — the teeth at the end of the comb — and their breadth of knowledge is uniformly deeper as a more pronounced 'backbone' is required to support and integrate the various specializations. An example might be, knowing all that there is to know about business, not just business finance; or knowing programming rather than merely Java Programming.

Being 'broken-comb-shaped' comes closest to the expectations that Vitruvius had for architects. We believe a designer's mind must reflect this same kind of integrated breadth and depth across knowledge domains. The challenge is how to achieve this knowledge profile. The modern education system actually impedes inter-disciplinary learning — the entire system is optimized to produce 'pole-stand' graduates. [Figure 3.4 shows a pole-stand, like one commonly used to display flags, with a small base of breadth knowledge supporting a disproportionate vertical pole of expertise.]

The optimal path to becoming a polymath — modern polymath or broken-comb professional — is to be a philomath. Philomath comes from the Greek and means "lover of learning." A designer's mind is an insatiably curious mind: constantly asking questions and seeking the knowledge necessary to find and understand answers. Philomaths have many traits that support their learning, but being vociferous readers, is primary. Philomaths, and aspiring designers, read widely across multiple disciplines. It is also essential to read for pleasure! As Alan Kay stated, "If you do not read for pleasure, you cannot read for purpose."

A designer's mind is full of metaphor, metaphor that is essential as a vehicle for exploring and understanding new areas of interest. A designer's mind is dense with connections among apparently disparate bits of knowledge; the source of insights, inspiration, and imagination.

Think different.

Designers Think Differently

This does not mean there is some kind of intrinsic difference in how their brains function or that there is some kind of innate talent that differentiates design thinkers from others. It does mean that designers ground their thinking in an alternative perspective or viewpoint that shapes their view of the world. Their understanding of essential concepts and the effectiveness of common practices has been shaped by history and shared experience.

Business and software professionals that wish to make effective use of design thinking need not adopt and master the worldview and knowledge of a designer, but they must understand it and recognize where it complements and contrasts with their own, traditional and cultural, ways of thinking.

Equally important is for everyone, including designers, to recognize instances where common words and common concepts disguise and obscure different, sometimes radically different, understandings and assumptions. For example, business, software, and design professionals all talk of 'systems' and even recognize design as the modification of those systems to alternative states — totally obscuring the fact that there are qualitative differences between the deterministic systems of business and software, ala Herbert Simon, and the complex or composite systems of the designer, ala Pelle Ehn.

In this chapter we have noted some of these fundamental differences: Designers think of design as a process of discovery, not creation; designers seek to find essence and facilitate its expression, and do not attempt to force fit theory onto reality; designers are philopmaths becoming polymaths — not ensiled specialists.

Chapter 4
Design Thinking

The Challenge of the Living

In Chapter 2 we presented a typology of systems using a four quadrant graph [Figure 2.1] and in this chapter we want to focus on the two quadrants at the right side of that figure — systems that are substantially artificial or human defined while incorporating human beings and other natural-complex systems as elements. We will henceforth refer to these systems as "living."

We can say that all artificial systems are 'designed' — that is, their present state is a result of intentional and informed decisions to alter their elements or relationships — usually employing engineering design. There is, however, a qualitative difference in the nature of the thinking required to design artificial-deterministic systems and artificial-complex systems. This can be illustrated by taking figure 2.1 and adding a gradient fill to the two quadrants of the typology graph that is lightest at the top and darkest at the bottom. We can label the lighter area 'engineering' design and the darker, 'artistic' design.

We use the terms engineering and artistic only as a marker of the primary origin of the thinking — perspectives, concepts, principles, and practices — about design that dominates the two categories. Engineering design, as discussed earlier, derives primarily from scientific disciplines while artistic design derives primarily from architecture and the applied arts. The two categories are not mutually exclusive. Specific aspects of art can be found in engineering and specific aspects of scientific formalism can be found in art.

When we talk of Design Thinking in this book, and when that term is used in the business press, it refers to the thinking that is prevalent in artistic design. Design Thinking is seen as an extension and enhancement of thinking about design; that is particularly useful for the design of complex and composite systems. Two observations support this claim.

First, is an observation about the elements of which a system is comprised — are they homogenous or heterogenous?

The elements of a deterministic-artificial system are all machines, and all relationships in the system are formulaic.

A computer system, the telecommunications infrastructure in an industrial country for example, is composed of physical machines like switches and circuits plus computer programs — virtual machines. Engineers, using engineering design, are very adept at understanding and building this kind of system; so good, that the rest of us take for granted that our cell phones will always work and unerringly connect us to the party we called.

All elements of a deterministic-artificial system can, in principle be known, enumerated, and specified. All relationships can, in principle, be precisely defined as mathematical formulae or functions. The thinking about design required to understand and build this kind of system can itself be formalized and reduced to rote method applied with sufficient rigor. Even the use of the system that results from human actions that are not known, can be statistically predicted with great accuracy. When individual humanity is replaced by statistical determination, the human has been reduced to a machine (deterministic) element.

Complex-artificial systems tend to have heterogenous elements. Some elements, like human beings, are complex-natural, while others, like a computer, are obviously artificial-deterministic. Because they have heterogenous components, we have labelled this type of system as 'composite'.

It may be possible, but would certainly be very difficult, to enumerate all the elements of a composite system. An example of the difficulty would be human components and the need to differentiate between humans of different genders and different cultures, not to mention all the idiosyncratic differences between individuals that might share a gender and a culture.

It is certain that you could not enumerate and reduce to formula all of the relationships that exist in a composite system. The complex elements, which are systems in their own right, have emergent behavior and are inherently non-determinstic and hence unpredictable.

The limited success we have had designing composite systems, like the International Space Station, which have complex elements — the astronauts — is predicated upon our ability to constrain human behavior with extensive and demanding protocol and procedure. In effect, they are successful to the degree that we turn the complex human components into mere machines.

The second observation concerns the two forces. We introduced this figure in Chapter 2 when discussing wicked

Patterns of Design Thinking

In the following chapter, we present specific elements of design thinking in a form called a 'pattern'.

Patterns provide an effective means to convey discrete bits of knowledge in an accessible manner.

Individual patterns provide focused discussion and quick points of reference. A collection of patterns can comprise a 'pattern language'. Individual patterns act as vocabulary words and the relationships among patterns form a rudimentary grammar.

Together they provide a 'language' for talking and thinking about design.

problems. One force arises from the fact that as we move from deterministic to complex systems the amount of knowledge required to understand and modify those systems increases, sometimes exponentially. Simultaneously the second force arises from the fact that we are less and less certain about the knowledge we possess — uncertain as to its completeness and its reliability.

Consider again the design of a computer system as an example. Because it is a deterministic-artificial system what we need to know is finite and restricted to a single area of expertise — the computer and the programming language employed to write the software that runs on the computer. We are certain of all the knowledge we utilize: only these precisely defined inputs in exactly this form; only this limited set of outputs in this defined format; and, only these trans-form algorithms stated in this context-free grammar. Only this set of immutable primitive instructions embedded in the physical hardware.

This is not to say that the design of artificial-deterministic systems is easy and free from complications. Our inability to produce 'bug-free' software or to guarantee that a given sequence of inputs will lead to the expected and correct outputs clearly illustrates that the design of this kind of system is hard. However, in principle, that hardness can be addressed and ameliorated with additional formalism and more rigorous method.

In contrast, consider the amount of knowledge, across disciplines, required to design landscape — e.g., around a home, a botanical garden, or a park. Climatology, weather patterns, soil and water chemistry, botany, etymology, ergonomics, culture, legal policy (e.g. liability, zoning and the use of insecticides and fertilizers), zoology, ornithology, color palettes, shape and layout aesthetics, hydrology, and more.

Our certainty about any of that knowledge is frequently tenuous. For one thing we cannot be equally expert in all those fields of knowledge and we are constantly aware that we might be missing some crucial bit of information that will make the difference between success or failure. Much of the know-ledge we utilize is imprecise; statistical or heuristic at best.

Some useful knowledge is unknown, by anybody. For example: I put up a hummingbird feeder and attract a small number of birds, then, wanting more birds, I put up several additional feeders in the same area only to discover — for the first time by anybody — that hummingbirds are territorial and one dominant bird will keep all but his friends

111

away from the entire area. Ten feeders, unless widely distributed, will attract the same number of birds as one.

The design of living systems presents many challenges with two of the greatest being: how to address the need for tremendous breadth of knowledge that is inherently uncertain; and, how to use that knowledge to understand the system well enough to untangle the many wicked problems that the designer must resolve.

Design Thinking, as we have defined it, provides the perspective and tools necessary to effectively design living systems. In the remainder of this chapter we will discuss Design Thinking, theory and practice, from four points of view: comprehension, communication, imagination, and, resolution.

Comprehension

Comprehension is understanding. As designer's, our need for understanding extends in three directions. First, what can we understand about the World in general and how can that knowledge help us understand the various things in the World and the myriad systems we will be asked to design? Second, what must we understand about a system, as a whole, such that we can effectively and positively alter that system, by design? Third, what do we need to understand about ourselves and our minds and how we affect what and how we design?

Worldview

We begin with the World and the nature of reality. We have already discussed part of this in our exploration of the etymology of the word design — the metaphysics of Parmenides, et. al., that argued against something coming from nothing and the notion that design was not creation but instead involved rearrangement of what is, in order for Form to assume appropriate shape.

This kind of world-view con-trasts with the mechanical deterministic worldview of the physical sciences and engineering. Where the latter focuses on stability and constancy, the worldview of design focuses on change and variability. The scientific worldview seeks correct, universal, and absolute answers — e.g. the speed of light, the law of gravity, or the Finite Element Mesh that guarantees a bridge will survive all identified forces. Design concerns itself with the

> "
> *The limited success we have had designing composite systems, like the International Space Station, is predicated upon our ability to constrain human behavior: turn the complex human components into mere machines.*

particular, the idiosyncratic, the best possible answer in a specific place and time for a specific audience.

Change, constant and accelerating change, has been a major concern of business professionals since the 1980s. The software world seriously addressed the challenges posed by change around the turn of the century: most notably in the case of 'Agile Development' where an early manifesto for the movement was the book by Kent Beck, *Extreme Programming Explained: Embrace Change.*

Our underlying worldview biases our thinking about problems and solutions. This bias is seldom consciously noticed. Like culture, it is presupposed and below the threshold of consciousness. Our ability to recognize problems and solutions is constrained by this bias in the same way that an urban dweller lost in the Australian Outback is likely to starve because they cannot, quite literally, see the myriad sources of water and sustenance that abound in even the most forbidding of landscapes.

The business or software professional that already recognizes the world as dynamic and constantly changing will find more common ground for discussion and mutual problem solving with colleagues proficient in Design Thinking; more so than with advocates of traditional engineering and scientific design.

Whole Systems

Design begins with a search for Form.

Design is about the alteration of a system in order to effect an alternative, preferred, state of that system. The concept of a 'state' implies stability and constancy; i.e. the system persists as it is until a change is introduced. Corollary to the concept of state is the notion of stability. A system is stable if it is in a state that tends to persist over time, unstable if it cannot maintain a state even though change, system rearrangement, arises from within, not caused by external forces.

Stability is a characteristic of whole systems, not individual elements or relationships. In fact, a system can maintain stability even if the state of any element or relationship is, individually, highly variable. For example — the complex system that is a human being maintains stability for many decades despite constant change in its structure, its organs, and its state. If, in the case of an illness, the human system is made unstable and at risk of failure, numerous mechanism exist that strive to restore stability.

113

An extension of the notion of stability is 'essence', a characteristic of a system that persists across state changes. Our human being, for example, is always a human being, in sickness and in health, for better or worse, etc. If change, the cumulative change from mutation perhaps, forces the human system to find a new essential stability, we would no longer consider the resulting system to be human. Australo-pithecus and Neanderthal systems are not, despite myriad similarities, Homo Sapiens Sapiens.

Designers think about this kind of meta-stability as **Form**.

Form is essence, the intrinsic nature of a thing. Form can be, and often is, hidden or partially expressed, like the Swan inside the Ugly Duckling. Form exists before the designer and the designer facilitates Form to express itself as Shape appropriate to a context. Form is generative in the sense that a single Form can be expressed in many different Shapes, all of which are nevertheless implicit in the Form. A simple example, a single color red. Red can assume a variety of shades or hues (Shapes) without ceasing to be Red. The essence (Form) of red is evocative but this too might take different shape depending on context — evoking passion, anger, fire, etc. in different circumstances. Shape also varies by culture: Red in China is festive, in the U.S. it is passionate. Black can be for mourning or celebration, as can White.

Design begins with a search for Form. A system has Form, as does each element and each relationship within the boundaries of that system. The designer must discern the Form of each. This poses an obvious difficulty, as even a small system with a few elements has an exponential number of possible relationships, meaning that the collection of Forms that need to be found becomes very large. Fortunately, the exponential number of possible relationships is bounded and limited by the essence, the Form, of the system as a whole.

Color, for example is a system and the essence of that system is a spectrum of light. Red is a subsystem whose essence is also a spectrum of light, but bounded more narrowly. The number of possible colors is large, but the relationships among those colors is not exponentially large. Instead, it is finite and easily described in any of a number of formal systems like CMYK, Pantone, NCS, RGB, and Hexidecimal.

We stated that Form is generative, can be expressed as Shape, each shape appearing to be different, but all sharing the same Form. For example, consider a Maple tree. The essence of the tree consists of its intrinsic ability to

Patterns of Design Thinking — Form
That all things have an 'essence', a Form, that must be discerned and preserved is a fundamental concept of design.

114

contribute color, proportion, fractal branching, etc. The absolute Shape of the tree will vary with context: it might be lopsided if part of it is shaded from the sun by another, more opaque tree or wall; or, if it finds itself in a bonsai garden it must assume a Shape that is consistent with its Form but at a different level of scale — its Shape is a miniature of its Form.

A business enterprise has a Form. The Form might be captured in a Mission Statement — but seldom is this really true. When a company attempts to articulate its Core Competencies it might come closer to discerning and stating its essence, its purpose — its Form. Often time, the Form, the essence, of a company is well hidden behind its shape. For example, the essence of most insurance companies and banks is "an investment company" and their ostensible reason for existing, insurance or banking, serve as little more than a subsystem that assures a revenue stream for investment. Similarly, is the essence of Facebook© the making of human connections, or the precision delivery of advertising?

The Form of a computer program is always a formal transformation machine, assuring that a given set of well defined inputs are inerrantly transformed into a set of defined outputs. A program that expands to become a composite system — with human users and a socio-political context — its Form can be much harder to discern. The evolution of operating systems is a prime example. In the beginning the essence was the management of system resources. Today the typical operating system is an amalgam of applications, resource managers, delivery platforms — i.e. Web browsers — and content: all with little or no discernible focus or Form.

Form is critical because it defines potential — the field of shapes that a system can adopt and retain its metastability. It is the Form of homo sapiens sapiens that allows humanity to adopt a wonderful diversity of shapes without losing our common human core.

Form is critical because it provides boundaries — limiting the range of change that can be introduced into the system without inducing the instability that destroys the system or forces the system to re-stabilize with an alternative Form.

Form is critical because Form is what Is — what the designer 'remembers' or 'reconstructs' as we discussed earlier when defining design and the Greek metaphysics presupposed by the word. The designer must discern Form before she can facilitate the expression of that Form as a desired Shape.
Arie de Geus authored an article in the Harvard Business

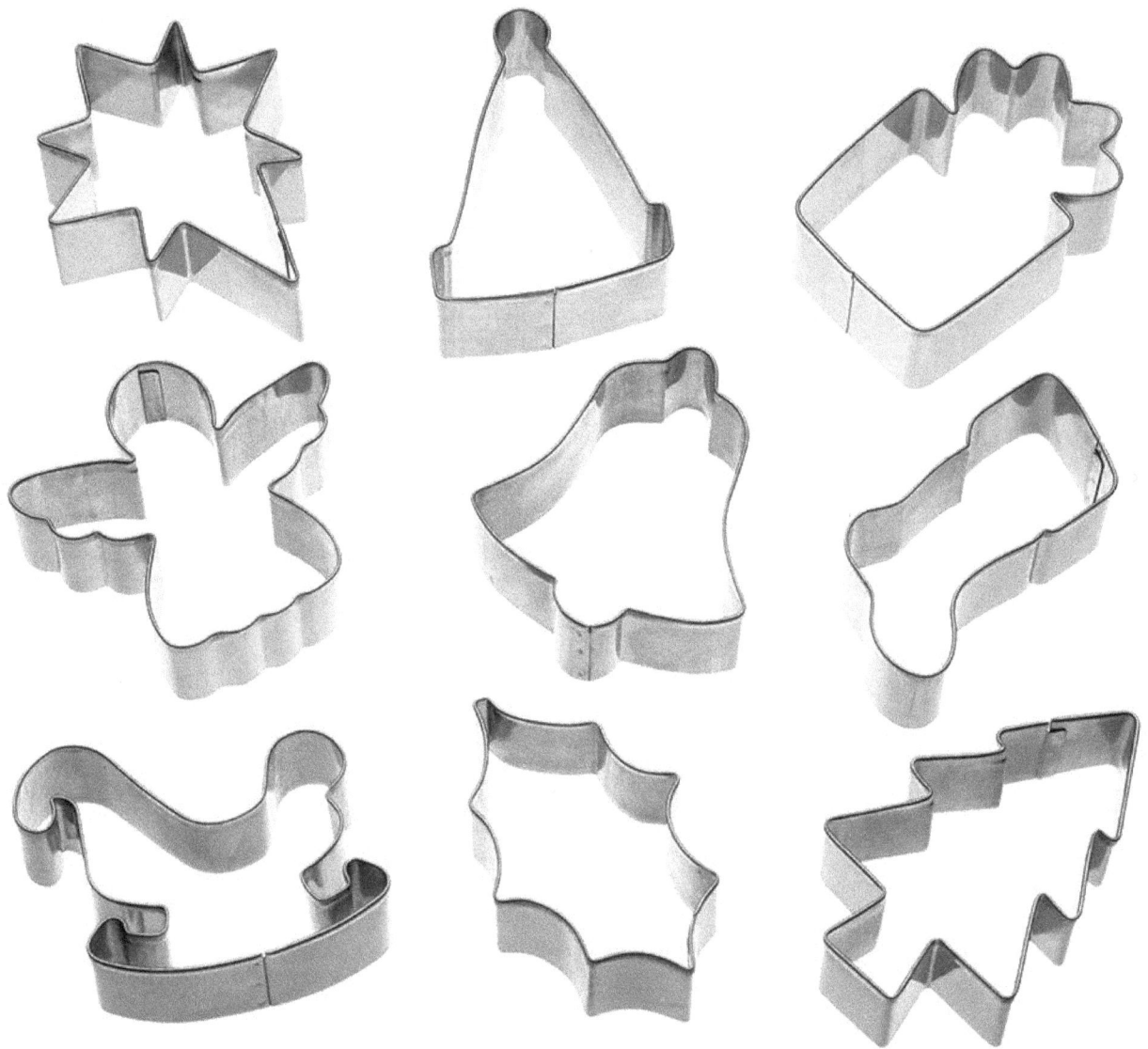

Figure 4.3 — Cake forms

Review (later expanded into a book) on *The Living Company*. The article noted how few companies survive for more than a century — when, because they are not biological, there is no obvious reason for them to die. Also noted were some exceptional exceptions: Japan's Sumitomo, beginning as a copper casting shop founded by Riemon Soga in 1590; and, the Swedish company Stora that began as a copper mine in central Sweden more than 700 years ago.

De Geus searched for the reasons why some companies were able to thrive for so long when the vast majority failed prematurely. The an-swer he found was a core set of principles that seemed essential to be a long lived company. One of those core principles was a sense of identity which is very close to what designers think of as Form. The others were values, e.g. human centric, and principles like fiscal conservatism. A long and prosperous business existence is dependent upon recognizing this core — the essential Form — of your organization and preserving that core despite what appear to be radically different Shapes that your company may take.

As examples of the change in Shapes assumed by a company, consider that Stora is now a major paper, pulp, and chemical manufacturer; or that the fur trapping, Hudson Bay Company is now a major U.S. retailer under the label Target.

The designer's task is to alter the enterprise system such that it assumes a preferred state — a new Shape — being true to the core essence, the Form. To achieve this goal, the designer recognizes that her role is facilitative, not creative (in the way we usually interpret that word as making something out of nothing). Using the analogy of agriculture — Form is present in the seed and the farmer facilitates the expression of that Form into the shape of a mature plant, not by altering the seed, but by altering other elements of the system of which the seed is but one element.

Patterns of Design Thinking — Unfolding
Design relies on a 'process' of "essence preserving transformations."

Designers, like farmers, facilitate the 'unfolding' — the natural expression of the Form contained within the seed into the mature plant. **Unfolding** has already been discussed, in brief, as essence preserving transformations. Design deals with a metaphysical world where nothing arises from nothing, but where everything is merely re-arranged. What appears to be novel or original is merely Shape, never Form. And even in this case the novel Shape, technically, is novel only to us at this moment in time. The Shape has probably appeared to others at other times but we have lost our memory of those times, allowing us to be surprised. Many readers have experienced this effect, when they reread, perhaps multiple times, a favorite book only to find themselves wondering about what happens next because their brain has conveniently 'forgotten' what they had read so many times before.

Unfolding provides the ground of action, the acts and activities that we undertake as designers. Seeing ourselves as 'creators' is very tempting, especially once we have established professions and academic institutions where one can gain immense amounts of ego satisfaction and peer recognition.

Christopher Alexander discussed this issue in *Notes on the Synthesis of Form*, as it was reflected in architecture. He contrasted the "non self conscious process" with the "self conscious process." The former is associated with buildings and built environments that arise from 'natural' processes and without a profession of architecture. As architecture became a profession, and especially when universities began to teach architecture as an academic subject, architects became self conscious about what they did. Instead of fit and liveness, architects gave precedence to abstract and arbitrary characteristics and the evaluation of buildings was reduced to consistency with theoretical principles that had little or no connection to the real world.

Alexander also discussed the concept of unfolding at great length in his work, *The Nature of Order*. Using a seed as an example, Alexander shows that a flower results from a sequence of transformations, each of which preserves the structure, what we are calling Form, intrinsic to the seed. This is the case even as the Shape, the expression of the Form, varies with each transformation.

Structure preserving transformations are also familiar to mathematicians. In algebra, for example, you can pose a complicated, difficult to understand and solve, equation; then apply any of a number of transformations, e.g. adding the same value to both sides of the equation, giving it the appearance of being a different equation.

Applying a sequence of these transformations can lead to a very simple shape of the equation, a shape that makes the resolution of the equation simple and straightforward. Unlike the mathematician, the designer lacks the luxury of a predefined, proven, set of transforms that guarantee preservation of structure, of Form. The designer makes changes to a system, perhaps guided by experience derived heuristics, and determines, after the change, if Form was preserved. This accounts for the trial-and-error nature of the design process — process being what designers do at any discrete time during the overall duration of an act of design.

A recognition, knowledge, and understanding of Form is presupposed and prerequisite to unfolding and to design. Discernment of Form, however, depends on our ability to transcend tendencies of the human mind that cloud our perception.

The mind/brain is a 'sense-maker' optimized to accept massive amounts of input data then synthesize and abstract that data to yield sensable information.

Presented with chaotic inputs, e.g. randomly lit pixels on a computer screen, the mind/brain 'sees' regularities where there are none. Gambler's facing random chance, discern "systems" that they believe will assure they beat the odds

Designers, like farmers, facilitate the 'unfolding' — the natural expression of the Form contained within the seed into the mature plant.

118

Figure 4.4
A chalice or two faces in profile?

Patterns of Design Thinking — Zen Mind
Accurate perception of essence
is dependent upon overcoming natural
tendencies of the mind/brain to project
or 'make sense' of the world.

and win consistently.

Faced with ambiguity, the mind/ brain will resolve it into certainty. This is the foundation of a class of illusions — do these minimal lines depict a chalice, or two faces in profile? Do these lines and spaces depict a closeup of the haggard face of a crone, or an elegant and beautiful woman standing upright?

When the mind/brain encounters the unfamiliar it does its best to 'recognize' what is perceived; usually by categorizing it based on a few prominent features. Often the results of categorization is less than desirable, e.g. stereotypes and various 'isms'. It can also be the foundation of an incredibly valuable tool, one that designers rely upon extensively — the metaphor.

The perception of Form, of essence, is made difficult by these various tricks of the mind. The designer is constantly faced with unfamiliar systems — a new client's business for example — and is tasked with making a change to that system that allows it to take on a new state, one consistent with its intrinsic nature, its Form. Often this occurs under deadline. The designer must understand this novel system well enough to do his job, and quickly.

The first impulse is to bring to bear all the powers of one's mind, but this can be a mistake. Remember those mind tricks and recognize that they can lead you astray, mis-perceive Form and mis-interpret shape. Designer's develop mental discipline that allows them to directly perceive Form.

A fundamental premise of most mystical traditions is that the World we see around us is an illusion. For example, our ordinary existence is filled with differentiated things and permanence while the mystic sees everything as a field of constant change. Mystics promote various disciplines, meditation being one of the most common, that "still the mind" — quiet the various tricks we spoke about — in order to allow direct perception. We call this Zen Mind.

Zen Mind is best illustrated with a bit of imagery — a mountain lake in the evening with a full moon in the sky above. The lake is perturbed by wind and birds landing or taking off, perhaps a monk tossing pebbles. The moon is reflected in the water but is distorted, its real nature cannot be perceived. If however, the lake was undisturbed, it will assume a smooth, glasslike surface and reflect the Moon accurately and completely. According to this Zen imagery, the lake is a metaphor for your mind, disturbed by various attachments to the World and mistaken notions of what

119

Figure 4.5 — A millipede.

Is and Is Not. If you wish enlightenment, to achieve a Zen Mind, you must still the perturbations, calm your mind until it no longer projects a reality to your senses, but simply allows direct and unfiltered perception.

Our intent is not to bring everyone to enlightenment any more than it is to make everyone a designer. We use Zen Mind as a reminder that designers should focus on seeing what is there, not projecting, superimposing, some arbitrary reality.

Enfolded into Zen Mind is a measure of the degree to which someone has become enculturated as well as their mastery, depth of their understanding, of design. Athletes speak about being, 'in the zone'. Kent Beck said: "There are three stages of extreme programming: out of the box, adapted, and transcended." Christopher Alexander spoke of a Pattern Language as a Gate, and noted that the practice of the *Timeless Way of Building* required, "Passing Through the Gate."

In all cases, what is being described is a state of mind where you cease to consciously think about what you are doing and simply recognize and take the correct action. It is the opposite of the story of the millipede who lost his ability to walk once he asked himself which foot goes first?

**Patterns of Design Thinking
— It Takes A Village**
Design projects required multiple perspectives, multiple areas of expertise, and many signers to assure success.

120

Communication

There is a tendency to individualize major accomplishments — the founding of a company, an empire, an operating system, a religion — even though we know it was a team effort. In business, in software, and in design; few if any accomplishments are the work of a single individual. Yes, it is true that a single designer might be able to complete a small design task — the creation of a logo for example — just as it is true that a programmer might, as an individual code an elegant algorithm. System design, however, requires, with extremely rare exception, the involvement of multiple people with multiple perspectives and areas of expertise.

Collaborative work, of any kind, is absolutely dependent upon communication. Communication involves many layers and takes many forms. Beginning with vocabulary, with words, and grammar; communication also involves symbols, some of which might exist below the threshold of awareness. All of these elements combine to form languages, languages with unique as well as common aspects.

Patterns of Design Thinking — Logos
Examines the necessity of words, of vocabulary, and the benefits and problems that arise from 'naming'.

Logos (Greek, meaning 'word') concerns naming and is closely related to the Confucian concept, "rectification of names". Confucius believed that meaning and knowing, along with harmony and social order, was dependent on each thing having its proper designation or name.

Naming is inevitable, both within ourselves as we think with vocabulary, and among ourselves, we need words to communicate. The legend of Babel illustrates the latter, because God confounded the language of the babelites, giving different groups different words for the same thing, making it impossible for them to communicate and coordinate their activities or maintain their social order.

121

Logos is intimately connected to Form. Design may begin with the search for Form but cannot be complete until that Form is given a name. We might perceive something without naming it, but we cannot think about what we have perceived until and unless we label, name, it. And we certainly cannot communicate except, we suppose, by simply pointing to what we perceive and hoping the other person's perception matches our own.

The name must be 'correct'. It must be appropriate for and consistent with the Form, àla Confucian rectification of names. We actually encounter the issue of inconsistency when we have a name before we have a Form.

Two examples, one from the business world and one from software. A wonderful little restaurant in Mt. Carmel Junction Utah advertises its "ho' made pies." The name arose when all the letters (home made pies) would not fit on a custom made sign, and only later did the negative connotation appear. The restaurant decided to use the connotation, gently, as a marketing tool.

Second, the term, 'Object', arose when a group of people, like Alan Kay, perceived a new Form of modularization. Software developers who did not share the original perception had to rely on descriptive language as they attempted to understand it. Unfortunately the language and the metaphors it employed, e.g. biological cell and homunculus, was inadequate for the task. The result was widespread misunderstanding and attempts to force-fit the new Form into familiar language as "animated data entities" or miniature COBOL programs (encapsulated data and procedure).

Although it seems that the correct name for a Form would be obvious, in practice there will be a convergence as different people, sharing the same perception but giving different names to it, come to understand the commonality behind the plethora of names and come to an agreement as to which is 'most appropriate' and how the nuances of difference might best be integrated to generate a more comprehensive understanding.

Glossolalia is defined as "speaking in tongues" and frequently associated with religious mystical experience. The experience is most often seen in groups who collectively establish a kind of altered state of experience prompting one or more individuals to amplify that experience and make utterances in a language unknown to the speaker and most of those in attendance. However, quite frequently, there are individuals whose state of mind allows them to translate the alien speech and make it intelligible. These events often generate advice and direction that the group, as a

Patterns of Design Thinking
— Glossolalia
Just as it takes multiple perspectives and elements of specialized knowledge — design requires making sense and finding commonality among multiple languages.

whole, uses to guide their collective actions going forward. A collaborative design group will, necessarily, speak multiple languages — each specialized area of knowledge using its own vocabulary, often including a multitude of neologisms and acronyms. Effective collaboration requires transcending the polyglot and establishing a common form of communication.

Carl Jung is famous, in part, for his work on archetypes and the collective unconscious. He provides us with a theory of how we can know, and even act upon, that of which we are not aware. The highly controversial Rupert Sheldrake suggests that shared morphology provides a medium for shared knowledge, also below the threshold of consciousness. Noam Chomsky suggests that knowledge of language is innate to our genetic structure. In all cases, knowledge that is below the threshold of consciousness is nevertheless present and, in many cases, usable and influential upon our conscious thinking.

Christopher Alexander argues that QWAN (a Quality Without A Name) is perceived or perceivable by anyone, from any culture, and any point in time. We are attracted to structures and environments that have QWAN, and indifferent to or repelled by those that do not. All without any necessary awareness of what we are seeing or why we deem it good or bad.

All of these ideas contend that we have access to a deep pool of knowledge, a source from which we can remember things, of which we are not consciously aware. But they also argue that we need to become aware of and to use this knowledge if we wish the products of our design effort to have certain, highly intangible, qualities like Beauty, Fit, and QWAN.

A design team that ignores these 'subconscious' symbols and languages is unlikely to be effective and actually risks offending those for whom the design was intended. Moreover, taking heed of archetypes and the 'collective subconscious' provides insights and rich sources of 'remembered Shape'. Taking advantage of this source can save time, minimize search paths, and assure desired qualities in our results.

A particular instance of the glossolalia problem arises between the design team and the client. Almost certainly, the two groups will use differ ent languages: the language of business or the language of computers and software, as opposed to the language of design. The problem reflects more than just language, it involves all of what we would describe as culture.

We began this chapter by pointing out the existence of a design culture and the need for those wishing to understand and utilize design thinking to comprehend that culture. Culture is essentially invisible, the complex web of behaviors and interactions you engage in every day are not thought about, they are as 'automatic' as breathing. Cultural conflict arises when two different groups, each engaged in its own 'automatic behavior' experience conflict but cannot pinpoint the source of that conflict. Conflict of this sort presents a significant challenge for designers working with computer scientists and MBA trained business professionals. The latter disciplines share a worldview that is almost diametrically opposed to that held by designers andleads to the need for professionals on both sides to, almost literally, 'change one's mind' in order to find the common ground necessary for communication.

The worldview of the design culture holds that reality is holistic, dynamic, complex, unpredictable, and necessarily ambiguous. In contrast, the scientific worldview shared by most computing and business professionals sees reality as complicated but predictable according to invariant, formulaic, rules. The scientific worldview is famously reductionistic and precise, tolerating no ambiguity. It is easy to see why 'abandoning' one worldview in favor of the other can be so challenging.

It must be said that the 'scientific' worldview is a subset of the design worldview. This assertion directly challenges the ego of those committed to the scientific paradigm. In 1947, John von Neumann, mathematician, computer scientist, and inventor of the still dominant von Neumann computer architecture, addressed the Association of Computing Machinery. He stated that future computers would have just a dozen instruction types, a number known to be adequate for expressing all of mathematics. He stated: "This number should not be surprising since 1,000 words were known to be adequate for most situations in real life, and mathematics was only a small part of life, and a very simple part at that." When his audience reacted with hilarity (a common response to a bruised ego) he further stated, "If people do not believe that mathematics is simple, it is only because they do not realize how complicated life is."

In this context, adopting the design worldview should not be seen as 'abandoning' the scientific, merely as a way of 'expanding one's horizons'. This does not make it any easier, but it should remove at least one source of angst.

Communication across this barrier can be accomplished, common ground can be established. Anthropologists have developed two approaches, **Participant Observation** and

Patterns of Design Thinking
— Participant Observation
A system cannot be understood from afar.
You must be in, and involved in,
the system to see it clearly.
— Thick Description
Composite systems cannot be specified
or reduced to requirements. Like cultures,
they can only be described — thickly.

Thick Description, that were, more or less, independently discovered by designers. Participant observation requires the design team, primarily, to become involved in the system that is the target for their design efforts. Not as mere observers, but as participants! The software world, particularly Agile software practitioners, have rediscovered this principle, calling it Gemba — from the Japanese. The "Toyota Way" also incorporates this principle in that approach to product design.

The outcome of participant observation, the support for communication between and among the design and client cultures, is not an almanac of facts, figures, and rules. Instead it is a literary narrative describing in detail what has been observed and noting any interpretations made about those observations. Interpretations are used as a means of dialog between observer and observed to assure understanding.

This kind of design approach contrasts significantly with the typical software development approach. The latter expects the client to extract a comprehensive set of "requirements" or specifications, none of which contain meaning or context, and the software team merely "builds to specification." It is not at all uncommon for the development team to be forbidden from contacting, observing, interacting with, or communicating with the business.

Design depends upon capturing a rich narrative, stories, constraints, hopes, desires, expectations, and needs — all of which is embedded in context. This narrative affords the designer an understanding of the system as it appears to those living in that system; the system as it is, from the observer's "objective" perspective; and, where the system needs to be altered to better suit the needs and wishes of the people in that system.

Obtaining this narrative seems, on the surface, to require immense amounts of time and resources. In fact it does not: at most it requires no additional time than that which is already expended on attempts to understand systems and depict what is desired. In software development, for example, the time spent creating a massive set of "requirements" is instead spent telling stories and sharing experiences. The latter are far more valuable than 'requirements' which can never be complete nor clear. Communication among everyone involved in the system at hand, e.g. the business, provides a foundation for design. Only after sufficient knowledge has been shared among everyone, is it possible for the team to concentrate on intra-team communication. Even then, communication within the team must constantly be refreshed and validated by conversations outside the team.

125

Figure 4.7 — Natural Stone Bridge

Central to this transition is a shared — among all the stakeholders involved in the system or enterprise — a 'theory'. This theory has three essential elements: 1) a common language; and, 2) shared models grounded in a common understanding of what a system is and what elements and relationships comprise that system; and 3) a collective understanding of the system and how it works embodied in a comprehensive set of stories along with a common metaphor/model of an element or a relationship.

Just as it is helpful to have a common and general model of a system, a similarly common and general model of a system element is desirable. The concept of an "object" as first proposed in metaphor — "an intelligent virtual computer," or "a nameable thing differentiated from other things by what is does, what it contributes, possessing the knowledge and abilities to fulfill those obligations." — is just such a model. Objects are familiar to software developers as a programming construct, which is inconsistent with the original intent and value of the object idea. The business community has a superficial understanding of objects, as named things like account, customer, or transaction. The object model was intended to provide a way of bridging the gap between domain expertise and programming expertise, creating a single concept and model that captured the entities familiar to the domain expert in a form that could act as a specification for a programmer who would ensure that the computer faithfully simulated that object operating in context.

The result was supposed to be a tool, populated with things and relations among those things that was familiar to the domain expert without any need for that domain expert to understand anything about the intrinsic nature of the tool or how anything was implemented inside the tool (computer).

We use the object concept as a metaphor and as a model. It builds upon the already shared understanding of a system as a set of elements and relationships among them. As a metaphor, 'Object' provides a tool for decomposing a complex system into its constituent elements and its discrete relationships. An object is any named thing that contributes to the system. An element object contributes outputs, or behaviors, a relationship object contributes the maintenance of a connection between or among elements.

As a model, 'Object', provides a concise way to capture the critical aspects of an element or a relationship: a short list of the contributions, the behaviors or responsibilities, that the object provides to the system; articulation of the knowledge required by the object if it is to fulfill its responsibilities; a protocol for communicating with the object; and,

128

enumeration of any changes in state that the object can, and is willing to, provide to other objects, via a notification process. Implicit in the model is a textual description of the object and any 'family resemblance' — i.e. behaviors shared in common with other objects — it has to other objects.

Alan Kay, coiner of the phrase 'object oriented programming', used the metaphor of a biological cell to illustrate his conception of an object. This points to another critical aspect of the object model: each object is autonomous and is intrinsically composable. Objects served as a basis for taking things apart, but equally important, a way of putting them together again in new and novel Shapes each of which preserves essential Form.

When discussing his concept of a pattern, Christopher Alexander also stressed the importance of:
"[using] them to create not just one design, but an infinite variety of designs, all of them free combinations of the same set of patterns" as having a public interface (analogous to the receptors on the surface of the cell) that allowed cells to interact with each other; an encapsulating membrane; and a lot of complexity inside that membrane that allowed the cell to do what it did."

The complexity inside of an object is arbitrary and may involve the interactions of numerous objects, each of which has the potential to be complex with its own interacting set of objects. At some point there are objects that are, somewhat arbitrarily, treated as atomic. Such an object might be a 'character' like the letter 'a'. But, if you look inside that object you will still see structure and abilities, but the complexity will be minimal. This leads to the notion that "everything is an object".

Juxtaposing the model of system and the model of object exposes obvious parallels. Everything is a system. Everything is an object. A system is composed of a set of elements and the relationships among them. An object is composed of communicating and interacting objects. Elements and relations may be systems. Objects may be complicated and complex. Systems are intrinsically mutable and constantly changing. Objects should be intrinsically mutable and capable of constant adaptation and evolution. Systems are nested. Objects are nested. Systems are self similar across levels of scale. Objects are self similar across levels of scale. Some elements may be seen as atomic. Some objects may be seen as atomic.

It is quite feasible to use "system" and "object" interchangeably. Doing so provides a pragmatic and simple vocabulary that does nothing to detract from the power and flexibility of either the system or object concept. **Everything An Object** expresses a pragmatic and simple way of documenting Form, naming it, and using the subsequent vocabulary for composing designs as well as decomposing systems.

The 'theory' of a system is not something that is easily, or even possible, to keep inside one's head. Instead, it is necessary for large parts of that theory to be expressed in tangible form, and these tangible forms provide the actual means for communicating, thinking about, and expanding the theory. This necessity has a direct and immediate impact on the environment where design takes place.

As early as the 1960s and 70s, people recognized the role of space and environment on individual and team productivity and work satisfaction. More recently, the Hasno-Platner Institute, the "dSchool" at Stanford, gave priority to the design of work and collaborative spaces and the first publications for general audiences concerned the design of workspace. Despite this awareness, the typical work environment is still a small individual desk space in a 'cubicle farm'. One of the largest challenges faced by agile software teams was convincing management of the need for an alternative workspace. **A Room of One's Own** discusses what is known in the design culture about the effect of space in supporting high performance teams.

We know many things about the kind of space that supports design. One, it is a public space. Most of the time, most of the people, in the room will be members of the design team but everyone in the enterprise is welcome in the room and will often have specific reasons to be in that space. Two, it must be an open space with lots of facilities — whiteboards, tables, visible supplies, prototypes, etc. — for the public presentation of shared know-ledge, of shared theory.

Three, it must be a dynamic space with people moving freely from work focus to work focus; with even the furnishings and compartmentalization be alterable to support different activities at different times.

And, fourth, the space itself must be a participant in the design process, capturing and expressing the theory of the design and the work progress towards realizing that design. Anyone, coming into the room should be able to look around and immediately observe and understand what is understood and what is happening. The client can determine whether or not shared theory is still understood as well as how it has been expanded since the last visit. The

Patterns of Design Thinking
— Everything An Object
Provides a single, shared, metaphor/model of elements and relationships comprising a system.

Patterns of Design Thinking
— Room of One's Own
Physical space enhances, or hinders, our ability to communicate and our ability to think.

130

manager can immediately ascertain the state of the effort and any potential problems or issues, without the need to stop work for a, seldom productive, review meeting.

Imagination

All of our communication, all of our theory building and modeling, provides a foundation for thinking about what might be. We must understand what is before we can think about what might be. We must understand how things work before we can determine what might be done differently. We must understand why things are what they are — part of that why is the essence, the Form of the system —before we can evaluate the success of any changes we make.

We will not have a complete understanding before we begin any design act. Overcoming this lack of complete and certain knowledge is precisely what design thinkers are good at. We must, however, have sufficient understanding that we can move forward; including, a pretty solid understanding of Form and a solid outline of our theory of the system. Even these fundamentals are subject to enhancement as our work proceeds. In the concluding section of this chapter we will return to the issue of foundational understanding and how it might change the way we think about "continual design."

Given a foundational understanding it is time to think about what might be, to use our imagination to discover/ remember and articulate new Shapes that our system might express.

Possibility is, of course boundless. A vast and seemingly trackless space defined as anything and everything is possible or might be. We could easily become lost in such a space and our ability to find our way is dependent on having some general sense of direction and some likely boundaries within which to focus our explorations.

Lead designer is a common role in design teams even though design teams generally lack the hierarchical structure of typical business and software teams. Design teams and, starting in the early 2000s, Agile teams are structured as "self-organizing" and peer-based, needing "leadership" analogous to the way a sports team needs a coach because they require more support for collaborative work by a group of peers, the need for a 'leader' remains.

Agile software development provides a similar structure,

Figure 4.8 — Set your imagination free
Illustration by Coconut-icecream, deviantart.com.

**Patterns of Design Thinking
— Tribes**
*A form of social organization based on
peers, consensus decision making
and situational leadership.*
— Design Brief
*A charge to the design group
that limns the collective effort.*

relying on self organization among peers while recognizing the need for a 'coach'. Business has a long history of exploring different management structures, all of which are likely to include a leader, a CEO. Societies also provide examples of how peer organization can be consistent with leadership roles. We talk about this in our pattern, **Tribes**. Although not unfamiliar to business, this type of team is atypical and inconsistent with traditional hierarchical, top-down control structures most commonly seen.

A major contribution of the lead designer is the **Design Brief**. A design brief might be seen as 'marching orders' — here is what to look for, where to look for it, how to know you have found it, and the shape your work should express — but it would be more proper to see the design brief as a nucleus around which the work of the team coalesces. Just as a raindrop requires a nucleus around which water vapor aggregates to form a droplet, so to does the work of the design team require a nuclear starting point for their work.

**Patterns of Design Thinking
— Prometheus Bound**
*Constraints are equally important
with expectations and desires
for a design effort to succeed.*

The team also has at its disposal an understanding of constraints (boundaries), both soft and hard. These came from the original communications between design teams and clients as discussed in the pattern, **Prometheus Bound**. An example of a soft boundary might be, "the client prefers primary colors over pastels." A hard boundary might be, "the client cannot spend more than $$$ on this design." Other variations of boundaries might include: absolute, relative, client originated, context derived, designer's experience, etc. Boundaries have the effect of narrowing the search space for a solution to the client's needs.

**Patterns of Design Thinking
— System Metaphor**
*The articulation of our developing
understanding of the systems Form,
concise and metaphorical,
used to guide our design work.*

A **System Metaphor**, a concise, but metaphorical description of the Form of a system, can often be found in the design brief. Kent Beck introduced the notion of system metaphor into Extreme Programming, but not as the Form of the domain system, but the Form of the software that was to be produced. In both cases, the metaphor was intended to guide our thinking about design.

Humans are absolutely dependent upon metaphor when attempting to understand anything that is novel to us. The scientist, for example attempting to understand the unknown structure of an atom, uses the metaphor of a solar system — the Sun as nucleus and the planets as orbiting electrons — to guide the development of new models and new mathematics for physics and chemistry. The designer and the software developer are similarly dependent upon metaphor.

Metaphor works by asserting similarity between something known and something unknown.We can then look at the

133

Figure 4.9 — The Keeper of the Threshold by Elihu Vedder, Carnegie Museum of Art.

known thing and use our understanding of it to find referents, or specific characteristics of the known. We then see
if we can find analogs of those referents in the unknown
thing. If we do find correspondences, the metaphor is
strengthened, eventually becoming a lexical term, an
equivalency. If we do not, the metaphor dies as unproduc-
tive and we seek an alternative.

The choice of metaphor is very important. Choosing the
wrong one can result in a waste of time at minimum and
irrevocable misunderstandings at worst. It is quite useful,

134

therefore, to find a useful metaphor for the system as a whole, its Form, and, perhaps, for the solution as a whole, the design.

Design is what occurs when anything is possible, it is, in fact, the effort of reducing the possible to the desirable. Design occurs at a time of liminality. The notion of a liminal time comes from the work of Arnold von Gennep, an anthropologist, and his work on Rites of Passage. When a person transitions from childhood to adulthood, for example, most cultures incorporate a Rite with three stages: Separation, where all that a child was is removed; Liminal when the child is neither what she was or yet what she is to be — where all things and all outcomes are possible; and Integration, where the adult is defined and the no longer child assumes the new role, the new self.

Designers take advantage of the liminal to explore with the freedom of imagination; rapidly conceiving of alternatives, of possibilities, of unrestrained brainstorming. It can be exhilarating. Soft-ware developers and the business clients who pay them, might find it challenging to accept and exploit the liminal. Historically, all the way back to Structured Analysis and Design, software professionals were told to model systems without fore- shadowing their implementation — to capture in the model what needs to be done absolutely independent of how it is to be done. This, of course, requires time and imagination. The developer is so used to seeing the world through the lens of a programming language and development environment that they have difficulty imagining alternatives. The business client is not sufficiently aware of why he should be paying for this time, seeking instead the most direct route from problem to solution.

Designers take advantage of the liminal to explore with the freedom of imagination; rapidly conceiving of alternatives, of possibilities, of unrestrained brainstorming. It can be exhilarating. Soft-ware developers and the business clients who pay them, might find it challenging to accept and exploit the liminal. Historically, all the way back to Structured Analysis and Design, software professionals were told to model systems without foreshadowing their implementation — to capture in the model what needs to be done absolutely independent of how it is to be done. This, of course, requires time and imagination. The developer is so used to seeing the world through the lens of a programming language and development environment that they have difficulty imagining alternatives. The business client is not sufficiently aware of why he should be paying for this time, seeking instead the most direct route from problem to solution.

Hailstones

A hailstone might be a better metaphor for design activity than a raindrop. Although a hailstone also requires an initial nucleus around which to form, the hailstone iteratively and incrementally builds upon that nucleus as it rises up and down within the cloud — until it reaches a size and composition that allows it to fall to the ground.

To be liminal is ambiguous. The generative power of design is found precisely in this ambiguity, in fact, all creative activities are firmly grounded in accepting and exploring ambiguity. This too is a hard lesson for 'scientific managers' in the business world and software engineers in the development world.

We capture more about the realm of the **Magical Liminal**, a pattern that illuminates the principle and outlines how to use that principle to establish techniques and tools that support imagination, free exploration, and the power of the liminal. This pattern celebrates ambiguity and provides insights of how to enhance your design by embracing it.

Patterns of Design Thinking
— Magical Liminal
Where our thinking and designing occurs after we have removed what was and before we coalesce on what will be.

The liminal is, in part, a world of pure possibility because it exists in the designer's mind and is not subject to the constraints of physical reality. Eventually what is in our imagination must be made tangible and must be deployed and integrated with a real world system. Design is not realized until it becomes real.

If you observe a design team at work you will see them constantly engaged in 'making things real', e.g. creating visual models on whiteboards or three-dimensional prototypes of the objects being designed. Doing so is an essential aspect of design. The Italian philosopher, Giambattista Vico asserted, *"We are sure only of that which we build"*. What we imagine possible must be realized, in some form, before possibility can be certainty. It is also true that we cannot be certain that what is in your mind is the same as what is in my mind until, and unless, we can share a sensible and comprehensible externalization and agree that what we see before us is in fact what we were thinking.

Show Me, is a pattern that examines the role of prototyping, of visual modeling, and other forms of externalizing what is in our minds in order to confirm our common understanding. An important corollary of externalizing our imagination is the fact that it allows that which is being designed to participate in the designing. A less anthropomorphic way of stating this principle: modeling and prototyping provide essential feedback for confirming our ideas and our thoughts.

Patterns of Design Thinking
— Show Me
"We are certain only of that which we build" [Giambattista Vico] and prototypes and tangible models constantly and continually affirm our understanding of what we are designing and designing for.

Evaluation. Values, shared values, are fundamental to any culture. How things are evaluated, deemed beautiful or ugly, useful or frivolous, profound or superficial, etc. is grounded in value. We have mentioned earlier the need for this kind of evaluation and the various concepts that have been used to capture it: e.g. QWAN, Beauty, Fit. We also discussed Alexander's distinction between self conscious and non self conscious cultures and their different foundations for evaluation. The self conscious culture evaluates

138

things in terms of conformance to abstract theory and idiosyncratic 'schools of thought'; while the non self conscious culture evaluates on the basis of fit and of appropriateness.

The end result of design occurs when a designed change is introduced into a system, causing a change of state, and the resulting state is evaluated as to whetheror not it accomplished the desired and expected result while maintaining the integrity and stability of the system as a whole. Intermediate design outcomes — prototypes, drafts, sketches, or other artifacts — must be evaluated against our emerging theory of the system and how we see our designed artifact supporting that system.

Designers utilize many different values or evaluation criteria as means for determining the 'goodness' of their work. In most cases, these evaluation criteria complement and extend criteria already familiar to business or software professionals. In some cases, what the designer values is sufficiently emphasized that it has the effect of replacing or overwhelming traditional business and software values.

Patterns of Design Thinking — Joy
If the outcome of design does not improve our human sense of self, enhance our participation in life, fails to bring us joy — we would deem that design to be a failure.

For example, **Joy**, as a criteria for ensuring the outcome of design enhances and improves the human condition is, for us and for most designers, absolutely paramount. The term 'joy' means much more than simply being pleased by or receiving pleasure from something. All kinds of nondesigned, and ill-designed things might give us pleasure.

Instead, we see Joy as an outcome from a design that enhances our humanity, individual and collective. Software developers tend to be so focused on meeting requirements, algorithmic elegance, efficiency, and correctness, that they seldom consider whether the software they create makes the user of that software feel better about themselves and their work. Similarly, business is often dominated by profit considerations at the expense of social and environmental concerns.

Patterns of Design Thinking — Fit
Any design solution must be incporporated into a system, effecting a change to that system, and must maintain the stability and consistency of that system. It must "fit in."
— Seed Recognizes Flower
The Shape (flower) of our design must be consistent with the Form (seed) of the system

Fit addresses two important ideas: congruency between problem and solution; and, appropriateness of solution for its deployment context. One way to evaluate a design is by the degree to which Shape, the result of the designer's effort, reflects Form. In many ways this is the most important criteria for evaluating design — is the expression true to the essence. A figurative way of stating this, and our pattern's title, is **Seed Recognizes Flower**.

One way to judge the appropriateness of a solution to its deployment context is by the degree to which the use of it falls below the threshold of awareness. The best technologies, for instance, are those that do not require us to stop

and think about what we are doing when we use them.
An old fashioned land line telephone requires no conscious thought while the typical TV remote requires significant amounts of attention to use correctly (unless you are under the age of 20). We address this aspect of fit in our pattern, **Invisibility**.

Until recently, design was seen as mere adornment, making something pretty by embellishment. As we move towards an understanding of design as essential instead of peripheral we risk forgetting that **Attractiveness** still matters. Attractiveness is a matter of perception but perception is an essential basis for human decision making. It is our perception of some thing, often an attractive feature, that enables us to see an affordance. Perceived beauty is a motivation for paying attention to something, attention that is required before we are able to invest the effort necessary to understand and see the value and utility of something.

Designing

We conclude this chapter with a short discussion of what kind of work effort is appropriate for design thinking and how design thinking might alter our conception of how that work is constructed and related to other work efforts. We obviously believe that any work or work effort, any aspect of life, or the systems within which we exist, will benefit from the application of design thinking. Very early in the book we noted that we are constantly engaged in changing ourselves and the world around us; and asserted that informed and intentional change was always better than the alternative. Since design thinking is defined as intentional and informed change, everything, essentially by definition, is enhanced by design thinking.

Our real concern however, arises from the fact that advances in technology, especially computer technology, has opened new domains where, we believe, design thinking can and will provide an important, if not essential, tool for assuring we will all inhabit a better world tomorrow than we do today. For most of human history, design has been grounded in what Alexander called the "non self conscious process".Design was not a distinct act or speciality or occupation; instead design was embedded in culture, guided by myth, ritual, and tradition. If we needed a new home, we did not concern ourselves with the 'design' of that home as we were assured that if we paid proper attention to ritual and followed the guidance of myth our efforts would result in something that we wanted and that was appropriate for ourselves and our environment.

Much of that non conscious form of design persists today. Less than ten percent of our built environment — houses, buildings, highway systems, cities, and infrastructure — is the product of deliberate and conscious design, i.e. is a product of an architectural process or the realization of an architect's vision. The same, with only the percentage being lower, is true of a business enterprise. Few enterprises are organized and implemented as the result of a conscious design process — instead they result from the application of conventional wisdom and business school taught models (myth and tradition) with little or no conscious thought.

Science and technology have made possible myriad things that have heretofore been impossible or impractical. One example, computer and communication technology has made it possible to scale the social and cultural organization of a tribe — consensus decision making, every one a peer, and leadership that is situational and ephemeral — making government, especially local government far more effective at far less cost.

Technology, including the Internet, the Web, and mobile platforms, has opened the door to enterprise designs that are radically different from anything seen before. That same technology makes possible an enterprise that effectively realizes organization structures that have been tried but proven impractical, like working from home or distributing collaborative work across continents and time zones. Despite the potential, there is little evidence of the application of design thinking, or any kind of conscious design, to the world of business.

'Living System Design', as a new discipline and design art form, is grounded in design thinking while incorporating advances in business thinking and software development practice is both possible and desirable. Providing a seed from which such a discipline will emerge, by design of course, is a primary motivation behind writing this book.

The emergence and practice of Enterprise Design will fundamentally alter the way we think of doing design, and software development. Instead of episodic, 'project focused', design effort, work will focus on the designed change of single elements or relationships comprising the enterprise system. Given that an element might be a system itself, we will still see variable scale in design efforts. But even here, the expected size of a design effort will be constrained to one or a few 'stories' describing a focused and immediate system change.

In this chapter, we discussed the importance of communication and the establishment of a common theory about the enterprise, its parts, and how those parts interacted to collectively accomplish the intent of the system. The very first design effort will require a fair amount of work to articulate that theory and establish the means and modes of communication. Knowledge of the system will grow from minimal to a level sufficient to support the planned design effort.

Design Thinking — its world view, the concepts and principles, and the practices — taken and applied together and in concert, provides a foundation for our knowledge about the enterprise system to be cumulative. This means that each subsequent 'project' will require less and less overhead for knowledge accumulation and assimilation. It also ensures that knowledge of the system is shared, like culture, among everyone in that system. No longer will critical knowledge be isolated in a particular design team or software development team or business team and only for the duration of that team's life together.

Design Thinking is a means for effective and lasting cultural change. An enterprise can transform itself into the living, adapting in real time, innovative, and sustainable entity that has long been the vision of business. For any of the preceding to be realized, it is essential that Design Thinking not be put into the straightjacket of method and methodology.

The entire concept of method, especially as it has been employed in business and software development, reeks of mistrust. Mistrust of people. Method is deployed as a means of compensating for perceived human failings and ambiguities. If you assume average and below average capabilities in your human workforce, method becomes a cheap way to obtain slightly above average results. Inexpensive when compared to the alternative — enabling, enhancing, and empowering your human capital.

Design thinking is predicated on the assumption that professionals can and will seek to become modern polymaths capable of working collectively and collaboratively on behalf of themselves, their clients, and all of humanity. Agile software development originated in just this kind of demand for and offering of respect. For many, these assumptions about designers and others adopting design thinking will be deemed idealistic and unrealistic.

We beg to differ!

Figure 5.1 — Sunflower in bloom.
Photo by Thien Gretchen, Texas, US.

Chapter 5
The Patterns

Patterns are known in the software world but are less familiar to those in the business and design communities. For those in the latter, allow us to introduce patterns and an explanation of why we have elected to use them in this book.

The idea of patterns began with Christopher Alexander, an architect. *A Pattern Language* (APL) is the second of a two book exposition on how to assure that built environments, from rooms to cities, had characteristics of beauty, fit, liveness, and QWAN (the Quality Without a Name).

The first book, *The Timeless Way of Building* (TW), contained the philosophy, the why of building with these qualities as goals, and APL was the application of the philosophy in 253 discrete patterns. Each pattern addressed a specific aspect or concern of building at various levels of scale from "1-Independent regions" to "253-Things from your life."

Kent Beck, a respected figure in the software community came across Alexander's work at the University of Oregon. The University of Oregon was partially designed by Alexander and is the subject of Alexander's companion volume to *A Pattern Language*, titled *The Oregon Experiment*. Beck joined a number of others, including Ward Cunningham, to present a workshop at an OOPSLA conference, circa 1996, in Washington D.C. This workshop resulted in the formation of Hillside U.S., a community dedicated to the promotion of "patterns of software". Hillside has sponsored a number of PLoP (Pattern Languages of Programming) conferences around the world: EuroPLoP, AsianPLoP, Sugarloaf PLoP, GuruPLoP, are among them.

Four members of that group — John Vlissides, Ralph Johnson, Erich Gamma, and Richard Helm — published Design Patterns in 1994 and a movement was born. Since then, several books and thousands of papers on patterns and pattern languages have been published. Patterns have been written about software, but also about organizational structures, education, fearless change, human interface design, barbecue, business models, conference organization, beauty & fashion for teenagers; almost any subject that attracted professional attention.

Business professionals working with software developers, and software developers wishing to better understand their business clients found patterns to be of use. Analysis patterns, marketing patterns, knowledge management patterns, banking patterns, monetary patterns, and business culture patterns came to be developed and shared.

Alexander's intent was to develop a "pattern language" which would be more than a collection of patterns — somewhat analogous to a collection of cooking recipes. Instead the patterns would form a vocabulary and relationships among patterns would provide a kind of grammar such that together they would provide a 'language' that architects could use to think about and discuss their work.

Alexander's pattern language was not a general purpose language or even a general purpose architectural language. Instead the intent of the language was centered on how to think about and build environments that had the quality of QWAN — the Quality Without A Name. QWAN evolved into the concept of 'liveness' in Alexander's later work and roughly means Beauty, Fit, and having Life.

Although the design community has not adopted Alexander's ideas of patterns and pattern languages, designers, especially industrial or product designers, do use a similar concept — the "design language". There are several parallels: a design language uses metaphor and standards where Alexander uses patterns to create a kind of vocabulary and suggestive grammar to outline design options and the criteria for selectio among them; each design language has an overarching purpose, or theme, the realization of which is the goal of using that language.

A design language or design vocabulary is an overarching scheme or style that guides the design of individual instances among a set of products or architectural settings. Designers wishing to give a family of products a unique but consistent look and feel, describe choices for design aspects such as materials, colour schemes, shapes, patterns, textures, or layouts as a design language. They then use the language to guide their thinking about and making the decisions they make when designing discrete objects in the product family. [See sidebar about the "Snow White" language used at Apple.]

Discrete 'vocabulary' items — patterns in a pattern language, design specifications in a design language — can be precise or ambiguous. For example, in "Snow White", a corner with a "2 millimeter radius" is very precise but a font expressing "cleanliness and order" is not.

Snow White

Frog Design created the "Snow White" design language for Apple circa 1982 to replace the original Apple industrial design style. Highlights of the language include:
· *Apple computers would be small, clean, and white.*
· *All graphics and typestyles must express cleanliness and order.*
· *Final products would be smart, high tech, and precision tooled.*
· *'No paint, less cost' rule.*
· *Minimal surface texturing.*
· *Recessed international port identification icons.*
· *Simple unadorned ports and slots.*
· *2 and 3 millimeter radii of front and rear rounded corners.*
There were many other, precisely detailed specifications in the design language.

"Light from two sides" from Alexanders pattern language is precise, while "Dancing In The Streets" is more metaphorical and ambiguous. When an element of a design language, or a pattern, is deliberately ambiguous, that element is intended to provide a framework for making a decision rather than the decision itself.

Why use patterns?

Alexander wanted to show architects how to construct buildings, parks, towns, and countrysides that would exhibit QWAN. This was an ambitious goal requiring the effective transfer of massive amounts of information. Alexander realized that the common method for communicating this kind of information, formula and/or method, would not be adequate: mostly because QWAN was complex with ambiguous and unknown elements.

A pattern is a compact way to communicate a concept or an idea, but not as a rule, formula, or discrete step in a method. A pattern provides a concise idea along with sufficient supporting and contextual information that the reader will understand how to use that idea; how to modify and adapt that idea to various contexts; and how to use that idea in combination with other ideas (patterns) to create new, whole, designs.

A design team establishing a design language has a similar objective. A design language is a compact way of summarizing and conveying large amounts of information or knowledge. You can use a design language as a aid to making decisions, an aid to imagination, without the need to recapitulate all of the knowledge and discussion behind each element of the design language.

Design languages and pattern languages are are generative, in that they provide a foundation for discovering, articulating, elaborating, or critiquing both theory and pragmatic application of the transmitted knowledge. Neither is intended to direct the design process; they are intended to help designers think about what they are doing.

Learning design thinking requires effort. For professionals in domains where design thinking is relatively unknown must master design concepts and knowledge essential to adapting that thinking to their domains. At first glance this might suggest a need to write multiple volumes, each focused on a particular aspect of design or specific element in a domain like business or software.

We believe that patterns provide a better approach. They are an effective, precise, and efficient medium of knowledge transmission. They provide a foundation for understanding problems and thinking about solutions. Patterns focus on an element of a design or an aspect of the design process: always with sufficient context to make sense of that element or aspect and understand how it relates to others. This context makes it possible to combine patterns in varied ways to provide powerful design solutions.

Patterns can evolve and change to reflect expansion of our knowledge. The structure of a pattern, including its evocative name, provide a handy index and facilitates the exploration of problems and leads to asking the kind of questions that have led to successful solutions. It is important to stress that a pattern does not provide a solution. It facilitates the designer's efforts to craft one appropriate to his needs.

Patterns

Each pattern provides a framework for thinking about a particular aspect of a design space, an aspect that encompasses some number of potential design decisions. A pattern actually captures a large amount of expert knowledge about what to think about, what things to take into consideration, when confronted with these decisions. A pattern is not a decision or a template for a decision, i.e. it is not a 'solution'.

A pattern is more akin to a story. Paraphrasing one of Alexander's architectural patterns, such a story might be something like the following.

Reflecting on our experience designing rooms, we have noticed that the QWAN or liveness (livability) of a room is enhanced when there are two distinct light sources. When light comes from two directions you limit some undesirable qualities like glare or harsh shadowing. You also ensure that more of the room shares a uniform and indirect light, softening the appearance of things in the room and making it feel more comfortable. A room usually takes the form of a cube, so you could have ceiling or floor light as a complement to window light, but we have found that this works only in exceptional cases; the preference is for light from two different walls. Two adjacent walls is preferred in some circumstances and two opposing walls in others. Of course you must take into account what, besides light, a window allows into a room — is it a beautiful vista, or the blunt and unappealing reveal of a brick wall of an adjacent building?

A common definition of a pattern is, "a solution to a problem in context."

This has led to a lot of misunderstanding of what patterns and pattern languages actually offer. Too often they are seen, and implemented, as a kind of solutions catalog .

A pattern is a compact, formatted, way of transmitting knowledge and experience.

Patterns contain: a discussion of a specific concept or aspect of a practice — e.g. architecture or design — that examines discrete challenges, where those challenges are encountered, what makes them challenging, how those challenges have been resolved and why those resolutions seem to have worked.

150

It is easy to see that a natural language narrative makes many of the details implicit and somewhat ambiguous. Alexander was trying to find a balance between the overly open format of a story and the overly explicit format of a specification. A pattern is a compromise. The structure of a pattern is intended to ensure enough of the story, and enough of the details in the story, are communicated while avoiding any sense that the pattern is intended to be 'The Answer'. A pattern can be seen functioning as a kind of checklist — did you remember to talk about this, explain that, or connect these ideas with those ideas?

The early adopters of patterns, outside of architecture, were classically trained computer scientists and software engineers. People like James Coplien and the Gang of Four (Vlissides, Helms, Johnson, and Gamma) authors of the first design patterns book, tended to see Alexander's structure as a specification. Some of them insisted, and still insist, that you cannot have a pattern that is not in "pure Alexandrian Form."

Most of the pattern authors came to recognize the need to adapt Alexander's structure and add, delete, or modify elements of that structure to facilitate what they were actually trying to communicate. As ideas about patterns evolved, multiple formats emerged but all of them intended to provide the clearest possible communication of a bit of knowledge and understanding.

Our pattern format includes the following:

1. A graphic icon that is intended to visually capture the focus of the pattern. These icons are used in various maps — especially the Mandala Map that will be discussed below — showing relationships among patterns.

below

Star Rating
Alexander used a three star system to indicate the maturity of his patterns; with three stars meaning his team 'nailed it,' two meaning more work was needed, and one meaning uncertainty about the pattern's expression.

We will mirror Alexander and one star will indicate something akin to 'draft' status, two indicates that refinement is needed, and three meaning we are pretty confident that we have it right.

2. A number followed by a name and number of stars [* * — see sidebar]. The number reflects 'type' or 'category', one way of interrelating patterns. The name is intended to be evocative and memorable — hearing the name immediately recalls to mind the substance of the pattern. The stars are a measure of confidence.

3. Pictures that capture the essence of the pattern. Pictures, like the name, are intended to be an evocative trigger, to 'recall to memory' the knowledge in the body of the pattern.

4. A thumbnail provides a means for quickly identifying when the pattern is useful (summary of problem and context) and the key aspects of the solution. The thumbnail is our own contribution to the patterns format style guide.

151

5. A context where a description of the problem space illuminates and helps to understand the nature of the problem.

6. An enumeration of forces, identifying discrete, but interacting, constraints or expectations that must be simultaneously resolved in any solution. A symmetrical relationship exists between the forces and the solutions that resolve them.

7. The problem itself, a succinct but clear delineation of the nature of the specific issues that might be appropriately addressed by the pattern. The challenge here is to describe the problem abstractly such that it reflects a problem space, but not so generally that it obscures the essence of the problem.

8. A solution follows, but again it is not 'The Solution', or even a family of 'solutions'. Using systems thinking vocabulary, the solution can be seen as an assertion akin to: "When encountering this problem we have found that modification of the elements or relationships of the system in this manner seems to provide a resolution, in context, of the forces that we believe led to the problem in the first place." The intent of a solution statement is to show how aspects of a problem might be matched to changes that can resolve the dynamics of that problem. It is a tool to assist the designer in thinking about their real and immediate problem and guide the exploration of a solution space.

9. A resulting context section describes the outcome, the consequences, of applying the pattern with an emphasis on how things will be improved.

10. Discussion, prose describing the pattern, elaborating the problem and solution sections, useful information peripheral but relevant to the pattern, and, often, examples and stories about uses of the pattern in various contexts.

11. Business Value. Discussion and examples of the benefits — cost, time, effectiveness — that are likely to accrue if the pattern is utilized in conjunction with other patterns and/or the value of the solutions that derive from the use of the pattern. The goal is to provide concrete evidence of potential business value.

12. Related Patterns notes instances where one pattern enhances, extends, or complements another. This is a second form of organization establishing relationships among patterns that serve as first order suggestions for the effective combination of patterns to generate powerful designs.

152

Pattern Relationships

Our intent is to provide the reader with a pattern language, not just some narrative and set of discrete patterns. The patterns we present provide a foundational vocabulary. It is not a complete vocabulary, as there are, potentially, hundreds of relevant patterns. As we noted earlier, relationships between and among patterns provide the 'grammar' necessary if the vocabulary is to be transformed into a generative language.

We have provided four complementary ways to establish relationships among patterns. We have included pattern names and terse descriptions in Chapter Four when discussing issues and ideas where the patterns are particularly relevant. For example: we spoke earlier about how design thinking challenges traditional organizational and spacial structures and noted how patterns, e.g. **Tribes**, and **A Room of One's Own** contribute to understanding and resolving those challenges. Similarly, our discussion of the need for diverse experts in self-organized teams is partially discussed in our patterns: **It Takes a Village** and **Tribes**.

Secondly, we have use the pattern numbers and associated colors to define four categories in which we organize the 29 presented patterns

100-199 Essence
These patterns distill the core worldview and values at the heart of the design culture. All of the other patterns are grounded in the Essence patterns.

200-299 Principles
Principles provide a bridge between Essence and Practices by distilling Essence into actionable directives that, in turn, provide the rational for individual actions, practices.

300-399 Practices
Guidelines for what to do, who to do it with, and where it might be done. These are not items on a checklist or steps in a method. They are suggestions derived from successful application.

400-499 Evaluation
A successful design, one exhibiting fit or Alexander's QWAN, has an ineffable aspect. These patterns provide focus on observable qualities that are primary indicators of design success.

A section of each pattern expressly states know relationships to other patterns, providing a third and explicit connection among patterns.

A final way of presenting relationships among patterns is a map inspired by a "Wheel of Life" Thanka painting above David's desk. This painting is in the form of a Mandala and captures with a detailed, but compact, 50 cm by 70 cm image an immense amount of knowledge about Tibetan Buddhist cosmology and mythology. [Figure 5.2] The innermost circle of the Wheel of Life contains icons representing the factors that give rise to the phenomenological World. These include envy, attachment, and lust.

We use a simplified version of this mandala to map a set of overarching and general relationships. [Figure 5.3] The core of the Mandala contains the icons for the Essence patterns, recognizing their generative nature and the fact that they are infused into and support all of the other patterns.

A large middle section is occupied by "Realms of Existence" — groups of patterns that are more closely connected to each other than any of them are to patterns in other 'realms'. Potential realms include the categories noted above: e.g. Principles, Practices, and Evaluation. It would also make sense to group one or more of the Essence patterns with those in other categories or realms based on how the latter directly derive from the former. Realms like Teams, Communication, Thinking Space gather patterns that directly make significant contributions to the stated Realm.

In Buddhism the realm of the gods, heaven, hell, and human existence. Our 'realms' are Principles, Practices, Teams, Imagination, and Evaluation. The fact that a set of icons, each representing an individual pattern, are grouped into a realm, suggests that they work collectively to establish and maintain the essence of that realm. Patterns within a realm are more frequently encountered with others in that realm, but remain connected to other patterns in the vocabulary.

The outermost circle gives the mandala its name, Wheel of Life, and represents the sequence of 'stages' from birth to death to rebirth. Our visualization captures a prototypical cycle of design activities. For the most part, the sequence is self-evident: beginning with Zen Mind and openness to understanding the nature and essence of the system to which you wish to apply design thinking. Design Brief and Prometheus Bound indicate the need to know fairly early in the process what is to be designed and boundaries that must be observed. Teams need to be assembled and think/work spaces established. Eventually designs are

Figure 5.2 — "Wheel of Life" Thanka painting above David's desk. This painting is in the form of a Mandala and captures with a detailed, but compact, 50 cm by 70 cm image an immense amount of knowledge about Tibetan Buddhist cosmology and mythology.

155

Figure 5.3
"Wheel of Design" — At the core of design
thinking is a worldview, a metaphysics,
and other aspects of a design culture.

156

implemented and require evaluation — which can lead to another pass around the cycle. While it is true that neither life nor design is linear in nature, some aspect of sequence helps in relating the patterns to specific activities or milestones. Our visualization captures this sequence while recognizing and illustrating that it is both cyclic and non-linear.

Our visualization can also be used as a visual 'index'. A quick glance at a stage of the design cycle or one of the realms, quickly leads to relevant patterns, even they had not already come to the readers attention. If a pattern is almost but not quite what you want, the relationships provide a key for finding others that might be more appropriate.

As a body the patterns provide a Design thinking framework. Individual patterns develop deeper understanding of both the framework and specific knowledge areas.

The pattern titles, along with the mandala map, provide an index that allows the reader to find specific patterns of interest — that are most applicable to the reader's current objectives. This eliminates the need to read all the patterns before you find what you need. Following relationships among patterns directs your reading with a constant focus on the most relevant knowledge. Eventually, as you incorporate the patterns into your thinking you will find yourself using them as vocabulary terms in interesting ways.

We present twenty-nine patterns in this book, but we fully recognize that this is not an exhaustive collection. Nor are the four categories complete. One category we considered but decided to leave for our companion website (design-thinking.systems), was Technique. Some of our first ideas for patterns in this category included: **Alignment**, **80/20 Rule**, **Attractiveness Bias**, **Gradient**, **Chunking**, and **Area Alignment**.

We do invite the reader to explore our website for additional patterns, hopefully many will be contributed by our readers, additional examples, and an ongoing commentary about the ideas in the book.

Essence

These patterns address the essence of Design and of the Designer's mind. Patterns in this category are presuppositional, acting as quasi-definitions and/or unspoken. Usually these concepts are cultural; which means they are typically found below the level of consciousness. Culture is seamless amalgam of perspective, attitude, values, world-view, and mental state that is taken as a given to those within the culture. They are seldom as obvious to those not sharing the culture.

The first pattern, **Form**, addresses the essence of that which is designed. **Unfolding** is focused on the process of designing. And, **Zen Mind** is concerned with the mental framework of the designer. The patterns can be difficult to understand. In part because they are abstract; and, in part because they address concepts that are substantially ineffable.

Patterns are supposed to reflect distillations of knowledge from multiple contexts. Our search for patterns began with observations of different designers and different types of designer (applied arts, architectural, software). It expanded with the recognition that everyone is a designer and all things are designed.

Any discussion of the ineffable will, by definition, involve knowledge or experience that is not easily put into words. The mental state of the designer approaching and engaging with a design problem is and example of the ineffable. The relationships between the designer and the designed is similarly difficult to address except via metaphor or koan-like assertions. The archer being one with the arrow is an example.

Our pattern, **Zen Mind**, uses the story of Sesshu and his work, the Long Scroll, illustrate the experience reported by many designers, particularly at the moment of clarity that immediately precedes articulation of the design. The mental state of Sesshu engaged in painting his scroll is an example of what many designers have experienced but few can articulate.

The five patterns introduced in this section are patterns of Designer's Mind. They are not patterns of how to achieve Designer's Mind. Just as there are many roads to enlightenment, the paths to Designer's Mind are myriad. It is not our intent to describe or define the Path, rather we are offering these patterns as a partial means to limn the Destination. The five patterns in this initial section are "used" in that someone seeking Designer's Mind will find them helpful in assessing, via introspection, if their Own Mind has characteristics reflective of the patterns we have observed in Designer's Mind.

Form ***

Thumbnail

If (any of these)
- your problem seems really complicated,
- how to proceed is not obvious, or
- your solutions do not seem to fit the problems;

then (all of these)
- acknowledge immutable essence,
- separate circumstance and essence, and
- respect simplicity.

160

Context

A dynamic reality where essence, Form, is constantly expressing itself as best it can in changing circumstances.

Reality is highly dynamic and intricately complex. Every act of design begins with a need to understand Reality, to isolate forces, find regularities, and recognize the ephemeral apart from the eternal. An elegant simplicity underpins and provides the generative force that gives rise to all that we, as humans, perceive.

Forces

Everything has an immutable essence. Essence is constantly trying to express itself. Circumstances impose constraints on expression. Designers can facilitate the expression of essence but only to the extent that their abilities, experiences and world view expose ways to alter circumstances; freeing essence to achieve full expression.

Problem

Everything has an essence, a form, that is expressed or made manifest in a particular context. The context includes the insights and abilities of the designer. The expression of form maybe incomplete or distorted by those circumstances. Circumstances change so a manifestation that may have been appropriate no longer fits. How can you assure that a manifestation, a design, is simultaneously the purest expression of essence, while being most appropriate for the immediate circumstance?

Therefore,

Form is the core coming to the surface.
— Victor Hugo

Solution

Use design thinking to recognize that behind apparent
complexity is the simplicity of a form, an immutable
essence that can be discovered by stripping away
the context that disguises the form.

Make the design consistent with the essence, the form,
and let it reflect itself in the manifestation.

Resulting context

The designer facilitated manifestations will reflect
the wholeness and simplicity of the essence.

Every design makes a change to a dynamic complex
system. Despite best efforts, the consequences of change
are ultimately unpredictable, making design a "wicked
problem" where the solution actually changes the problem. Good and great design will enhance the stability of
the system while enhancing our understanding in ways
that allow the designer to constantly evolve and improve
the design. Even poor design creates an opportunity

to increase understanding, expose previously unknown constraints, and clarify essence in support of redesign.

The most important aspect of the resulting context is the awareness that all design is interactive.

Pattern Description

This pattern asserts that there is an essence, Form, in all things and that this essence is manifested, in full or in part, in various circumstances. Designers facilitate expression of Form to the extent of their abilities.

Discussion

The idea of an essence in every thing we see in the world around us is fundamental to all but the most objectivist of philosophies. Japanese culture, and their concept of Kata provide an example. Kata is usually translated as "form". There is an umbrella term, shikata, that appends the prefix shi — the root meaning of which is a combination of "support" and "serve" — to form, thus yielding a "way of doing things." with special emphasis on the form and order of the process. "Way" has two connotations: how Form comes to be expressed and the behavior employed to bring about the congruency of Form and context. Boyé Lafayette De Mente [2003] discusses kata extensively:

> *"Some of the more common uses of kata include yomi kata "way of reading", kangae kata "way of thinking", and iki kata "way of living". ... There are dozens of other kata. In fact, there is hardly an area of Japanese thought or behavior that is not directly influenced by one or more kata.*

> *When used in the Japanese context the shikata concept includes more than just the mechanical process of doing something. It also incorporates the physical and spiritual laws of the cosmos. It refers to the way things are supposed to be done, both the form and the order, as a means of expressing and maintaining harmony in society and the universe.*

> *The absence of shikata is virtually unthinkable to the Japanese, for that refers to an unreal world, without order or form.*

> *Early in their history the Japanese developed the belief that form had a reality of its own, and that it often took precedence over substance.*

163

They also believed that anything could be accomplished if the right kata was mentally and physically practiced long enough.

To the Japanese there was an inner order (the individual heart) and a natural order (the cosmos), and these two were linked together by form – by kata. It was kata that linked the individual and society. If one did not follow the correct form, he was out of harmony with both his fellow man and nature. The challenge facing the Japanese was to know their own honshin, "true" or "right heart", then learn and follow the kata that would keep them in sync with society and the cosmos.

Zen priests teach that mental training is just as important, if not more so, than physical training in the achieving of harmony and the mastery of any skill. ...

The ultimate goal in traditional Japanese education among the samurai and professional classes was for the pupil to become one with the object of his training. The goal of the swordsman was to merge his consciousness with his sword; the painter with his brush; the potter with his clay; the garden designer with the materials of the garden. Once this was achieved, as the theory goes, the doing of a thing perfectly was as easy as thinking it."

— Boyé Lafayette De Mente 2003

The notion of a soul (with religious connotations) or a self (more secular) as the essence of a human being is almost universal. Animism and pantheism suggest that all living things have the equivalent of a soul — a bit of anime. A metaphysical thread running through the Vedas and Buddhism suggests that all matter, down to individual quanta, is infused with some proportional amount of 'intelligence'.

Everything, not just material objects and living things have an essence as well. Relationships among things also have an essence. In this case what is meant by essence is really more a sense of 'true nature' along with the sense that something is correct or appropriate when its expression conforms to its true nature. Behaviors and patterns of behavior also have an essence and are held to be appropriate or proper when the overt behaviors are consistent with an ideal or essential nature. The British, for example might compliment someone's behavior with the expression, 'good form'. This example illustrates the use of the term, 'form', as reference to essence or true nature and we see that the expression of form can be seen as positive (good) or negative (bad).

Essence, Form, is intrinsic to a thing, and is not, usually, directly perceived. Only when essence is manifest, as form, relation, behavior, etc., is it sensed, observed, appreciated, or evaluated. We often use terms like 'shape,' 'appearance,' 'structure' and even 'form' as synonyms for essence, Form, conflating two concepts that should be distinct.

Essence in Context

The shape of a tree is dependent on where its seed took root. Soil conditions, exposure to light as a result of surrounding trees and landscape. Elements suspended in the water that nourishes the tree and the frequency with which that water is provided also affect how the tree-that-was-implicit-in-theseed, is able to manifest itself. The origin of the seed, the qualities it inherited from the tree that generated it, affect the potential of the seed. All of these factors constitute the 'context' that constrains the ability of the essence to manifest itself.

What is true of the seed is equally true for any essence, and Form.

Manifestations of form are constrained by context. Context can inhibit the extent to which an essence manifests itself and can also contort or distort that essence, making it difficult to perceive without a well trained eye.

Designers attempt to facilitate the manifestation of essence and thereby insert themselves into the context in which that manifestation emerges. The abilities of the designer, their training, their experience, the degree to which they have the well-trained-eye, all become contextual boundaries.

Designer Role

Individuals in traditional design disciplines (applied arts) have a very different concept of their role, vis à vis their design outcomes, than business consultants and software developers, including human computer interface 'designers'. Design, as a verb, has two opposing, and perhaps irreconcilable, meanings: design as facilitating the expression of essence; and design as the deliberate construction of form.

Applied artists, are more likely to see their work in terms of facilitation — assisting the innate essence to express

165

a form that is most appropriate for a given context — by adding, modifying, replacing, or deleting some aspect of that context. Essence is respected and context is adapted.

Business engineers and software designers (from programmers to human-computer interface designers) in contrast, take the context, in the form of absolute requirements and specifications, as a given and seek to find a form that will best fit the context. Essence is irrelevant. This process, not surprisingly, gives rise to 'designed solutions' that are orders of magnitude more complicated than the problems they address. Such solutions are also brittle — even minor changes in the context (requirements) can have devastating impact on the viability of the initial solution. Despite such obvious problems, 'design as shape construction' continues to be the dominant perspective in business engineering and software, largely because 'construction' seems to be amenable to formal methods and managed processes. As organizations begin to explore and attempt to learn from the applied arts, they will need to reconsider their approach and their conception of the nature of designing.

Simplicity

When you see things as a whole, you see simplicity and elegance. Both science and design assume this to be true: the physicist seeks the elegance of an equation, e=mc2, that simplicity contains all of classical physics; the designer seeks the elegance of an expression that is the essence.

That which appears large and complicated, does so because the perceiver fails to differentiate the essence of the system apart from the individual essences of each element and each relationship within the system. *"The whole is other than the sum of the parts."* [Kurt Koffka]. The system in and of itself is a unity, a whole, and is simple enough to grasp.

166

Related patterns

Zen Mind enhances our ability to discern **Form**. **Unfolding** explores how essence becomes manifest in ways that preserve that essence. Care must be taken to assure that names, words, used to identify and discuss **Form** are, in fact True Names, as explored in **Logos**.

Form is whole and can be seen as whole, **Gestalt**. **System Metaphor** is, like **Gestalt**, a tool for pragmatic thinking and talking about **Form**. **Russian Dolls** discusses the preservation of **Form** across levels of scale, i.e. how **Form** can be represented in an abstract model that is consistent across those levels. This same model is presupposed in **Everything an Object**. Essence may appear in many forms without losing its core, because the context involves an observer and different observers pay heed to different aspects, different **Personae**.

All of the evaluation patterns share the premise that simplicity is complete expression of essence with no extraneous factors, a criteria for determining QWAN.

Form is perceived with a **Zen Mind** and the designer uses **Logos** to facilitate **Unfolding**.

Illustration

Along the Pacific coast of the United States are groves of majestic redwood trees. These trees can have trunks that measure 10 feet (3 meters) in diameter and reach a height of more than 100 feet (30 meters). A subspecies, the Giant Sequoia, will have diameters exceeding 30 feet (9.1 meters) and heights of 150 feet (45 meters).

Little redwood sprouts look almost like any other pine seedling. Often only an expert botanist or very experienced gardener can tell, simply by looking, what kind of adult a baby pine is destined to become.

The most interesting thing about redwoods is the mystery of where they come from. It is not a mystery today, of course, but in the not so distant past, it was unclear how these trees reproduced. In the redwood groves it is not uncommon to see a circle of small trees around the trunk of a dead or fallen tree. These were called "fairy rings." It was fairly easy to trace the roots of the trees in the circle to the boles on the trunks and exposed roots of the original tree. Modern DNA science proves that these new trees are clones of the original, identical in DNA composition.

The mystery is where the trees came from that were not clones. It was a mystery because it was not easy to find, or even see, the seeds of the redwood tree. Redwood seeds are so small that a million of them would weigh about 8 pounds (3.6 kilos). (In contrast, a million sunflower seeds would weigh about 150 pounds, almost 70 kilos.)

Despite the size difference, the tiny redwood seeds contain the Form of the redwood tree. Form is preserved, both when a mature tree produces new seeds, containing the innate Form, and when a tree clones itself without the seed as intermediary.

Fairy rings also show how Shape results both from Form and from context. The various trees in the ring — all of them with identical DNA and therefore identical essence or Form — rapidly start to exhibit individual differences. These differences arise from context, different amounts of sunlight, water, competition with other plants, or individual encounters with insects, disease or herbivores.

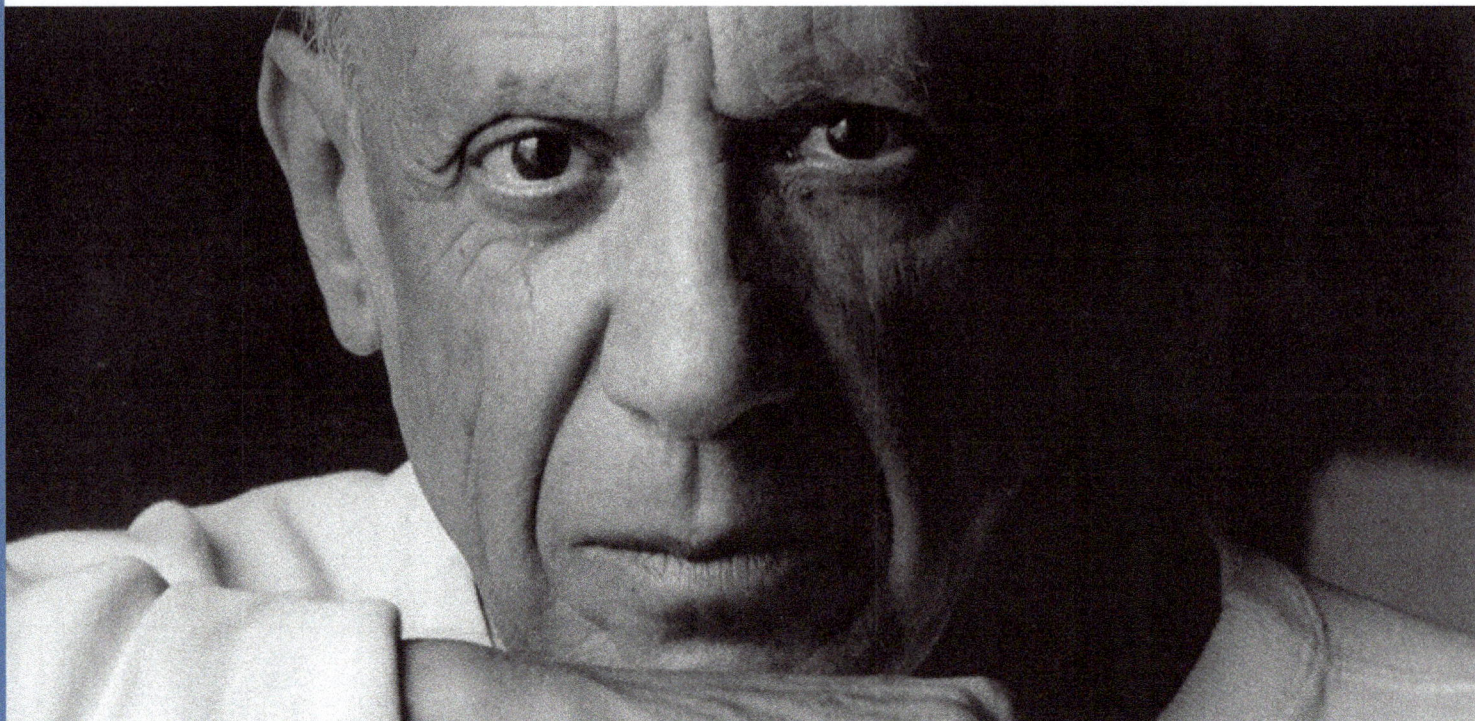

🔹 Unfolding ***

Thumbnail

If (any of these)
- you are not sure of the way forward,
- you tend to equate design with planning, or
- things are getting complicated;

then (all of these)
- let the designed be the designer,
- assure essence preserving transformations, and
- weed your garden.

Context

Design is directed activity, often by teams with different perspectives and possibly conflicting judgements. Designers must not only discern Form and the means that allow that Form to best express itself, they must simultaneously develop and follow a process that will not interfere and will contribute to effective expression.

Forces

Outcomes reflect the processes that generate them. Every thing has an essence and this essence wishes to be expressed, as completely and as faithfully as possible. Contexts offer opportunities and impose boundaries that affect the degree to which an essence can be expressed. The designer has a skill set and a body of experience that support his ability to facilitate the expression of essence. The designer is part of the context and imposes constraints on the expression of form that arise from his personal limitations — e.g. insufficient skills or experience, lack of self awareness, resistance, fears, ego, etc.

Problem

It is difficult to discern and lay out an explicit path that leads from essence to expression. The information necessary to identify all the critical decisions and actions required is incomplete, at best. There is little if any assurance that the final result will be 'Essential'.

Therefore,

Become who you are.
— Pablo Picassso

Solution

Allow the essence, the Form, to express itself, by Unfolding.
Begin with the assurance that you have understood the
essence of a thing and that you understand the environment, the context. Allow discrete, usually small, transformations, with, also discrete and usually small, alterations
in the context, each focused on allowing a new shape while
preserving essence.

Stop when the essence tells you it is 'as good as it can be
in the circumstances'.

Resulting context

A world where designed artifacts express essence and are
congruent with the world in which they are expressed.

However, the expression of Form has been constrained
by context, so being congruent does not mean that Form
has been optimally expressed. If you are dissatisfied with
the design, you should look to ways of modifying the context so it can be a better host for the form that expressed

172

in it. This adds a second dimension to the design effort, one that could be addressed at each increment of the iterative design process.

Pattern Description

The pattern shows how design relies on a natural process, unfolding, which is a sequence of essence preserving transformations. The designer assists by making appropriate alterations to the context assuring the fullest possible expression of the essence.

Discussion

We see two different approaches to building, or constructing, something. One focuses on fitting a solution to its context, as a whole, and seeking characteristics like beauty and QWAN. The other is concerned with the abstracting from the world a set of requirements that can be satisfied and building to requirements. Christopher Alexander's, Timeless Way of Building, captures the essence of one while, Herbert Simon's, The Sciences of the Artificial, captures the essence of the other. Our work shares the worldview of Alexander.

Alexander expresses his ideas about process most clearly in The Nature of Order with his extensive discussion of the organic, biological, process by which a seed transforms into a flower.

Complementing Alexander's ideas about unfolding, Richard Gabriel once wrote an essay, the "Designed as Designer" demonstrating how the thing being designed is an active participant in the design process.

Chaucer tells us, "an ook cometh of a litel spyr" putting into words a phenomenon we see around us every day — the emergence of something like the mighty oak tree from a mere sapling, and before that a tiny seed, an acorn. Modern biology tells us that all living things arise from a process of self-directed division and differentiation driven by our DNA — subject to environmental constraints that trigger or inhibit genetic expression.

Biology says that the essence of any life-form is sufficient to assure expression of that essence. Nuances and details, the kind of thing that allows for individual variation among a class of life-forms, are enabled by connection to the environment. Different environments have the effect of shaping different outcomes. Our pattern pre-supposes this biological model and extends it to apply to design and the product of design. Specifically, we see unfolding as universal, even for things we typically think of as non-biological, like a design. We are arguing that a design exists as a kind of seed and that it contains an essence, akin to DNA, that allows itself to unfold, to undergo a sequence of essence preserving transformations. Just as in biology, the extent to which the outcome of a transformation preserves fullness of the essence is dependent on environment factors. This makes the role of a designer more akin to the role of horticulturist, aiding growth, expression, by making appropriate changes to the environment, context, that constrains unfolding.

The only constant is change.

Unfolding occurs, but somewhat differently, over long time scales — this kind of unfolding is 'evolution'. Change in any dynamic system is constant and reciprocal, i.e. an element might unfold to a shape which then causes the context to vary, or a change in context affects the way in which an essence is expressed.

'Artificial' elements of a system — policies and procedures, products, bridges, buildings, logotypes, chairs, vacuum cleaners, computers, and software — change so slowly that they are usually perceived as static. A system is able to evolve, transform itself over time, is directly proportional to the number of artificial elements it contains. When the context and natural elements change at a different rate than artificial elements, the system as a whole will contain an increasing number of 'misfits, inconsistencies among elements and conflict between context and element. A differential pace of change can also occur between natural elements and their context — witness the dinosaurs vis-a-vis the rapidly, almost instantly, changing post-comet environment.

Unfolding over time, evolution, is optimized when the system and most o fits elements are capable of unfolding — transforming from state to state while preserving essence, or Form.

One more important consequence of our approach to design, is the nature of the 'target', of that which is designed. We see design as focused on an existing reality, not the construction of an artificial replicant of that reality. Design directly changes the world.

Design should yield 'living' results. By that we mean designs that are sensitive to their context at the moment

174

and over time. These elements unfold from Form to expression iteratively and in response to contextual changes that enable alternative expressions. Further, there should be consistency in rate of change in element and context.

Our insights parallel those expressed by Alexander, for example his discussion of unfolding as a basic property of the nature of order. Alexander, however, was concerned with structure, and structure preserving transformations, metaphorically the same as an equation that is too difficult to solve being transformed into another expression by adding, subtracting, dividing, or multiplying two sides of an equation by the same factor for example yielding a new expression that is easier to solve. A set of allowable transformations assure that the "Truth" of the original equation is preserved at each step of the 're-expression process.'

In partial contrast, our presentation of unfolding as "essence preserving transformations" focuses on essence and the faithful expression of that essence. Essence is always expressed in context and the context imposes both opportunities and constraints. There is an intimate connection between essence and context, both affecting the other. One, essence is immutable. Only context is malleable and it is only context that can be altered by the designer. The designer is part of the context and is also mutable. The designer can change, adding skills, learns from experience, and internalizes insights arising from acts of design.

Related patterns

Designers, as effective participants in **Unfolding**, should possess a **Zen Mind** in order to clearly perceive essence, **Form**, and the totality, **Gestalt**, of context.

Embodied Mind expands our notions of where thought and action originate or reside, usually the brain or mind, to incorporate the body, as an organism, and actions of the body, e.g. kinesthic knowledge. Experiencing design, particularly experiencing **Unfolding**, allows the designer to gain insights, and knowledge, neither of which are necessarily mental.

As an 'essence' pattern, **Unfolding** informs and influences all of the other patterns, bringing to them an awareness of the distinction between the natural and the artificial, the importance of designs that are 'alive', and other aspects of fit, congruence between thing and context.

175

Illustration

A time-lapse film of the emergence of a flower from a seed is the ideal visualization of the concept of unfolding. As the aril splits and the seed within begins to expand and differentiate into stem, petal, and, eventually, flower cells you see a recurring motif as newly differentiated parts separate and expand — they unfold.

Observing a bonsai artist at work is the perfect metaphor for how a designer interacts with the designed to obtain the desired results.

A seed or seedling is placed in a nurturing environment where it can express itself, unfold, just as its nature, its Form, demands.

The bonsai designer adds nutrients and exposes the seedling to sunshine to facilitate this expression. She might orient the seedling to the sun in order to encourage it to bend or branch in a particular direction as the plant seeks the optimal amount of light.

Like any system, design involves adding, deleting or altering an element. The bonsai system includes elements like branches, leaves, stems or trunks but also includes context, the container, perhaps rocks or moss, or figurines. The artist adds some of these elements, one at a time, or alters one of them — trimming a bud to encourage the growth of another element — also one at a time.

After each change the system, as a whole, is evaluated by comparing its Shape with the artist's understanding of the system's innate Form. The artist, the designer, must understand the Form so as to recognize that Form expressed as Shape. The designer also has a conception, an idea, of what might be the optimal Shape, the most suitable expression of Form, for a given circumstance or problem.

A Bonsai pine, in a context that simulates a seashore — with known patterns of wind and waves, time of year, and orientation to the sun — constitutes a statement of the design problem.

The designer manipulates the system, most importantly the elements of the pine tree itself, until is actual Shape matches the designer's conception of Shape-in-Context.

◎ Zen Mind ***

Thumbnail

If (any of these)
- you are lost in a plethora of trees,
- you know the "Devil is in the details," but would prefer not to go to Hell, or
- you fear failure;

then (all of these)
- apprehend the forest,
- master Non-Attachment, and
- be the Form.

Context

Our senses create a world of appearance, what a Buddhist would call Maya, or illusion. Our mind constantly interprets, analyzes, and attempts to "make sense" an overwhelming number of discrete inputs. Our mind differentiates, classifies, parses and analyzes — creating an internally consistent model. The analysis behind the model is subjective and influenced by the cultural and historical context in which it occurred. That is why so many people, for so long, believed the Earth to be flat.

Design demands we see through Maya and recognize the Essence — the human behind the facade of 'client', the emitter originating the sense input, the Form immanent in the element.

Awareness clarity and understanding are essential for any design activity or decision, and all are realized to the extent our open and enquiring mind supersedes our calculating mind. Beginnings are often times of anxiety and pressure. You can be tempted to anticipate understanding that is merely a projection of prior knowledge or see only those problems you already know how to solve.

Forces

Clarity of understanding is essential because you cannot build on false premises. There are many forces that conspire that prevent understanding: ego or false confidence, the inappropriate language of vocabulary, poor names, and simple miscommunication. Essence is often disguised or hidden behind a facade of illusion. Insufficient knowledge of context distorts meaning. Life and its myriads of demands are distracting. We fail to recognize and tend to project the world view that comes from our culture, because our own culture is usually below our threshold of consciousness.

Problem

We are so accustomed to the illusory world around us and so confident that we understand that illusion that we fail to see the reality behind it.

Therefore,

Solution

Still your mind. Leaving attachments and false understandings behind so that the real presents itself to you without
filters or distortions. Having achieved this state of mind
nurture its persistence so that it could be practiced in all
your other activities. Be like the enlightened being who
sleeps when tired, drinks when thirsty, eats when hungry.

Resulting context

You're 'in the zone'. You see correctly, you act correctly,
and you think correctly, all without effort, or conscious
attention. As exhilarating and desirable as this state might
be, it does not in itself result in an implemented solution.
Your 'perfect' understanding may or may not be capable
of direct implementation. There can be a significant gap
between concept and ink on paper; between what should
be done and the expressive capabilities of your computer
and the possibilities hardwired into computer circuits.
The value of the principles and practices patterns that
follow derives, in large part, from their power to facilitate
'translation'.

Pattern Description

This is a pattern about a state of mind or being. When one is in that state of being, one is highly sensitive to surroundings, is able to listen, and to see clearly the reality behind the illusion. Ego is removed, and the designer acts on the basis of need and correctness, in conformance with the Form rather than on the basis of willful desire. The designer becomes the instrument of the designed, engaging in a dialog and assisting the self-expression of Form.

Discussion

The pattern might appear mystical in nature mostly because it is associated with traditions and philosophy, like Zen that are often perceived as such. The 'state of mind' discussed in the pattern is actually quite common, and most of us have experienced it. It goes by many names, 'in the zone' and 'flow' being among the most common. It is also the state of mind that comes with mastering something, like riding a bicycle or playing chess — the point where you simply do what is correct without 'thinking about it'.

The limitations of our conscious mind are well known, Miller's "magic number seven, plus or minus two" is a frequently cited example. Less familiar are the capabilities of our non-conscious mind: the ability to process millions of simultaneous sensory inputs, to recognize and respond to thousands of highly dynamic variables (internal and external), vivid and detailed memory, and recognition of familiar things, like your father's face, even when you have fleeting and miniscule data points with which to work.

Transcendence is another term descriptive of the state of mind in this pattern and transcendence is oft advocated as an essential step in the quest for mastery. Kent Beck, for example, state that there were three stages of Extreme Programming: "out of the box, adapted, and transcended." Christopher Alexander noted that is was not possible to practice the timeless way of building until you had mastered the pattern language, which was but a gate, and the passed through the gate.

Despite our familiarity, often non conscious, with the state of mind advocated in this pattern, it remains 'mystical' in flavor. Perhaps this is due to the lack of 'procedure' in descriptions of how to achieve this state of mind.

The most common metaphor used to introduce the way in which a stilled mind is achieved, is a lake reflecting the Moon. Until all of the waves and ripples in the surface of the lake are smoothed out, stilled, the Moon cannot be reflected, perceived, completely and with clarity. Missing from the metaphor, however, is how one identifies the source or a perturbation and once identified, how is it countered.

This step towards a stilled mind is also quite simple, and very well known and is fundamental to our understanding of experience.

Designers are expected to design — frequently, constantly, in diverse contexts, using diverse media, and always subject to feedback and criticism. Poets write poems and accept criticism. Zen practitioners meditate, take actions to still their mind, and receive feedback. (If the stories of Zen practice are to be believed, often with a cudgel to the side of the head.)

Learning from experience is, typically, not part of the education of business professionals and software developers. Richard Gabriel makes a point of this by comparing his education as a poet and his education as a computer scientist. Mastery of poetry required writing a poem a day, at minimum, but computer science required writing a few dozen, toy programs. Cultivation a Zen Mind is not only the right thing to do, it brings with it many tangible benefits.

Part of Sesshu's Long Scroll

A stilled mind reflects a whole, a gestalt, which, in turn, provides the context for understanding the discrete, trees in a forest instead of a forest that is a complicated collection of a multitude of trees. A gestalt provides the context that allows correct interpretation and implementation of individual details by allowing you to focus on the detail without losing sight of how that detail conforms to the whole.

The non-conscious mind is capable of integrating vast volumes of sensory inputs. As problems increase in scale and become more complicated and dynamic in nature, the number of variables multiply beyond the ability of a human mind to simultaneously comprehend them. Your non-conscious mind however does this as a matter or course.

What is difficult or impossible for the conscious is child's play for the non-conscious. You do need to operationalize the non-conscious, establish a stilled mind, but that is the result of practice. When you are 'in the zone', have a stilled mind, you open up the possibility of 'doing the right thing,' instead of striving 'to do what is right.' A stilled mind reflects a whole, all of the relevant factors affecting an action or a decision, a kind of situational omniscience. This is not the 'omniscience' of memorizing Wikipedia, but the omniscience that comes from allowing your non-conscious awareness to integrate all that knowledge and effect an immediate, usually also non conscious, response.

183

A corollary of doing what is right, is the absence of YOU. It is not your ego that is responsible for the doing. It is the situation and all of the factors operative in that situation that are expressing themselves. You are merely the instrument. YOU are not responsible, it is not YOUR doing. Professions as diverse as warfare, flower arranging, and brewing and serving tea, are exemplars of egoless action. As Lafayette De Mente points out:

> "The ultimate goal in traditional Japanese education among the samurai and professional classes was for the pupil to become one with the object of his training. The goal of the swordsman was to merge his consciousness with his sword; the painter with his brush; the potter with his clay; the garden designer with the materials of the garden. Once this was achieved, as the theory goes, the doing of a thing perfectly was as easy as thinking it."

Doing the right thing with a stilled mind can result in what appear to be superhuman effort. Sesshu was a Zen master and an artist, a Sumi-e landscape painter. The following illustrations are from Sesshu's Long Scroll — a landscape watercolor that measured 14 inches (~40 centimeters) by 50 feet (~15 meters).

At the end of the scroll is the inscription, "Painted by the aged Toyo Sesshu, who formerly held the First Seat at Tendo Temple, on a peaceful day in his sixty-seventh year, or the eighteenth year of Bummei." Sixty, plus, square feet of exquisite detail in ink on rice paper, allowing no mistakes, in a single day is, if not superhuman, extraordinary!

Related patterns

Zen Mind focuses on a state of mind that transcends language, **Logos**. The two patterns are nevertheless complementary, because once you have perceived the reality of something you must still articulate and communicate that perception using words and language.

A principle pattern, **Magical Liminal**, describes a situation where **Zen Mind** is particularly valuable. In an anthropological rite of passage the liminal state exists until the ones performing the rites choose, and impose, what is required to establish a desired outcome, to incorporate the one undergoing the ritual into a new role with a new identity, or self.

The same thing can happen in design, the designer lacking a **Zen Mind** imposes a preconceived outcome. The power of the liminal comes from being aware of all that can be and all the ways to affect an outcome, the same kind of situational omniscience that comes from a stilled mind.

Unfolding requires 'essence preserving transformations' and these transformations are supposed to be driven by the essence, not the designer. **Zen Mind** is a prerequisite if the designer is to understand, simultaneously, the essence and the totality of the context in which it is expressing itself so that she can facilitate, but not impose, the outcome.

In some sense this pattern related to all of the other patterns in this book. **Zen Mind** focuses on the mental state of the designer, a state that is important and useful while engaged in the activities and making the perceptions expected in each of those patterns.

Essence which is **Form**, is accurately perceived with **Zen Mind**. Perception is communicated with **Logos**. **Zen Mind** is conducive to assuming the role of facilitator and provides the completeness of knowledge that allows **Unfolding** to be, in fact, a sequence of essence preserving transformations.

Stories

Stories about Zen Mind, or aspects of that state, are abundant. Central to most is the idea of clear perception, the ability to see past illusion and assumption to Reality as it is.

For the designer, this translates to the ability to discern Form without being distracted or misled by Shape or mere appearance. Designer's work with systems and must be able to distinguish elements of that system before they can discover Form, of the system and each element.

A favorite Zen, originally Taoist, story that illustrates both the ability to discern Reality and to successfully decompose systems at their "natural disjunctions" is 'The Venerable Butcher". The story of the Zen (originally Taoist) Butcher illustrates what results from actions arising in the context of a stilled mind.

"Having reached the venerable age of 67, the court butcher decided to retire. He had cut meat for the court

185

for more than fifty years, using the same knife without the need to sharpen it. The Emperor decided to recognize this remarkable feat and during the festivities he asked the butcher to explain why the butcher's knife never needed sharpening.

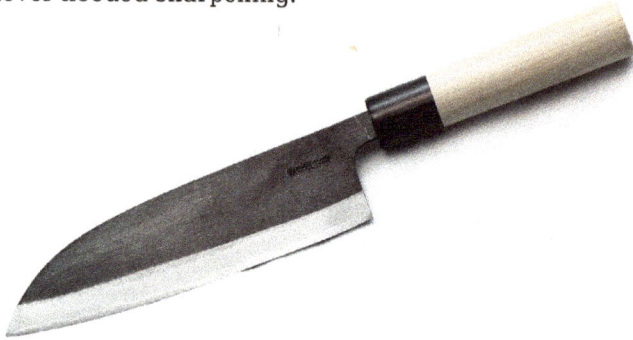

The butcher thought for just a moment before telling the Emperor, "I simply cut where the meat wasn't."

Other traditions have similar stories of perception.

A young lady and her father approached a sculptor who was just finishing a statue of a prancing stallion. The girl asked the sculptor, "How did you know that the horse was in that block of marble?"

The father quickly shushed her and asked the sculptor instead, "How did you carve that magnificent statue?"

The sculptor replied, "No, your daughter is correct. I saw the horse and merely removed all of the marble that was not part of it."

Logos ***

Thumbnail

If (any of these)
- you need to communicate,
- you need to think, or
- you need to understand and connect with others;

then (all of these)
- identify the roots and essence of communication,
- collectively establish an open, living, language, and
- shape your mind with this language.

Context

The world!

For approximately 25,000 years humans have been dependent on language to communicate and think. We make sense of the world around us by partitioning and naming; yielding vocabulary. Understanding is partially expressed by subjecting vocabulary to grammar; yielding models such as sentences. Meaning and knowledge derives from artful integration of sentences, context, and viewpoint to create stories. All of this is fundamental and essential for every aspect of any human effort, including design, and any kind of thinking, including design thinking.

Forces

Language separates us by disguising our commonality with the appearance of unique identities.

Language is based on on vocabulary, which can mislead as well easily as inform, as nouns state what 'is' and uses parts of speech to assert relationships. Vocabulary can mislead as easily as inform; as Korzibski famously noted, "the map is not the territory."

Miscommunication is a constant possibility as speakers of each language infuse their words with context, historical and cultural, that is not shared among everyone.

Design, or any other form of cooperative collaborative work, depends on the ability to harness the power of language while simultaneously countering all of language's pitfalls.

To be talked about, or thought about, a thing must have a name. The name should reflect the essence of the thing, i.e. be a True Name, but the arbitrary nature of words allows multiple 'names', most of which reflect the world-view of the namer instead of the essence which is named.

Words are essential to thought, and communication is next to impossible without them. Possession of words, a language, does not assure thought nor communication and can, in fact, result in the contrary.

Words have the ability to shape minds and through them, outcomes.

Problem

We need language but language separates us. Language and naming, words, are absolutely essential but as dangerous as they are beneficial: dividing but also capable of uniting; obfuscating but also capable of illuminating; sowing confusion but also capable of communicating understanding.

Therefore,

189

Solution

Sensitize yourself to language. Become consciously aware of how language and naming, words, affect your thoughts, your understanding, and your interactions. Choose the languages you speak and the words you employ.
Strive for clarity and nuanced precision.

Resulting context

The conscious and deliberate use of language allows us to transcend mere information and leads us to clarity and increased understanding.

A common language will allow us to see past the words and recognize ways in which we are the same, increasing our mutual empathy.

Having established a common language, care must be taken not to allow that language to become a divisive force. Your language will define its own words, its own vocabulary, which helps within your group and culture, but separates you from other cultures. The example of jargon and acronyms known only to 'insiders' is an example.

190

Every language encapsulates worldview and perspective. Each sentence in the language is like a portion of a hologram — each piece incorporates the whole — such that each language focuses our attention and thinking, like blinders.

Language, like blinders, support focus, which is good, but at the expense of blinding us to the broader context and the possibilities therein.

An example of how developing a language increases one way of communicating at the expense of others is the manner in which infants learn language. Infants can produce every sound in every language. But as their skill within a specific language increases, they lose this ability. Adults therefore have great difficulty learning the sounds in a second language learned as an adult.

Pattern Description

The pattern begins with the observation that language is essential, inescapable. To achieve clarity, the pattern asserts that awareness of language and its conscious use is prerequisite to grasp the world. Grasping, understanding, gives us a tool that is critical for consciously shaping the world and our, humans and humanity, place in it.

Discussion

Language separates us, beginning with the multitude of languages spoken. Today, there are about 7,400 natural languages spoken by ethnic groups and at least that many technical languages, spoken within a specialized domain or profession. And there are thousands of variations within each technical language — e.g. within the professional or technical language of business there are variants for banks and for retail, and even variants among individual banks and individual retailers. All of these different languages are used to separate one group from another and use the language to identify who is in the group and who is not.

Cooperative endeavor is grounded in common language. "Behold, they are one people, and they all have the same language ... now nothing which they purpose to do will be impossible for them." Genesis 11:6. Confounding language, however, pretty much assures nothing will be accomplished.

Myths about the confounding of language are found in many cultures and probably reflect an awareness of a cusp

191

in language development that was not totally positive. At some point in the development of language, words lost their direct connection to the world and became arbitary sequences of sound. The sounds ceased to be the thing itself and became a representation of that thing. Because the sequence of sounds was arbitrary there was no reason to choose one sequence over another and as different groups adopted different sound-words language became confounded.

Languages that are arbitrary and symbolic weaken and break the connection between the name, sequence of sounds that is a word, of a thing and the thing itself. Names become 'incorrect'. "If names be not correct, language is not in accordance with the truth of things. If language be not in accordance with the truth of things, affairs cannot be car ried on to success." (Confucius).

Words have power, and for a long time that power was 'magical'. Words have long been associated with magic, in everything from casting spells to gaining power over someone. Saying Voldemort's name invoked his presence; anyone knowing your True Name, has power over you. Abusing the power of words results in harm. Mesmerize is used as a synonym for hypnotism but derives from the name of a famous 'spellbinder' and spells are sequences of words. Words are used, everyday, to influence and alter our behavior. Words 'change minds'. Words can induce altered states of consciousness, e.g. the mantra intoned by one seeking enlightenment, the Zen Koan, and the Tantric Buddhism of Tibet. Words, coupled with proven bio-feedback techniques, have proven effect on human neurophysiology and in healing.

Words shape our beliefs and our opinions. If we are exposed only to one set of words we are unlikely to have any beliefs or opinions that are not consistent with those words. For example: television networks, news-papers, and magazines have a 'point of view', a bias, if you will. The words they use reflect that bias. If you have but one source for information your thoughts will reflect that bias, simply because those are the words you use to think.

Belief, in the form of religion, is determined by words. Words are so important in this context that debates over the proper word to be used in a given situation, or the ostensible meaning of a word, easily devolve into violence.

Design teams that succeed in creating and using their own, shared, language will also develop their own pat-

192

terns of usage, their own idiom, their own body of stories, and their own "theory". Peter Naur defined 'theory' as a shared mental model, developed and shared by a team, but persistent only in the brains of the team members.

As necessary as a common language is for a design team, the development of one will de facto isolate that team from other design teams and even from future incarnations of the same team. The last point can be illustrated by noting that the design efforts of Apple have been guided by at least two, quite different, design languages. The language appropriate in an earlier context was supplanted by a new language more in tune with its own contemporary context.

Teams can use their language as a means of identification, branding, leading to competitive advantage. But they must always maintain sufficient self-awareness to detect divergence between language and context and/or between language and reality in order to remain relevant.

Related patterns

Glossolalia is grounded in Logos and extends it by articulating the need for multiple perspectives, often originating in language, and polyvocal words as foundations for creative thought.

Magical Liminal exemplifies the power of words discussed in Logos. In a rite of passage identity is removed by taking away words and things named by words; and incorporation is accomplished by giving new words, often including a new name, to define an outcome in the mind of the individual undergoing the rite. In the liminal, you have no words but all words might be yours and your identity depends totally on which words you choose (or are chosen for you).

Logos has little direct effect on two of the 'essence' patterns (**Form** and **Unfolding**), but **Zen Mind** is in many ways the antithesis of **Logos**, in that a **Zen Mind** is a state without words, a state of direct perception of what Is.

All of the other patterns are written in language and the reader is encouraged to think of them in the context of what is said in **Logos**. Applying all of those patterns will also involve using words and Logos is an indirect influence.

In **Logos** we say that communication is 'almost impossible' without language. **Embodied Mind** is, in part, an example of how communication, knowledge, and understanding are

193

obtainable without the mediation of Language. For example, kinesthetic knowledge which comes from the body and its movement not from the mind and its words.

Stories

Numerous stories exist about the origin of language and the confounding of language, all of which emphasize just how critical language is to thought and communication.

From the Rg Veda:
> "When men, Brhaspati!, giving names to objects, sent out Vak's first and earliest utterances. All that was excellent and spotless, treasured within them, was disclosed through their affection."
> "Where, like men cleansing cornflour in a cribble, the wise in spirit have created language, Friends see and recognize the marks of friendship: their speech retains the blessed sign imprinted."
> "With sacrifice the trace of Vak they followed, and found her harbouring within the Rsis. They brought her, dealt her forth in many places: seven singers make her tones resound in concert."

From the Hebrew Bible:
> In the beginning was the Word, and the Word was with God, and the Word was God. He was with God in the beginning. Through him all things were made; without him nothing was made that has been made. In him was life, and that life was the light of all mankind.

The power arising from the acquisition of language is illustrated by the tale of Sigurd who acquired the language of the birds by tasting dragon blood.

> When Regin makes a sword for Sigurd that lives up to his standards, he requests that Sigurd fulfill a vow and kill Fafnir, who is hiding treasure. After avenging his father and other kinsmen, Sigurd agrees to attempt to kill the dragon. They arrive at the spot where Fafnir guards the treasure and Sigurd delivers a fatal blow to the dragon. Before Fafnir dies, they have an important conversation that reveals the truth to Sigurd about the treasure. With this enlightenment, Sigurd takes a taste of the blood of the dragon and can hear the birds speaking of the two men. "There sits, Sigurd, roasting Fafnir's heart. Better he should eat it himself." ... "There lies Regin, who wants to betray the one who trusts him." ... "He should strike Regin's head off; then he alone would control the huge store of gold." With this advice and the other words from the birds, Sigurd

drew his sword and cut off Regin's head and took all the gold from the treasure that Fafnir had previously guarded.

The Hao, a Polynesian people, tell a story of an angry God that "chased the builder away, broke down the building, and changed their language, so that they spoke diverse tongues" — a story with remarkable similarity to the Tower of Babel story in the Bible.

People First ***

If (any of these)
- the system replaces the person with a datum,
- you adapt human behavior to conform to machine limitations, or
- your employees come to work just to collect a paycheck;

then (all of these)
- recognize design is by and for people,
- leverage human abilities, and
- empower people.

196

Context

Whenever you are engaged in an activity that is intended to effect a change in circumstances. Every action you take affects people: at minimum it affects you, yourself. In design, business and software, actions affect hundreds to millions of people, if not everyone.

You are a human being engaged in design and therefore intent on bringing about change in the World around you. Your morality includes an awareness that your designs will impact people, linked to a commitment to positive, life affirming, effects.

Forces

We are keenly aware of how any change in environment or circumstance effects us as individuals. We are seldom as sensitive to how changes effect others. As professionals we can be so focused on abstract goals — e.g. sales, profit margins, algorithms, data structures — that the effect of our design on humans (employees, users) is obscured. The demands imposed by learning professional theory, practice, skills and knowledge inhibits our gaining an understanding of humans and human capabilities.

Problem

Business and, more so, technology is premised upon abstract models of human beings at the cost of capturing all that is interesting, complex, or unique to humans. Systems, conceived, designed, and built using abstractions are not 'habitable', causing problems for the business as well as everyone that is forced to interact with those systems.

Therefore,

197

Solution

Put people first. Discover and utilize capabilities that are unique to human beings, not replicable by artificial systems, and conform your designs to humans instead of humans to your designs.

Resulting context

A world that affirms the huA world that is easier and more direct but also much more complicated and challenging because a focus on human beings introduces a significant degree of ambiguity to an already challenging act of design.

Acknowledging human beings increases complexity because people are idiosyncratic and unpredictable. They can be obtuse or, conversely, insightful and perceptive. Individuals and groups can seek different goals, embody different values, and have different world views.

Designs that succeed in placing the human first, tend to become intuitive and 'invisible' creating an example of a wicked problem, where the solution changes the nature of the problem.

198

Pattern Description

This pattern emphasises the need to take people seriously because they truly are the core of every design. Design is done by people and people are affected by all design. The pattern suggests that failure to understand people and their capabilities can be very detrimental to design outcomes.

Discussion

It is very common for managers to assert that people are essential — both employees and customers or clients. "People are our most important asset," is an oft heard management phrase in this regard. This phrase captures, somewhat ironically, a major issue in how management really thinks about people. The phrase equates people with an abstraction — an asset. As an abstraction, asset, captures only those attributes that people have in common with buildings, raw materials, and equipment — attributes that include none of the unique factors of being human. Nor any of the unique and incredibly valuable capabilities that humans, alone, possess.

Abstraction is a general problem. 'Customer' is also an abstraction. 'Manager', for that matter is an abstraction. When we substitute abstractions for reality we lose significant, often critical, understanding of the things behind the abstraction.

As business entered the computer era, abstraction became even more of a problem. The computer, actually the limitations of the computer in dealing with data and information, forced the abstractions to be even more constrained and artificial. The business might abstract a living human customer to a few facts, but the computer abstracts that same customer to artificially organized bits of data distributed across multiple data structures. Meaning is lost.

Designers need to understand people and the things that people can do, can contribute to the system being designed. Applied artists, those traditionally considered as designers, already do this, albeit often non-consciously. A design decision as simple as picking a color is done with an awareness of the affect of that color on human thought and emotion.

A lot of design work has this characteristic, but even traditional designers need to understand more of what

199

humans do, what humans contribute, and how humans react to various elements of a design, of an altered system.

A huge moral imperative is advanced by this pattern. As business and software professionals seek to utilize design thinking, they need to reflect on what they are really doing when they re-design a business, or re-design a software application. They are directly, immediately, and not necessarily positively affecting people and the lives of people. This is of particular importance because much of business, and almost all of software, has been 'designed' to defaults that actually harm people.

Business, for example, deals with abstractions like employee and manager. They use these abstractions, along with procedures, business plans, policies, etc. to 'design' the business.

The humanity of both managers and employees are lost in the abstractions. As a result people come to work, often reluctantly and motivated only by the need for a paycheck. Work is an environment that actively diminishes their humanity and tries to make them into 'little machines' following instructions. Managers are not able to take advantage of human capabilities, especially individual differences among human employees because human resources insists that only job categories, an abstraction, not humans, matter. This makes the manager's work more difficult and less rewarding than it could be.

Software can make things worse. Imagine sitting in an office working with a client to complete enrollment in a program where the software requires you to enter the exact same bit of information, something as basic as a name, multiple times. It is frustrating and demeaning — showing no concern at all for the human, only the convenience of the machine. The software could have been designed and implemented differently.

If the moral imperative is not enough to motivate business and software professionals to engage the human elements of their work, perhaps business survival and the relevance of 'software engineers' might.

The Internet and mobile platforms along with the availability of the tools and applications they spawned is a disruptive force for both business and software. Disruptive to business because it is so easy for anyone to become an entrepreneur. Innovators like those behind YouTube, Skype, or Flickr quickly create new businesses, and new business categories, and directly pose challenges. And the ease of introducing change means that traditional

200

business like telecom, or even mobile phones, are constantly challenged — look at the changing fortunes of companies like RIM and Nokia in the 2010s for examples.

The profession of software engineering is at risk when a few kids using tools like HTML and Javascript can accomplish in days or weeks what it takes a traditional software engineering team months or years to complete.

But the core challenge from both of these disruptive forces is the human element. Increasing numbers of individuals have access to the tools and resources required to support their creativity, their innovation, their place in the world. Moreover, these individuals are still in touch with their humanity and the humanity of those for whom they are creating. They create things that appeal to them, as humans. Their model of users or consumers of their work is another human being who shares the interests and enthusiasms of the creator, designer. This is in direct contrast to products from traditional business that are driven by abstract lowest common denominator models of customers.

A generalized disruption, with significant implications for human concerns, is the change from an era of mass production to mass customization. When Henry Ford had a near monopoly on automobiles, he could ignore human differences and get away with saying that, "you can have any color you like as long as it is black." Microsoft could add massive numbers of features to products like Word, in order to appeal to the widest audience possible even if it meant the software was over complicated and buggy.

Today, however, and because of the Internet, it is possible to "find your market" even when your product is highly specialized. But once found, you must appeal to that market in very personal, human-centric, ways. You will not be able to do this unless you understand people.

This is more of a challenge to established, traditional, businesses and professions than it is for the individual entrepreneur. The entrepreneur can be economically successful with a very small customer base and with an understanding of the human that does not surpass his understanding of himself and his likes and dislikes. The enterprise needs a far greater understanding of people and needs to find the means for designing products and services in such a way that they can be customized to appeal to multiple simultaneous markets instead of one mass market.

Related patterns

Humans are essential to design, and therefore every aspect of design, and all and every pattern that supports design thinking. Some of the patterns deal more directly with aspects of people. For example, people experience **Joy**. **Embodied Mind** is concerned with the minds of people, and the archetypes noted in **Forever Jung** are those found in human minds. When engaged in **Participant Observation** you are trying to understand people as they understand themselves. And **It Takes a Village** of people to design.

Illustration

In the 1960s, the business world was adopting computer technology to automate any process or procedure that they could. One example, shared across most business, was the processing of accounts receivable. A company would send out bills, demands for payment, that included a stub with information about account, customer, and amount demanded.

The customer would then write a check, frequently stapling it to the stub to insure both were process together, and mail them back to the company; sometimes folding the paper documents to fit the size of an available envelope.

When the company received the payment, data from the stub and the check would be entered, manually, into the computer and the payment would be recorded and applied to the proper account. The manual processing of payments took a fair amount of time and was tedious and subject to human error, misreading or mistyping information. At this time, programs or machine instructions, and a great deal of data, was entered into the computer using Hollerith cards — stiff paper with punched holes representing characters. An idea arose: print the bills on Hollerith cards, with most of the information needed to record a payment pre-punched.

When the customer sent back a check, only the amount paid would have to be entered on the card, all other information already present. The bill would serve as the data entry source and a great deal of time and effort — for the company — would be saved.

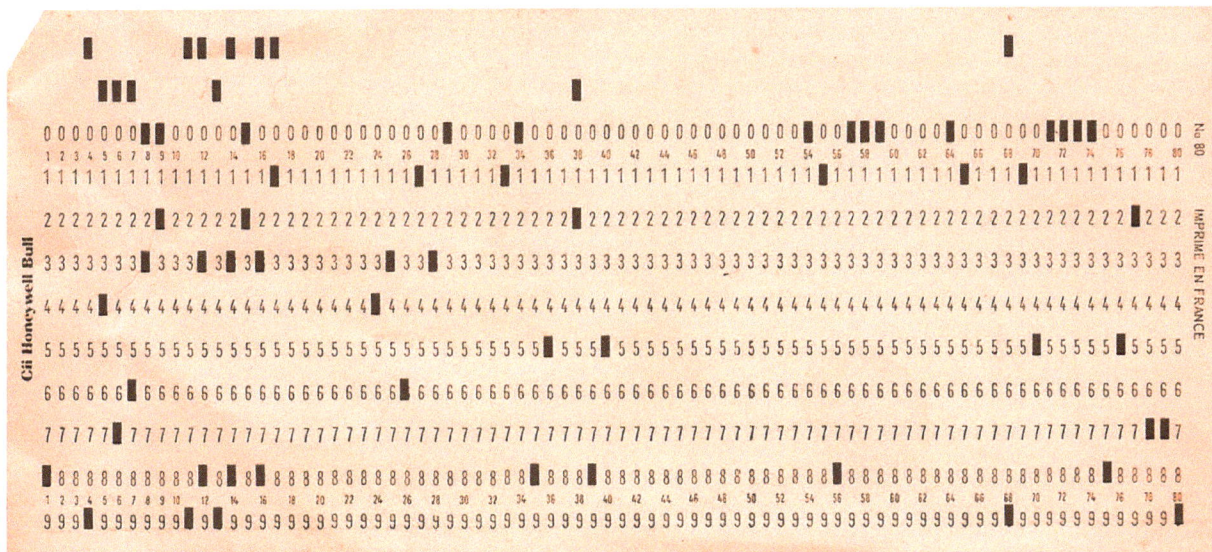
A Hollerith card

Hollerith cards were very effective, machine readable, means for entering information into a computer — if the cards were maintained in the same environment as the computer. Humans however had a tendency to put the cards in damp pockets, or back pockets and sit on them introducing deformations. Some people would staple them to the checks the remitted; others might fold them to fit an envelope. All of this made the cards unreadable by machines.

Companies took to printing the phrase, "This is your payment card, do not fold, bend, staple, or mutilate" prominently on the cards. Humans were being asked change their behavior to meet the needs of the computer! This reflected a general, almost universal, attitude that the machine was more important — and far less malleable — than humans, so when there was conflict, the human had to accommodate the machines.

The reaction was predictable, people do not like to be discounted, nor should they be. An explosion in popularity of tee shirts bearing the phrase, "I am a human being! Do not fold, bend, staple, or mutilate" ensued.

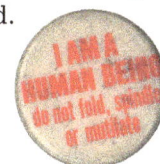

203

Principles

Principles act as bridge between theory and practice.

Communication is the core of design theory: designs are intended to communicate a message; design is based upon the designer's ability to communicate with that which is being designed; and, everyone involved in a design effort, from client to users to members of the design team, need to communicate among themselves. A 'designful mind' supports one's ability to communicate, especially communication between the designer and the designed. The first patterns in our book, the essence patterns, address a particular form of communication, a dialog between the world and the mind of the designer that expands the designer's awareness, perceptions, and understanding of the world.

The principles patterns focus on specific aspects of theory, including designful mind, and on finding an appropriate balance between the abstract and general and the explicit and concrete. Concrete ideas are required if we are to define actions, things for a designer and a design team to do. Abstractions are required because there is no single 'correct' action that necessarily follows from a principle. A single principle makes possible many practices. There can be multiple means to the same end but each alternative is expected to be consistent with the principle on which it is based. Skilled practitioners, like skilled craftsmen, must define their own practices and tools. As context, the degree and breadth of skills available to a design team, client awareness, and the domain of focus act together to define a unique challenge for the designer. The designer's ability to find or adapt an appropriate action depends on their comprehension and application of principles.

A balance is required — the designer needs a set of practices most appropriate for the situation, but those practices must remain consistent with the principles and through the principles to the theory of design.

Communication is key and a common thread throughout our Principles patterns. We present two groups of communication-centric patterns, one focusing on communications leading to understanding, comprehending, and that which is designed. The second group focuses on how to share, to communicate, that understanding with others. **Gestalt**, **Russian Dolls**, **Magical Liminal**, **Forever Jung**, and **Personae** are included in the first group. **Embodied Mind, Glosso-lalia, Everything An Object**, **Thick Description**, and **It's About Time** comprise the second group.

Gestalt ***

If (any of these)
- you are lost in the details,
- you need to understand how the tree fits in the forest, or
- your problems look like your answers;

then (all of these)
- become mindful and put the microscope away,
- grasp wholeness, and
- articulate your understanding.

Context

You are gathering a lot of information and trying to relate and fit all the pieces together. Because the information comes from many sources, many perspectives, the same things seem to have different meanings in different situations.

Forces

There is a lot of information. You encounter the information without any preimposed order, without any pre-established connections so each bit of information is independent and unrelated, or with only local relationships. The amount of unrelated data items you can hold in your mind at any one time is very limited (Miller's Magic Number 7, plus or minus two). Key relationships may be hidden, making it difficult to make necessary connections. The information and relationships among them are dynamic.

You may not see the obvious because of your perspective. You might project your own biases. You can make premature conclusions or extrapolations (blind men and elephant). You might be distracted or insufficiently mindful to observe and listen correctly. Your brain can 'autocorrect', smooth out minor inconsistencies, keeping you from seeing what is really there. You see answers instead of questions.

Problem

There are so many, apparently independent, bits of information available that you cannot see a coherent whole, an essence. Equally possible, your own predispositions lead you to seeing whole that is really just a projection of a shape of our own creation.

Therefore,

The whole is other than the sum of the parts.
— Kurt Koffka

Solution

Experience a Gestalt by allowing commonalities to form patterns that allow the essence of the whole to emerge and reveal itself.

As a unity, a whole, it is simple enough to grasp and establish the wholeness preserving abstractions that can be used to articulate and share with others.

Resulting context

Seeing the gestalt is important because the whole mirrors the essence; much the same way as a map mirrors a territory. The gestalt provides a frame of reference and suggests explorations.

The gestalt provides a critical guide, but only a guide. The designer or design team must still do the work of filling in details, making connections, and validating insights. Like a metaphor, a gestalt suggests commonalities and connections to knowledge already possessed by the designer. Metaphors suggest referents that can be compared, thereby increasing its power, or suggesting the need for an alternative.

208

Pattern Description

This pattern focuses on how a holistic view provides an essential guide as you engage the problem and limn design solutions. Gestalt deepens your experience.

Discussion

A gestalt is something that comes to you as a result of careful observation with an open mind. It is not something that you conceive and project onto reality.

Once you've had the experience, you make sense of that experience with abstractions that can take many different forms including: metaphores, models, or concepts. It is expected and every one having this experience might form their own abstractions but in interactions with others that have had that experience a common means of expression will emerge by consensus.

The word Gestalt comes from the German where it means essence or shape of an entity's complete form.

Human beings tend to be prisoners of their idiosyncratic perspective. Moreover, we are aware of this and often speak of the need to transcend our individual perspective.

For example: we might be in the process of making a decision, strongly influenced with immediate concerns.

It is common to remind ourselves that we should, "consider the big picture", i.e. the gestalt or whole picture, before making our decision lest we be misled into what will turn out to be the wrong or less optimal action.

One of the major differences between Western 'scientific' medicine and, for example, Ayurveda or acupuncture, is the symptom-symptom-modification perspective of the former.

The holistic perspective does not necessarily make traditional approaches to healing better, but they do, unquestionably, lead to insights and effective treatments that would never have been discovered from the scientific perspective.

Our expertise can also trap us within a narrow perspective. For instance an investment advisor might be so focused on profit margin and key business ratios that they miss the significance, often social or human consequences, of making certain investments or business decisions.

Software engineers are so focused on understanding how a program will execute within a machine that they lose sight of how the use of the program redefines, too often negatively, the role of the employee using it.

Related patterns

A gestalt is a revelation of **Form** which cannot be experienced without a **Zen Mind**. **Gestalt** is preserved at levels of scale as discussed in **Russian Dolls**. Particular care must be taken in forming abstractions see **Logos**. **System Metaphor** is an expression of **Gestalt** and consistency between the two is expected. One criteria for evaluating a designed outcome is the degree to which the **Gestalt** is evident in that outcome. We discuss this in **Seed Recognize Flower**.

Story

Few stories illustrate the need for a gestalt as does the ancient tale of the blind men and the elephant.

A group of blind men encountered an elephant for the first time.

One man examined the elephant's trunk and concluded, "Oh, an elephant is very much like a snake." Another examined the tail and stated, "no, an elephant is much more like a rope." A third man grasped a leg and was certain that, "an elephant is really more like a tree."

The fourth man placed his palms on the side of the elephant and definitively stated, "you're all wrong; an elephant is like a wall!"

Each observer was trapped in his own perspective and could see only what that perspective was capable of revealing. None of the observers could see the elephant in its entirety — all lacked the critical gestalt view that would have tied the individual perspectives into a whole that would reveal the real nature of the elephant.

Designers are necessarily concerned with 'whole elephants'; and not just the 'elephants', but the entire eco-system of which the elephant is but one element.

Less metaphorically, if your intent is design an enterprise, your perspective must encompass the enterprise — and — the culture, society, and regulatory environment in which it operates.

![Russian doll icon] **Russian Dolls** ***

If (any of these)
- you need to partition your problem,
- partitioning introduces confusion, or
- you do not see how your skills apply;

then (all of these)
- recognize the commonalities across partitions,
- leverage the power of fractal self-similarity, and
- refine your skill set for graduated application.

Context

Design occurs at different levels of scale. An architect designs cities as well as buildings. A graphic designer produces marketing campaigns as well as brochures. It is not necessary for a designer to learn different design concepts or theories just because they are working at one scale instead of another. The project is in progress and the design is evolving. Attention, necessarily, shifts from the general to the specific and then back again, visiting many points inbetween.

Forces

The world is too large to contemplate as a whole and we must partition, decompose, it into segments that are tractable. The segments, however are still related to the whole, and still must be understood in the context of the whole. The world is very large and decomposition is recursive, but even the smallest segment, perhaps a single design product, is connected to its context, which is connected to its context, all the way back to the world. We have a tendency to see things that differ only in scale as being, somehow, fundamentally different. We also have a tendency to use different vocabulary when we are working at one scale than we do at another, which masks the underlying similarity.

Problem

If you believe that the context you are working in is qualitatively different than the one you were working in a moment ago, or yesterday, you get confused; or, perhaps you feel inadequate, that the skills you possess do not apply somehow in this context like they did in the last.

Therefore,

Solution

Seek elements and relationships that are common across partitions, particularly partitions of scale. Find an abstraction or a metaphor that captures the essence of that commonality. Use that abstraction to separate variations that occur from varied context from those that occur solely from scaling.

Resulting context

The power of the Russian Dolls metaphor is how it reveals a common thread that can be utilized across contexts and regardless of scale. This thread is a prototype for establishing a "design language" — commonly used to assure identity across a product line. Designers then use this language to guide future efforts.

Pattern Description

Russian Dolls asserts that there is a self-similarity that prevails across levels of scale. This self similarity is captured and expressed in a metalanguage. The meta-language opens your mind to the manner in which your knowledge is equally applicable, regardless of scale.

214

Discussion

Russian Dolls provides a metaphor for the self-similarity that we assert exists at all levels of scale, that applies in every partition or segment that comes to be as a result of decomposition.

In a Russian Doll, the innermost doll will have mere suggestions (simple lines and dots and solid colors) of a face. As each doll in the nested set gets larger, there is more room to add detail and nuance, until the topmost doll will show eyebrows, eyelashes, corneas, and pupils in place of the simple dot of color on the innermost doll. Despite the difference in detail, in resolution, each doll in the set depicts, recognizably and unmistakably, the same whole.

General Systems Theory (GST) provides an example of a metalanguage, or meta-concept of the sort advocated in this pattern. The Universe is a system. We subdivide, decompose, the Universe but each partition remains a system. It does not matter how many levels of decomposition we descend, the end result is still a system.

GST further asserts that all systems, regardless of scale, satisfy a common definition: "A system is a collection of elements and the relationships among them." We use this meta-definition to guide our explorations, seeking the elements, which are system of arbitrary size, and the relationships that illuminate our problem and our solution. Our task as designers is guided by this same meta-language, as we seek the essence of each element or relation and consider how we might assist each to express itself in a different manner, such that the whole is in better balance truer to its own essence.

Related patterns

Russian Dolls introduces the notion of a meta-language and meta-concepts that we use to think with as we design, connecting this pattern to both **Logos** and **Glossolalia**.

Everything An Object extends **Russian Dolls** by proposing a specific meta-language analogous to the systems language discussed above.

Story

The first Russian nesting dolls were, according to one theory, inspired by this old Russian nursery story.

"Once upon a time, a long time ago, there was a very little girl named Oksana who loved to run down the mountain. But she never went alone. Oksana always took one of her sisters with her. There were wolves on the mountain.

One day, all the women in her family were busy making brightly colored scarves to wear in the coming festival. Oksana's big sister had lovingly made a very small scarf, just the right size for Oksana. "There you go, my little sister," smiled Oksana's biggest sister as she tied Oksana's new scarf under her chin.

Oksana was very happy. She gave her biggest sister a hug of thanks and danced outside. Oksana swirled and twirled and spun around. The ties of her scarf danced in the breeze. It was such a lovely day. Swirling and twirling, she moved farther and farther away from home without even noticing. Inside the house, the next to youngest sister stood up and stretched. She leaned out the window to take a deep breath of clean mountain air. Way in the distance, she could see a colorful speck swirling and twirling in the breeze. Her eyes narrowed. What was it? Could it be? Oh no!

Shouting to her mother and grandmother and sisters, Oksana's sister flew down the mountain. Her sisters, mother and grandmother, all attired in their colorful scarves and peasant costumes, ran quickly behind her. When they all reached little Oksana, they hugged her tightly, each enclosing the other within her arms.

Oksana's eyes widened nervously when she realized how very far away from home she had wandered. If not for the love of her family, she would have been alone on the mountain. If the wolves had noticed, well, better not to think about the wolves."

It is easy to see how this mythical group hug inspired the Russian Dolls we know today. Less obvious is the self-similarity principle that is the core of this pattern. This principle is revealed by the fact that each woman and girl in the story wore essentially the same costume and colorful scarf.

The costumes, with their color schemes and patterns,

provided a constant reminder of what it meant to be a woman and girl in Russian peasant culture.

The culture itself regenerated itself over time and generations, in part, by replicating the attire worn by members of that culture. Subtle variations in the costumes also recapitulated, symbolically, the journey from girl child to maiden, to mother, to elder, so each person could 'see' — be reminded of — from whence she came and what awaited her in the future.

A simple bit of self-similarity with powerful and effective results.

Magically Liminal ***

If (any of these)
- you are staring at a blank page,
- you have too many answers, or
- you are paralyzed with anxiety;

then (all of these)
- embrace the liminal,
- observe all that might be, and
- incorporate the emergent 'right' answer.

218

Context

Anytime there is an open design decision, involving anything from the outcome as a whole to a detailed part of a single design product. You know what was and why it can no longer be, but that which will be is nebulous, is potential.

Forces

The anxiety of the blank page, the hesitation, the fear, familiar to every author, designer, business engineer and software developer. Even when you are certain you know what will be on the page, there is hesitation because once you make the first mark you are to some degree committed but are not yet sure you are doing the right thing.

The vastness of the sea of potential solutions is intimidating. We might prematurely limit our search for the 'right' solution only to areas that are consistent with our existing knowledge and experience.

The client can usurp the designer's role, and overly constrain the solution space, by making decisions or specifying outcomes instead of letting them emerge.

We are so accustomed to being 'rational' beings that it can be hard work in 'magical' realms where the rules are removed and everything is, quite literally, possible.

Problem

Each new design problem demands an objective evaluation and analysis. In varying degrees, objectivity is achieved when the designer is able to 'separate' himself from his default mindset, experience, and skills. The more novel the problem the greater the separation and the accompanying "separation anxiety."

You must put something on the paper, but you resist doing so, you procrastinate, perhaps because you feel you have nothing to put down, perhaps because your rational mind posits too many solutions.

Therefore,

Solution

Recognize and embrace the power of the liminal creating a bridge from confusion to solution. Liminality allows outcomes to reveal themselves to you, to emerge from the 'everything is possible'.

Resulting context

Once you have detected emergent designs, you must begin the process of incorporation, i.e. making sensible, that which you have perceived. You are translating — in the form of drafts, sketches, or prototypes — the imaginary into the expressed, allowing each expression to be evaluated and refined until it fits its context and becomes a design that you can realize, make real.

Pattern Description

If you are uncertain, because your mind is blank or because you have too many answers, as to how to proceed, the pattern suggests you take advantage of a liminal state where answers emerge, present themselves for execution. The pattern suggests the need to support such a space and to allow designers to experience it.

220

Discussion

The liminal is a place where everything and anything is possible. Entering the liminal requires separation from old habits and default ways of thinking about problems and design solutions. Successful traversal of the liminal requires a "guide" and for the designer this guide is provided by your mostly non-conscious self — the synthesis of your experience and knowledge. As a designer you are an observer of the everything possible with the sensitivity required to recognize emergent solutions. This is creativity — remembering what has been forgotten and what is being expressed in a context sensitive manner.

Perhaps the best description of the liminal comes from Arnold von Gennep and his analysis of Rites of Passage. The rites studied by von Gennep involve humans changing their status and their role in a society: e.g. child to adult or secular to sacred. Rites of passage have three phases – separation (from what was), the Magical Liminal (Clifford Geertz called this, "the betwixt and between"), and incorporation (the new is made manifest and tangible).

The liminal is not only a state of betwixt and between, neither this nor that, it is also a state where anything might be. It is magical, in the sense that the rules and laws that govern everyday reality are suspended and everything is, literally, possible. It is a place where everything, including the designer's sense of self, is in flux. 'Magic' makes a playground for the imagination. Unfettered imagination is an important foundation for creativity, for discovery of design.

Related patterns

Zen Mind is essential in the **Magical Liminal**.
The designer benefits from the liminal to the extent that they put themselves in the position of an observer, allowing 'all that is possible' to present itself for review and possible selection to be a design outcome. It is a place of egoless omni-science and nonattached action.

The liminal is a place where **Form** may be observed. There is a 'language', **Logos**, at play in the liminal but it is a language of symbols that utilizes a grammar of myth and primordial story, captured in **Forever Jung**.

Illustration

David and the Phoenix by Edward Ormondroyd is a story
of parallel 'rites of passage'; one is the transition from
childhood to (young) adulthood experienced by David,
the other that of the Phoenix from the end of one life to
the beginning of the next.

Most of the book is concerned with the period of the
"magical liminal" the time between one stage of life and
the ensuing one; the time of betwixt and between, the
time when it seems that anything is possible.

David and the Phoenix spend this time engaged in
"alarums and excursions," visiting Gryffins (and their

kin, the Gryffons and Gryffens), Fauns, Sea Monsters, a Banshee, Nymphs, and Leprechauns. Also the most mysterious and magical of all, "The Scientist."

It is the "power of the possible" that makes David's adventures magical. The liminal time is a period to explore, to wonder, and ultimately to choose among myriad options in order to establish one's self as it is to be. David, primarily because he has seen and experienced the 'magical' and the 'scientific', is able to find an appropriate balance between a rational, but non-judgmental, non-dehumanizing, adult and the whimsical, naïve, and blindly accepting child.

Forever Jung**

Thumbnail

If (any of these)
- you see beauty but do not see where it originates,
- you sense familiarity with that which you have never seen, or
- you fear the unknown;

then (all of these)
- recognize symbols and biological forms,
- find the truth in myths, and
- understand that it is only your conscious mind that confronts the Void.

Context

You are designing for humans and the language of the human unconscious is symbolic and archetypal. You are in the liminal state and many things are presenting themselves to you and you 'recognize' many of them but do not necessarily understand them.

Forces

The unconscious is not idiosyncratic. It is shared, 'collective'.

Your design will be grounded in the symbolic, archetypal and evocative unconscious.

You have little, or no, knowledge of the unconscious and how it works.

You fear the unknown.

Everyone will continue to be uncomfortable with your work until it resonates with the archetypal and the symbolic.

Problem

You need to use the unconscious but may not understand what it is and how it affects your work.

Therefore,

THREE PRINCIPLES

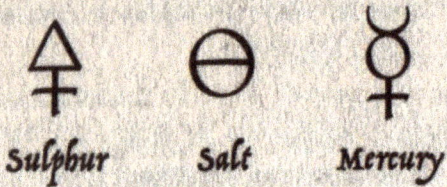

Sulphur   Salt   Mercury

THE FOUR ELEMENTS

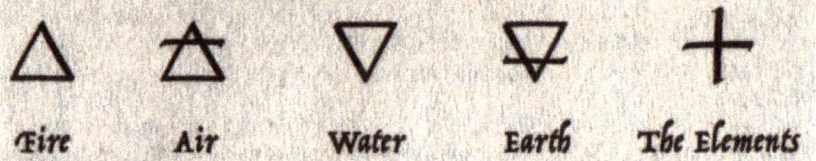

Fire   Air   Water   Earth   The Elements

PLANETS & METALS

Moon   Mercury   Venus   Sun   Mars   Jupiter   Saturn
Silver   Quicksilver   Copper   Gold   Iron   Tin   Lead

Solution

Incorporate the archetypal and symbolic in your design.

Resulting context

Connecting your design to primordial archetypes speaks to people in a direct and immediate manner. This dramatically increases the power and effectiveness of your design.

But, "with great power comes great responsibility." Archetypes can be either 'good', reflecting human affirming values and memories; or 'evil', symbols that invoke fear or base instincts. Propaganda is design infused with 'evil' archetypes. The designer is in a position similar to that of a statistician, using your craft to inform and enlighten, or to deceive and enslave.

Pattern Description

Understanding and appreciation of design is dependent on the unconscious mind, and this pattern asserts the need to understand and utilize the collective unconscious.

Discussion

We know that designs are appreciated, in part, because of factors that cannot easily be articulated, frequently because they exist at levels below our threshold of consciousness. Our pattern asserts the need to understand and address these unconscious factors before we will be able to generate appropriate designs.

Carl Jung has explored psychology to find universal sym-bolism. Joseph Campbell has explored myth to expose universal stories and relationships. Both men are attempting to explore and explain the unconscious and to reveal how the unconscious influences, and sometimes, determines, our reactions to the world around us. The same world into which our designs will exist.

The work of Jung and Campbell clearly demonstrate that much of the unconscious is shared across individuals and cultures. All cultures have an origin myth. The spiral is a symbol that is held to be significant in all cultures, including prehistoric ones, e.g. in cave art.

We named our pattern after Carl Jung because he is the person most readily associated with the study of symbolism and the collective unconscious. But many others have followed in his, and Campbell's, footsteps, expanding our understanding of how symbology affects us and cataloging both symbols and myths.

Christopher Alexander, engaged in a parallel quest, trying to understand why some designs, towns, buildings, rooms, gardens, etc. are universally recognized as 'good' or 'beautiful'. He asserted that this phenomenon was the result of the degree to which a design had QWAN (the Quality Without A Name). He sought the underlying principles behind QWAN in Nature. His work led to the discovery of fifteen properties that he believed, in combination, accounted for QWAN.

Others, D'Arcy Thompson for example, have explored Nature to find essences of shape and form and relating them to concepts and aesthetics. For example, the shape of a Nautilus shell is consistent with the Fibonacci number series, and the hexagon shape of a honeybee's comb results in the maximum amount of honey storage using the minimal amount of wax. Humans, and we suppose other organisms, see elegance in these forms. We appreciate and resonate to them. We are often pleased, especially if we are scientists, to see our theories and our mathematics confirmed by Nature — who originated them in the first place.

It is easy to miss a connect-ing thread. Shapes and forms, fundamental to biology, are reflected in the symbols employed in the subconscious, that, in turn, inspire conscious thought. Design decisions are enhanced to the degree that you can follow this thread back to biological origins. If 'good' design is as dependent as we believe it to be on understanding the unconscious and then utilizing that understanding in our work, designers should be knowledgeable in this body of work — at minimum they must be familiar with it.

Related patterns

Forever Jung provides an understanding of symbols and mythical stories that play such an important role in **Magical Liminal**.

Symbols provide the vocabulary and myth the grammar, **Forever Jung**, that comprise a language, **Logos**. It is a language that is qualitatively different from our ordinary technical and natural languages. Nevertheless, it is a language that must be incorporated, **Glossolalia**, and utilized by the whole team, **It Takes a Village**.

The symbols and mythology of **Forever Jung** are used to define or delineate a **Personae**.

Embodied Mind expands consciousness beyond the brain and into the biological where the same primordial forms that inform the subconscious, **Forever Jung**, influence the mind as a whole.

Story Telling, and **System Metaphor**, will increase in effectiveness to the extent they incorporate symbols and myths as talked about in **Forever Jung**.

Illustration

Altered States is a movie based on a Chayefsky novel of the same name. It tells the story of a man seeking the "primeval mind" the collective subconscious. He travels to Mexico and partakes of hallucinogens with aboriginal people, experiencing symbol filled visions and engaging in primitive, animalistic behavior. Later experiments involve taking an LSD-like substance while immersed in a sensory deprivation tank. Visions are experienced in this situation as well, visions filled with archetypal symbols, evocative of stories and myths.

The symbols and the myths seem to be universal and they exert their evocative power even when there is no clear evidence that the symbol, or the myth, had ever been encountered or prior to the vision experience.

Abundant evidence exists that all cultures, in all places and all times, have believed in a supernatural realm filled with symbols and 'magical' beings. In many cultures, a visit to this realm, in the form of a "vision quest" is essential to the transition from childhood to adulthood. And, although there is certainly variation in the set of symbols acknowledged by different cultures, there is also a large subset that is consistent across cultures.

Symbols are not exclusively visual images, myths are not restricted to narrative stories. Almost any sensory stimulus can assume the role of symbol or myth.

The power of symbol arises from the meaning, emotions, and memory they evoke. And this power is, in turn, dependent in part on the context in which the symbol is deployed. Finding the correct symbol for the correct context is one of the perfectible skills of the designer.

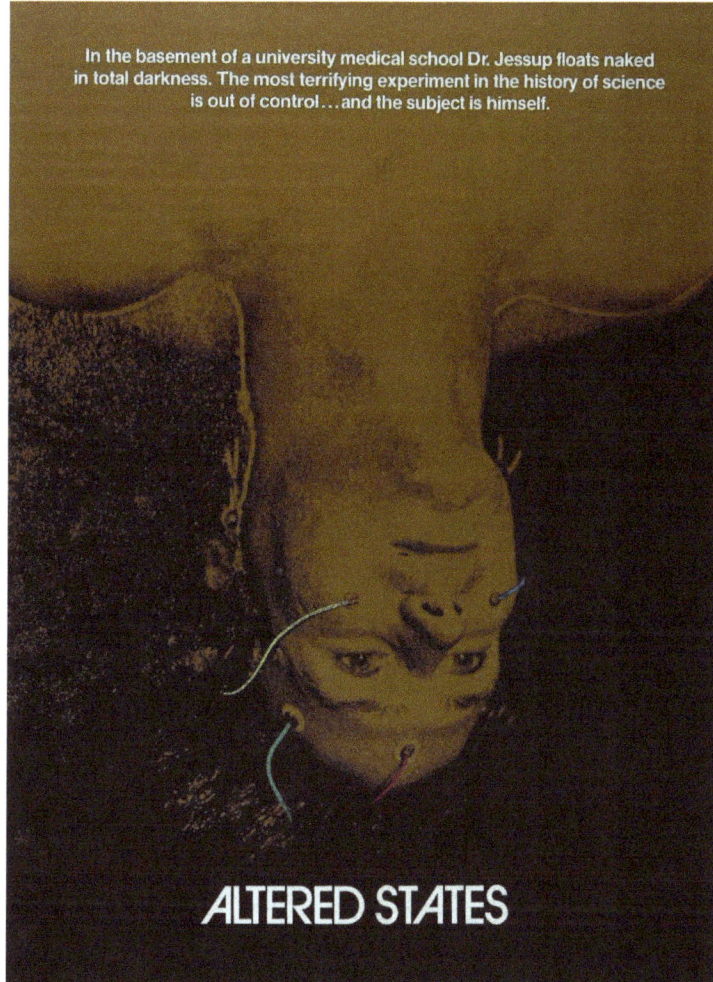

In the basement of a university medical school Dr. Jessup floats naked in total darkness. The most terrifying experiment in the history of science is out of control…and the subject is himself.

ALTERED STATES

In the movie, our hero reaches a point where he is at risk of losing everything, his body, his mind, his life — and it is a symbol, a simple tactile embrace, that saves the day. This is the power of symbol in context.

I'M READING A GREAT MANAGEMENT BOOK ABOUT THE RULES OF LEADERSHIP.

ALLOW ME TO PUT THAT IN CONTEXT.

THERE ARE PROBABLY 10,000 BOOKS ABOUT LEADERSHIP, AND EACH ONE HAS A DIFFERENT APPROACH.

AND THERE ARE MILLIONS OF REAL LEADERS, OF WHICH NO TWO ARE ALIKE.

MOREOVER, EVERY SITUATION IS UNIQUE AND REQUIRES A DIFFERENT TYPE OF LEADER.

AND YET, THIS ONE AUTHOR HAS FOUND A MAGIC FORMULA TO TRANSFORM YOU FROM A GULLIBLE BABOON INTO A GREAT LEADER.

AND THAT MAKES SENSE BECAUSE ALL GREAT LEADERS THROUGHOUT HISTORY ACHIEVED SUCCESS BY READING A RANDOM BOOK.

I DON'T LIKE CONTEXT.

IT ISN'T POPULAR.

Personae **

Thumbnail

If (any of these)
- you find it difficult to fit essence to context,
- the context seems to be demanding too much or too little, or
- you can't adapt your designs;

then (all of these)
- use personae to custom-fit essence to context,
- objectify persona, and
- re-express essence instead of adapting design.

Context

You understand the essence, the form, of a thing and the context in which it is to be expressed. You are trying to find an expression of the form that best fits the context.

Forces

An essence can be complex, with a multitude of aspects and characteristics.

A context imposes opportunities for expression but also imposes constraints that inhibit expression.

Fit requires an optimal balance.

Problem

There is a misfit between essence and context and it is difficult to find an expression that achieves the appropriate balance.

Therefore,

Masked, I advance.
— René Descartes

Solution

Use a persona, an expression of essence that is customized to the context in which it appears.

Resulting context

The use of a personae adds emphasis and highlights what the designer needs to focus on in the current context. It should be seen as a megaphone.

The use of personae, masks, like the use of archetypes presents the designer with a moral challenge, assuring the mask is not used to deceive or hide. Additionally, care must be taken to assure that the persona is indeed true to the essence behind it, as undistorted an expression of Form as is possible.

Pattern Description

The pattern identifies an issue, difficulty of finding an expression that best fits a context and suggests that the concept of 'persona' can resolve the issue.

232

Discussion

Persona, and the plural Personae, is a term derived from the Greek, via Etruscan and Latin, meaning "mask" and referring to the masks used in classic Greek theatre. The use of masks provided multiple benefits: it allowed a single actor to play multiple roles; the mask could exaggerate characteristics of the role, reinforcing the playwright's message in the minds of the audience; and; amplifying the voice of the actor. Amplification played two roles itself, one drawing attention to characteristics of the role as expressed by the actor's voice, and overcoming the limitations of an age without electronic amplification.

In Jungian psychology, the concept of persona is associated with the need to express one's innermost self in ways appropriate to a social context. Much of what we appear to be is not intrinsic. Most of our behaviors, our values, our world views and our ideas come to us from culture and is persona, not self. The same self, born and raised in a different culture would express a persona consistent with that culture. Persona is a kind of intermediary between self and context.

For Jung, a strong persona was flexible, adapting easily to changes in the context. Over identification with a specific persona could cause psychological harm because the individual could lose the distinction between themselves and the world they live in — becoming all persona and nothing but persona.

If we make the analogies, self to essence and culture to context, we can illuminate a common design problem: finding an expression of essence that retains fidelity to essence while simultaneously satisfying the constraints of context. Context may demand an expression that emphasizes certain aspects of essence or may deem certain aspects as irrelevant and distracting, and expect that they be hidden. The demands of context are dynamic as the context is dynamic, and that is why you need to have a flexible persona, or multiple personae — allowing constant refit of essence to context.

For example, the essence of the butterfly is in the egg. The egg must express itself, in context, before the butterfly is realized. The demands of context require that the first expression is a caterpillar, emphasizing some aspects, e.g. color and motility, while totally hiding others. The next context demands aspects that were more evident in the egg — a cocoon that acts like the boundary of the egg, separating and protecting developmental activities from environment. When the butterfly finally emerges its context changes rapidly, from purely local, and relatively stable, conditions at the point of emergence to the expansive and dynamic conditions of the garden.

Nature knows how to preserve the essence of the butterfly as it is expressed as egg, larvae, caterpillar, cocoon, and butterfly — the designer needs to learn Natures lesson and the concept of persona is the key.

The pathology of persona identification also has an analog in design. It is very easy to mistake a persona for the essence behind it, and try to modify the persona to fit another context instead of allowing the essence to re-express itself in that context. An actor becomes identified with a single role is said to be 'typecast' and casting directors, blinded by the type find it impossible to modify the 'role' to fit the film, with the result that the actor is out of work.

Related patterns

A mask made explicit and visible aspects of the character that would otherwise need to be inferred, but they always revealed **Essence** — thereby connecting **Personae** to **Form**.

Each mask is a thing in and of itself; reflective of essence but separate from it. So to, a persona is a 'thing' with its own characteristics and meaning-in-context. **Personae** affect, sometimes opening new possibilities, sometimes establishing limits for how we use **Everything An Object**.

Prometheus Bound deals with boundaries and **Personae** expands our understanding of those boundaries by, for example, revealing that a given constraint applies to a specific persona, and not to the **Form** or essence.

Personae are intimately connected to **Unfolding**, as each identifiable stage in the varied expression of **Form**, e.g. 'child' to 'youth' to 'adult' to 'elder', reflects a distinct persona. Although a mask may hide rather than reveal, like the feared psychopath behind the mask of next-door neighbor; design is primarily concerned with the use of **Personae** to reveal and adapt **Form** to particular circumstances for some particular, ennobling, purpose. **Fit** and **Seed Recognizes Flower** assure that Personae are effective while remaining consistent with the essence preservation implicit in **Unfolding**.

Story — The Mask

Once there was a king
who was so nasty and mean
that it showed clearly on his face
and in his attitudes. So much so that
everyone in his kingdom hated him, but more than that
they feared him. Oh they respected him, for he was their
king, but when he would ride out among the people with
his face all contorted in mean and nasty ugliness, people
would scatter and run away.

If caught off guard they would bow low averting his eyes
in silence, the dislike and fear of him showing on their
faces. And the king would mumble, mutter or sputter
mean things to them. No one spoke to him not even a
'good day, sire'. After a while the king grew even angrier
with his subjects because of how they seemed to hate
and fear him. Finally he called his wisest wizard to him
and said, "I am tired of how the people treat me, use your
magic to make them nicer people, I command it."

The wizard thought a long time and said the king would
have to do exactly what he told him to do, with no questions and to the letter. He asked the king if he was willing to do that. "If you will not, it is hopeless" said the
wizard. The king agreed. "Fine he said, whatever you say,
I will do. Anything that is necessary to get those rotten
people to treat their king they way he deserves. He grumbled a bit more under his breath and settled his face into
his ugliest meanest grimace.

The wizard went into a high cabinet and took down a box
which he carefully opened. Inside the box was a mask of
the king's own face. It was so like the king that the king's
mouth fell open when he saw it! Except for one small or

235

not so small difference. The expression on the mask was smiling and friendly — almost radiant, instead of grouchy and mean and nasty. The king hardly notice the difference of the expression "Where did you get such a mask?' he asked. "Never mind the where," said the wizard, "it is a magic mask.

Here is what you must do, as you agreed with no questions asked: You must put this mask on and not take it off for 100 days." "What ... why ... ehhhm, I ... it isn't my way to grin like that, they will lose respect ... grumble ... grumble ... grumble I can't do that ..." "Never mind the protest", said the wizard, "you agreed. Put it on." Well the king grumbled but he did put it on. That day as he rode through the kingdom a few appeared to glance up at him in surprise, for never had they seen the king smile before. After a few days a few brave ones smiles a small smile back. And a week later one actually stood and smiled and said, "Good day to you, Sire." This surprised the king and he did not know what to say, but he did not grumble mean things at the man. Word began to spread, the king had had a change of heart. People began to stay where they could see him when he rode by, some bowed and then looked up and smiled at him. Ah, thought the king, this is how a king should be treated. Perhaps my subjects are becoming nicer people, perhaps they are not as rotten as they were a while ago. This continued.

Each day more people spoke to the king, smiled and even waved as he rode by. And the king ... well he began to wave back and to offer his own "good days" and "how fare ye's". And the people began to tell him how life was for them. As the king heard sad stories of poverty and illness, he began to order that the people receive more of the bounty of the land, that they have the services of doctors and that disputes were settled fairly. Oh, the people came to think highly of that king. They brought him fruits and vegetables, and flowers from their gardens and the king in turn came to really love these people who had become so lovable. He would stop by a peasant's home and sit on the stoop chat and taste a cake or such that a good wife had baked.

The king and his people loved one another. And the King began to feel guilty. He cared so much about these people now and he knew he was deceiving them with the mask. They liked him better, he thought because of the beauty of the mask, but it is not me and I can not longer deceive them. Although the 100 days were not quite up, he knew he had to remove the mask and be honest with his people and if they would no longer love him, he would have at least have had these past days. So, he went into a large hall, and looked closely into a large mirror at his face.

The mask was smiling as it had on the first day he put it on. he regretted having to take it off, but he could no longer fool the people he had come to love. He reached up and pulled at the mask and it peeled off in his hand. When finally he got his courage up to look again at his mean contorted face, he saw ... a miracle. For in the days he had come to love his people, his face had changed and now it matched the mask in every respect. It was beautiful, and smiling and looked as he felt at that moment. He wept and touched his laughing face.

When next he went out among the people his heart was light for he knew he was himself, true and true enough. And that king and all the people of his kingdom lived a long and contented life.

Embodied Mind***

Thumbnail

If (any of these)
- you cannot find the right words,
- you are told is obvious, but it is not, or
- you are told to "just do it";

then (all of these)
- look for where the knowledge is really stored,
- acknowledge the value of doing, and
- communicate on multiple channels.

238

Context

Situations where you are trying to understand
how knowledge is communicated or the best ways
to communicate knowledge.

Forces

Humans in industrialized societies think and communicate almost entirely in terms of words and language.

Human beings have more channels than language used
to hold and communicate information or knowledge.

Problem

You cannot express, in words, what you need to communicate or you observe an exchange of information but do
not see how it was done.

Therefore,

Movement is life —
without movement
life is unthinkable

MOSHE FELDENKRAIS

Solution

Recognize that the mind is not the only place where information and knowledge are found and does not provide the only means for transmitting or receiving knowledge.

Resulting context

When you recognize that communication transcends the use of the five senses and that knowledge and experience are 'remembered' quite differently than, for example, rote memorization of multiplication tables; you are ready to bring all the other patterns to bear and craft designs that utilize all the channels of communication available to you.

Pattern Description

The pattern asserts that there are multiple channels by which information and knowledge can be conveyed and all of them must be utilized if you are to achieve full and complete communication.

Discussion

Mind is associated with brain and it is commonly acknowledged that the brain can be seen as having two halves, a right and a left. The left associated with words, language; the right with space, emotions, and relationships. The first step towards understanding the nature of an embodied mind is to remind ourselves that both parts of the brain are integrated and must be accounted for.

The brain resides in a body, and is not isolated from that body. The brain shares a complex chemistry and a 'hormonal stew' with the rest of the body and thinking, and therefore understanding and communication are affected by that chemistry.

More importantly, some knowledge is not found in the mind at all, but is actually located in the body. 'Muscle memory' and 'kinesthetic knowledge' are two examples, often noted and discussed. Knowledge stored in the body is 'wordless'. It cannot be captured or conveyed using words. It can be talked about, but cannot be expressed. Think of something very ordinary, something you do every day, like walking across a room. Where is the knowledge that allows you to do that? How would you express, in words, what it is that you do when you place one foot in front of another?

We can talk about such knowledge. We can even pretend that the knowledge is captured in words and then use those words to instruct a robot, for example, such that the robot can simulate walking. This does not mean that the robot knows how to walk.

Similarly, you learn to ride a bicycle as child and then stop for a number of years. If, at some later point in life you want to ride again, you rely on the memory of your muscles to do so. You do not attempt to recall the words of instruction given to you so long ago. Not only would it be difficult, the words would not do you much good because they were given to you in the context of childhood and are understood in that context.

We acknowledge some aspects of embodied mind already. Industrial or product design, for example, will consider how something feels, in the hand and by the hand, as well as abstractions like shape and color. Apprenticeship is based in part on an understanding that many of the skills used, by a tradesman are best learned by doing, by allowing the body to acquire and retain knowledge that cannot be communicated, in words, from master to apprentice.

We are just beginning to understand the extent to which mind is embodied, the physical body, of course; the environment in which the body operates, including culture, almost certainly; the universe, a kind of quantum consciousness, maybe. Whatever the case proves to be, meaning, understanding, and knowledge must be seen as transcending the mind and the words, language, used by the mind.

Related patterns

Embodied Mind points to channels of communication other than language, **Logos**. Much of **Thick Description** is concerned with the use of language to help us see, indirectly, behind the words to a fuller understanding. **Forever Jung** posits a means of communication that is not language based, as does **Embodied Mind**, and both suggest that **Glossolalia** needs to be extended to include non-verbal means of communication.

Story

Marsha Ivany's right shoulder was frozen. At 54, the retired teacher and recreational equestrian couldn't move her arm; lifting bales of hay was impossible, riding had become challenging, and even daily activities were prob-

242

lematic. The problem was so bad that Marsha consulted a surgeon, who felt that surgery was the only way her shoulder would release. She opted to try the Feldenkrais Method® while waiting for the operation.

Halfway through her treatment of twice-weekly sessions, Marsha went on a cruise and lapsed back into her holding and pain patterns. Frozen shoulders have many components and are not something that can be resolved in a few short sessions. The nervous system must accept new patterns that are layered one on top of the other so that eventually the whole problem can be resolved. Treatment must be maintained until new habits become automatic. Like many physical challenges, a frozen shoulder involves a trust issue. The body is afraid to let down its guard because the next movement could be painful, so the nervous system becomes hyper-vigilant. Because of this we have to focus on very small changes. Each new movement is slightly challenging but within reach and presented in such a way that the nervous system accepts it without tightening up again.

Often we have to "trick" the nervous system into allowing new movements. In Marsha's case, if we couldn't easily move the arm we would find a way to move the body around the arm. If there was pain in one area we would look for other areas that were pain free and focus our attention there or do unusual movements that didn't have a history of pain attached to them so that we could find a pain free pathway. Once we had a path we could reconnect the dots so that other options became available.

After four months of treatments, Marsha experienced significant improvement that progressed beyond relieving her frozen shoulder. With increased body awareness, she

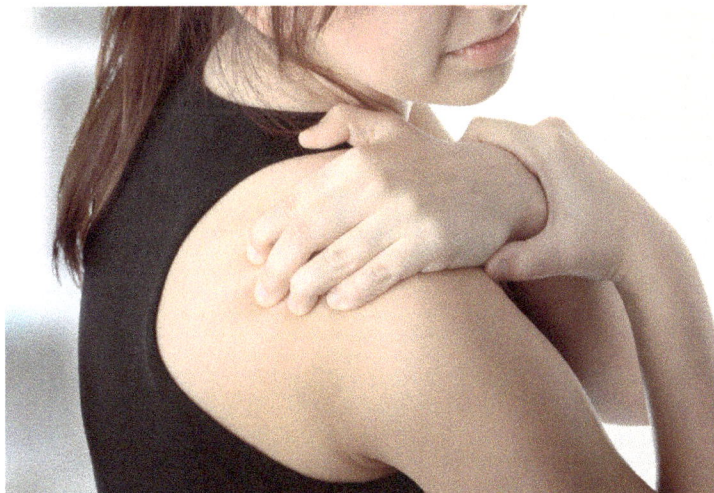

fine-tuned her repertoire of movements and was able to take riding to a new level.

Marsha returned to her medical doctor, who was amazed the Feldenkrais Method had worked. Mobility had returned and Marsha found it easier to ride and to practice Pilates. She was able to use the shoulder in a more natural fashion. Surgery was no longer necessary!

Two years later, Marsha finds that when she is learning something new her shoulder may still roll forward, but without pain. She has time to remind herself that this is an old habit pattern, and she slows herself down to make adjustments so that she is using a healthy movement pattern instead. Although she still notices "signs of aging", she feels she has the tools to deal with everything better: her posture has improved, and she is going to age gracefully.

Making the impossible possible,
the possible easy, and the easy elegant.
— Moshe Feldenkrais

"When I said you should improve security, I meant 'put a latch on the door'."

Glossolalia ***

Thumbnail

If (any of these)
- communication is fraught with misunderstandings,
- your work fits your style more than the problem, or
- you are working in an unfamiliar domain;

then (all of these)
- understand how language shapes thought,
- wake up! be curious! abandon complacency! and
- learn to speak in tongues.

Context

The designer's ability to utilize the generative power inherent in the liminal state, where everything is possible, is framed (bounded) by their own language.

Forces

Language constrains thought.

Our innate ability to recognize sounds and master multiple languages diminishes as we focus on the familiar language around us, first with natural language and then with the technical language associated with different domains and specializations.

Juxtaposing words in a single language opens possibilities for creative thinking, and when the words and grammatical constructs come from multiple languages, creative thought is significantly enhanced.

Mere translation or definition of terms in a 'foreign' language provides insufficient understanding for the designer to see the myriad possibilities, the 'anything' is possible, that is the generative power of the liminal unless it is metaphorical, in which case it unlocks the full power of language; inspiring and informing design.

Problem

How can we recognize and overcome the influence and bias, the limitations, inherent in language? Language is a tool for thinking, perhaps the most powerful and influential tool available to human beings. Language is used to name things, describe them, and construct complex thoughts involving interacting and interrelating things.

Infants are born with the ability to recognize and respond to all the sounds utilized by any language, but quickly all but those consistent with the language of the home and culture in which they live. This is the first example of how language constrains innate abilities. As we age, our abliity to learn new languages diminishes, depriving us of the unique world views and richness of concepts that are found in different languages.

As we develop a professional specialization and master the language of that profession, we find our ability to communicate across specializations increasingly difficult.

Language is integral to culture, as discussed in Thick Description, and, in fact, is often the clearest manifestation of the worldview at the core of culture. Language provides the vocabulary and concepts that are available to think with — a modest form of the Sapir-Whorf hypothesis. For example, how do you conceive of something that has no name and no words to describe it?

Designers are charged with the task of exploring possible solutions but cannot do this if they are subject to the constraint of a single language and worldview. Culture is not simply ethnic in origin. Different domains, business versus design, have associated cultures and languages. Even when working within a single ethnic culture, designers must be capable of using the language intrinsic to the cultures of the various domains of their clients.

Therefore,

247

Solution

Develop an ability to 'speak in many tongues'. This ability is grounded in an awareness of how languages vary and how those variations affect thinking. A 'flexible' mind results and the designer has access to realms of solutions otherwise hidden from them.

Resulting context

When designers employ multiple languages, their communication becomes free flowing exposing more ideas and potential solutions, while increasing the probability that 'best' solutions are revealed. Cross-fertilization across specialities and domains generates insights and deepens understanding; and playing with metaphor opens rich and exciting new worlds, rife with possibilities.

A syncretic (blended) language emerges and forms the core of a culture of design, respect, and joy. The language evolves and deepens as additional problems are encountered and resolved using that language.

But care must be taken to recognize that this new blended language may only be shared by those that participated in its creation. The language must remain open and 'living', constantly integrating new languages and responsive to changes and reformulations of itself. Otherwise there is significant risk that each design team will create an idiosyncratic language that separates the team from other designers.

Pattern Description

Designers, and those that wish to join the design culture, must transcend the limitations that arise from being mono-lingual — both in terms of the technical languages of their clients and, to a lesser degree, in ethnic natural languages — by developing the ability to 'speak in tongues', glossolalia. The natural curiosity of the child is required. Corollary to this is a willingness to play, to explore and imagine and simply take things less seriously than that to which we are accustomed. An open mind, deferral of judgement, is essential. Curiosity, play-fullness, exploration, and imagination thrive when critical assessment is postponed.

Curiosity is a thirst to understand that which is strange to us and we employ metaphor to quench this thirst. A metaphor proposes that this strange thing might be like this familiar thing, providing a bridge to understanding by positing questions that affirm or contradict the metaphorical juxtaposition. Fluency in multiple technical languages can be gained simply by reading. But you must read widely and read for pleasure. Alan Kay once said, "Those that do not read for pleasure, cannot read for purpose." Although non-fiction might be read simply for pleasure, it is usually fiction that fills that role. One of the benefits of reading fiction is the flexibility of the language that can be employed and the depth of understanding that comes from prose that is akin to poetry, seldom found in non-fiction writing and almost never from academic and technical writing.

For a child, imagination requires little more than a cardboard box — as illustrated in this Red and Rover cartoon.

249

Discussion

The amount of knowledge available in the world today is staggering to contemplate. And more is being added every day. Specialization, knowing all that there is to know about an increasingly narrow segment of the totality of knowledge has been a common way to cope with this challenge.

Specialization has its consequences. Those engaged ineach specialized area form a language and with it a culture. Gaining fluency in that technical language takes up most of an individual's university education and it becomes pragmatically difficult to master more than one technical language; there simply is not enough time. This, in turn, makes it increasingly difficult for specialists in one area to communicate with specialists in another, they think in and speak different languages.

Paradoxically, we are aware that the most fruitful, the most generative thinking arises from crossing disciplinary boundaries, by surmounting the difficulties of using different languages in our attempts to understand a common world.

Attempts to cross disciplinary chasms might take the form of translation or, more commonly, using metaphor to introduce concepts from one domain into another.

Translation brings problems. Companies attempting to enter international markets are very familiar with the danger of literal translation. One humorous example: the U.S. deodorant manufacturer that chose an octopus to symbolize the power of its product — "strong enough for an octopus with eight arms." Unfortunately, in Japan octopi have eight 'legs.' The purpose of the product was hopelessly muddled and it failed to gain a market.

Translation is notoriously difficult, an art form when done well, as words are not interchangeable. Words gain their meaning not only from their definition, but from the context in which they are used. Contexts can, and often do, completely redefine words even so far as to invert their meaning.

Attempting to adopt concepts from another domain, and use them metaphorically can lead to results that are just as misleading as translation. Because the new terms are, at first, perceived as metaphors their creeping lexicality fails to be seen. Soon they are treated as fact, not metaphor, and they influence thinking in the new domain in deleterious ways.

For example, business borrowed the notion of a system from classical physics. In physics a system is deterministic in nature and governed by formulaic laws. Business systems, because of the metaphor, came to be seen as machines (complicated but deterministic systems) and an entire discipline of 'scientific management' grounded in the machine metaphor came into existence.

It took decades for business to realize that the enterprise was indeed a system, but not the system of classical physics, but a complex adaptive system instead.

The problems of translation and metaphor can be avoided if individuals commit to being 'modern polymaths'. A polymath is someone who knows all that is to be known and the last person acknowledge as such was Leibniz. A modern polymath is more accurately described as knowledgable in multiple domains with a deeper understanding of one. The term "T-shaped individual" is a commonly encountered label for someone with both breadth of knowledge (the crossbar of the T) and a deeply understood specialization (the vertical upright of the T).

It is the breadth of knowledge of the individuals that

251

allows the formation of linkages across disciplines such that a diverse team, speaking many natural languages and many technical languages, is able to transcend specialization and communicate among one another. Without individual breadth, teams are merely collections of specialists speaking their own languages — babbling at each other without communication. The team's capabilities arise from using their individual breadth of knowledge to form a cross-disciplinary language and culture.

A cross-disciplinary language and culture is essential, but because it is embodied in a specific group of people, it too has the potential to be idiosyncratic and self serving. A design firm, for example, can develop its own language and culture that differentiates it from other designers. It reflects the self consciousness that Alexander decried in schools of architecture. Designers and those entering the design culture must be constantly on guard and alert to prevent this kind of devolution of their

language. The language itself must be open and capable of expansion and evolution. The power of the language comes from this openness. This implies that there should be few restrictions on accepting new concepts, new words, into the language. English, for example has essentially no rules for adopting new terms into the language thereby allowing all kinds of words, from myriad sources, into the language, even when they ostensibly represent the same concept or thing, are deemed synonyms. This creates an immense potential for nuance and precision of expression. This in turn sparks thinking about the 'why' of word selection which leads to the exposure of alternative intents and alternative meanings — fodder for creativity similar to that grounded in ambiguity.

Glossolalia can counteract business tendencies that are ultimately detrimental to the enterprise.

One example. Most businesses become what they are through an accretion of historical decisions, decisions that reflect both the nature of the individuals making the decisions and the circumstances prevailing at the time the decisions were made. These decisions are reflected in the language utilized by those in the business and forms part of the business culture. The language persists and continues to shape the enterprise even when the essential nature of the enterprise has changed. This leads to a loss of identity. The lack of correspondence between language and essence creates a misfit that is perceptible to clients and markets, causing harm to the business. Change is inevitable.

Essence preserving change, Unfolding, is inhibited when the language of the business is static and grounded in history.

A second example. We think with language and if we have but one language to think with, our thoughts tend to be habitual and repetitive. Instead of finding solutions appropriate to problems, we tend to use old solutions that appear to be close matches. We cannot see beyond our language. Programmers illustrate the power of habit when they gain fluency in a programming language only to have the same style and idiom appear in their code, even when writing in a different programming language. The old adage, "If you have a hammer, every problem looks like a nail," captures how habitual language precludes creative solutions.

Glossolalia advocates multilingualism (technical and natural languages) in both individuals and teams. Richness of expression expands the space in which possible solutions might be found and increases the potential of finding appropriate solutions. Integrating multiple world views, new dimensions, and alternative perspectives is, quite literally, mind expanding; is exhilarating and leads to feelings of **Joy**.

Related patterns

Glossolalia relates to **Thick Description** as part-to-whole; with language as one aspect of culture.

Appropriate and effective use of **System Metaphor** is enhanced by **Glossolalia** — knowledge of multiple languages, by individuals and within teams, contributes a rich source of metaphor and metaphor derived insights. The same rich vein of metaphor enhances **Story Telling**; in turn facilitating the development of a common language for the design and domain teams, one that allows specialists to communicate effectively across their domains of expertise. **Fit** and **Invisibility** are enhanced when the common language emerging from **Glossolalia** simultaneously transcends and extends the language employed by experts in a given domain.

The **Joy** we experience when we are designing, or evaluating a design, can arise from an apt and revealing metaphor or the appropriateness of a "well turned phrase" — the likelihood of both increased by **Glossolalia**.

Language, **Glossolalia**, is key for detecting and supporting **Unfolding**, by providing a common perspective and common constraints for ensuring that **Personae** remain consistent with **Form**: that essence preserving transformations are true and appropriate.

As we develop a common language, as we merge and integrate multiple languages and craft insights metaphorically derived from juxtaposing vocabulary from divergent sources; we are effectively establishing a new **Gestalt**. This emerging **Gestalt** is shared by designers and all the denizens of the designed domain.

Stories

The power that comes from possessing a common language and the loss incurred when languages are confounded are common themes in mythology and literature.

Odin kept track of mortal affairs by listening to the accounts of his two ravens, Hugin and Munin. Dag the

254

Wise, legendary king of Sweden, used his tame house sparrow to fly about and bring back news of his subjects. The figurehead that graced Jason's ship, the Argo, was carved from a tree in a sacred grove and could itself understand the same language of the birds as Odin and Dag the Wise.

Sigurd, sitting naked in front of a fire cooking Fafnir's heart (Fafnir was a dragon), for his father-in-law Regin, who was Fafnir's brother. Before the heart is fully cooked, Sigurd touches it with his finger, resulting in a burn. Sigurd puts the finger in his mouth and thereby partakes of the blood of Fafnir, instantly acquiring the language of the birds. Listening to the birds, Sigurd is informed of Regin's intended treachery and cuts off Regin's head and takes Fafnir's treasure.

The language of the birds is not only a shared language, it is also the proto-language once spoke by all humans as well as all birds. When humans possessed this language they had great power, but lost that power when language was confounded, as the story of Babel illustrates.

Design teams rapidly create a common language, and argot or, more accurately, a creole, that blends together vocabulary and usage and wisdom arising from the specialized language of multiple specialized professions and domains. This will happen if the design team provides an appropriate environment.

Once, in a small community in Southern Utah, United States, guidance and governance was grounded in a monthly religious practice involving glossolalia.

One Sunday the congregation was meeting as usual and, also as usual, at the appropriate moment, a congregant began speaking in a language known to no one else. When finished the group waited for another member to rise and interpret the message, but no one did. The silence wore on for some time before the elders decided that the message was not going to be translated and the meeting was dismissed.

Later that month the community experienced a serious, but entirely preventable, setback. They coped as best they could, but event caused some significant problems. At the beginning of the religious service the following month, a congregant arose and tearfully confessed that she was supposed to be the interpreter the previous month, that he had understood the message. But she was shy and afraid and did not truly believe that God had chosen her for this task, so she kept silent. The setback experienced by the community would not have occurred had she fulfilled the demands of the spirit she experienced.

This story illustrates: how essential knowledge is enmeshed in multiple specialized languages; the importance of each linguistic speaker to contribute to the whole conversation; and, perhaps most importantly, the importance of an environment that enables each person to feel confident and empowered to make his or her contribution.

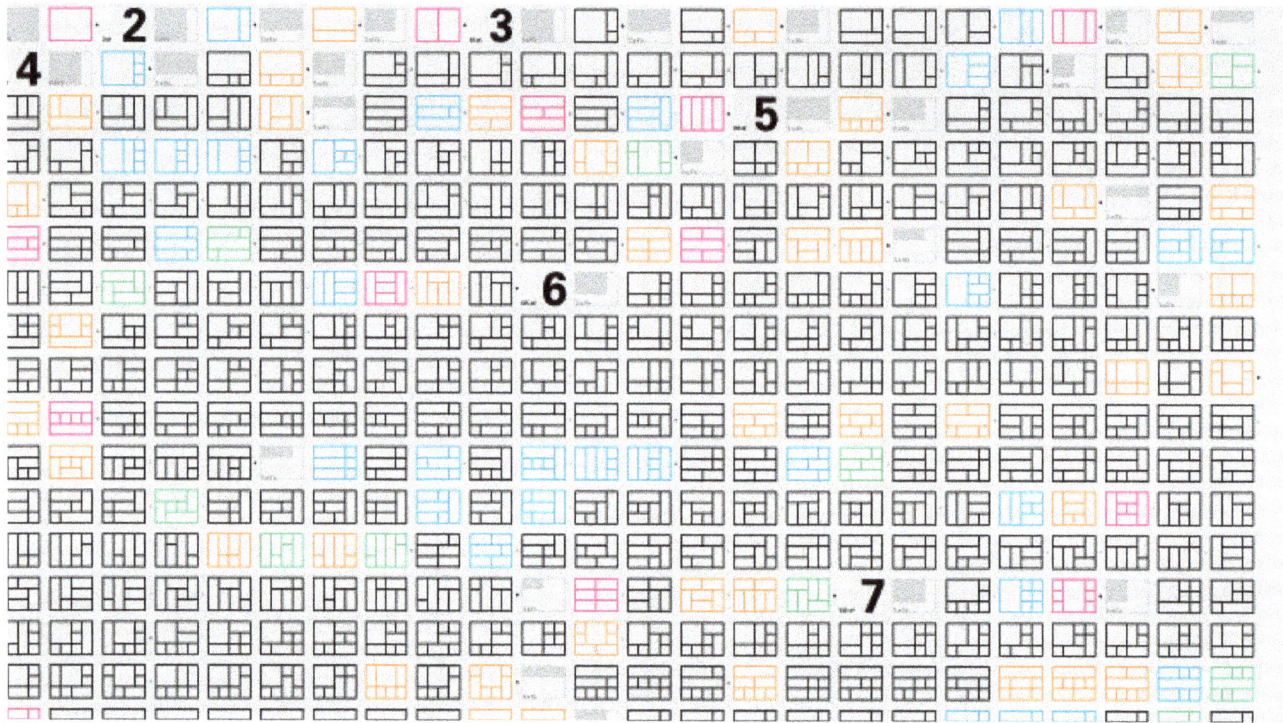

Everything an Object **

Thumbnail

If (any of these)
- you are lost in complexity,
- the whole cannot be held in your mind, or
- you cannot see clearly;

then (all of these)
- devise a simple meta-language,
- use it to partition the world into self-similar subsets, and
- use its terms to establish perspective.

258

Context

You are lost in complexity. There are no clear boundaries, nothing is differentiated from anything else. The volume of details exceeds your ability to juggle them simultaneously in your mind.

Forces

Humans are limited in the amount of information they can hold in their conscious mind at any one time, so decomposition of large and complicated domains is required before you can proceed.

Communication is facilitated when the vocabulary employed in the meta-language is familiar to, shared by, all the members of the team.

The meta-langauge and its vocabulary must be 'neutral', not imposing a special world view on its users.

Problem

You cannot move forward until you can make sense of the complexity you face. You need a way to differentiate or distinguish. You lack a starting point for your thinking. You are caught up in that which you see and cannot find a perspective.

Therefore,

Solution

You need to partition, to decompose, a large domain into smaller, mentally tractable domains. A metalanguage, equally accessible to diverse specialists, will provide means of communication supporting the need to decompose large and complicated domains. Your meta-language should not impose cognitive burden.

Employ a meta-language (we use 'meta' in the sense of 'pre') with a simple and familiar vocabulary — e.g. Object, Behavior, and Message — that, when integrated with technical and natural languages, supports discussion of things and the relationships among them.

Resulting context

Adding the "object language" to teams repertoire provides a tool that facilitates inter-speciality communication. An obvious example: bankers and software developers can use a common vocabulary of 'accounts', 'transactions', and 'ledgers' to bridge the communication gap that arises from the languages each uses in their own profession.

260

Use of the Everything An Object pattern, and the meta-language suggests, maximizes the ability of poly-vocal teams with multi-disciplinary expertise to communicate the 'what' and 'why' questions behind every design without becoming bogged down in details of 'how'.

Eventually, however, the what and why will need to be tangibly expressed and the 'how' will impose a new set of constraints for the design. An example is the need for the 'account' we understand to be realized using the data structures, operations, and control structures imposed by a programming language. The stories we tell that capture what and why need to be converted into the narrative — do this then do this — demanded by the computer.

The Everything An Object abstraction allows you to see clearly, to find the objects and the relationships among them. Clearly exposing relationships increases your awareness and helps you recognize their importance — something that is central to many Asian points of view. The use of an abstraction often has the side effect of distancing your direct experience and therefore your emotional connection to what you are seeing. You can become less emotionally involved and might not want to lose that kind of connection.

Pattern Description

The pattern begins with the assertion of a need to decompose large complicated domains. It then suggests that a meta-language be devised and integrated with natural and technical languages to provide a common basis for discussing things and relationships among things.

Discussion

Decomposition, dividing the world into subsets, sometimes repeatedly, until we have a subset that bounds those parts of the world of immediate interest and is small enough that our minds can think about all the things in the subset, and all the ways that the things interact, without losing sight of the whole.

There are many approaches to decomposition, the most common of which is reductionism. The large and complex is understood of something simpler and the next level of decomposition. World ---> Things ---> Elements (atoms) ---> Elementary Particles ---> Quanta. General Systems

Theory offers a simpler alternative, one where there is no qualitative change in the kind of things we encounter, at each level remains constant. World (system) ---> collection of systems ---> collection of systems ---> collection of systems ---> ... ---> collection of systems that we will treat as if they were elementary, i.e. when we no longer care about the systems within.

About sixty years ago, a few people in the software world began using the concept and term, Object, to partition the world into discrete things. The 'world' of interest was a subset of the World that might have subsets within it. Object and System are complementary terms and can be merged. World (an Object) ---> collection of Objects ---> collection of Objects ---> ... ---> collection of Objects that we will treat as if they were unitary.

Everything An Object captures this aspect of decomposition, we partition the world, but at every level we encounter the same kind of thing — objects.

Objects offer a powerful way to decompose the world into discrete things, while retaining the ability to put them together again. As Plato, circa 400 BC said:a{-First,}perceiving and bringing together under one Idea the scattered particulars, so that one makes clear ... the particular thing which he wishes ... {Second,} the separation of the Idea into classes, by dividing it where the natural joints are, and not trying to break any part, after the manner of a bad carver ... I love these processes of division and bringing together ... and if I think any other man is able to see things that can naturally be collected into one and divided into many, him will I follow as if he were a god.

The "one Idea" spoken of by Plato is the criteria for distinguishing between one Object and another. A criteria that allows us to see and partition at the 'natural joints' is essential. 'Behavior', what a thing does is a very useful partitioning criteria, one we already employ in our everyday lives. In everyday life we distinguish between a Wolf, a Wolf-Dog hybrid, and a Dog based on the different behaviors of each.

Once we have our behaviorally differentiated Objects it can be useful to "separate the Idea in to classes." A class is a set of objects that we believe are more similar to each other than to other objects. A class usually has its own name. The rationale for this aggregation into classes, and possible taxonomy of classes, is initially based on behavior as well, but may also be based on observable characteristics. Once we have identified Dog, we can cre-

262

ate a taxonomy of kinds of dogs based on characteristics like long or short hair, color, big or small, etc.

In addition to knowing things, objects, we want and need to know how they interact with each other. The only thing we know about an object is what it does, its behaviors, so the most obvious means of interaction is by one object soliciting the behavior of another. It does so by sending a Message, an invocation of a specific Behavior. Object, Behavior, and Message then become the three defined concepts or terms in a metalanguage (again we are using 'meta' in its original, Greek, sense of 'pre', not the contemporary usage of 'above').

Our meta-language is integrated with our everyday languages, technical or natural, such that we can begin talking about relationships among objects, sequences of interactions, 'intent' or 'purpose' of those interactions and relationships, anything we need to know or talk about.

We gain a powerful simplicity from our integrated languages. We can look at a sequence of interactions, for example, and call it a 'Script' and think of it as if it were an object with behaviors and capable of sending and receiving Messages.

When everything is an object, we see underlying commonalities and each discrete thing can be understood in terms of them. The concepts and terms from our meta-language allows us to talk about very different kinds of things as if they were all of the same kind. Using a meta-language creates a 'distance' that helps see, because if your are too close to something you cannot see it clearly. The 'distance' allows everyone to see the same thing, helping us communicating our understandings without getting colored by meanings implicit in our individual languages. We communicate clearly and simply. In this way our integrated languages provide us a way to express understanding, in a parsimonious manner, facilitating a more complete communication and understanding.

Related patterns

Everything An Object extends **Logos** with the notion of a meta (pre)-language. **Glossolalia** asserts the need to use multiple languages and **Everything An Object** provides a bridge that can be used to convey meaning across those languages.

The meta-language of **Everything An Object** provides

a tool for seeing the essence preserving transformations of **Unfolding**. A tool also used in **Seed Recognizes Flower** where your concern is whether or not the transformations did, indeed, preserve essence.

When you say that a thing is an 'object', and objects communicate with messages, you are using concepts from **Everything An Object**, metaphorically and this enhances **Story Telling**. A play is an object, as are each of the characters, each crop, the set, even the audience. This is an example of the 'distance' that allows you to talk of things that are dissimilar in detail in various technical languages as if they were all instances of the same kind of thing.

Personae arise when different clients of an Object are interested in and utilize different subsets of the Behaviors of that Object and Behavior and Object are concepts from **Everything An Object**.

Story
In Complexity All Stories are True? by Tenneson Woolf

Like many, last spring I became fascinated with the story of Malaysia Airlines Flight 370. Alarmed. Concerned. Sympathetic. Sorrowful.

The flight was an international passenger flight leaving from Kuala Lumpur, Malaysia, and scheduled to arrive in Beijing, China. The flight was lost. Incredulous as this sounds in an age of advanced radar and satellite imagery, the flight was lost. There were 239 people on board.

Did it crash into the sea? Was it hijacked? Was it a terrorist attack? Did it explode? Speculation on news programs ran rampant for a number of months after the disappearance. Though this disappearance led to the largest and most expensive search in aviation history, that continues now, no evidence has been found or shared to confirm any of several possible stories about what really happened.

The unexplained disappearance of this plane strikes me as being rather complex. Without intending to overlook the basic tragedy of 239 lives lost, most likely, there is a key learning for me from this event that is related to complexity. Is it that in complex circumstances, all stories (OK, many stories) remain simultaneously true. There can be much posturing about a preferred story, and the selective attention to data that supports that story, but it

A decomposing leaf

remains that all stories are true. None of the stories can be disproven.

Let's back up a bit and link this to participative leadership.

In the Cynefin Framework developed by Dave Snowden, there is an important distinction between four environments: simple, complicated, complex, and chaotic. In a simple environment, one story tends to be true.

A causes B. It's very linear. Little discussion is needed to confirm the narrative. Smoking causes lung cancer.

In a complicated environment, a few stories are true. There is still linearity. A more involved algorithm per-

265

haps, but the narrative is still clear. Smoking increases the chance of lung cancer. So does exposure to secondary smoke. So does exposure to a polluted quality of air.

In a complex environment, all stories remain true. Meaning must be negotiated. Must be a conversation, in which many narratives are relevant and simultaneously plausible. What promotes good health? Yes, of course, exercise. Yes, of course, a proper diet. Yes, of course, rest. And yes, of course, avoidance of habits such as smoking.

Despite these many affirmations, in a broad enough conversation, there will be people that know of others living a long, long life despite the absence of exercise, a proper diet, rest, etc. Despite the habits of smoking, and other patterns that correlate with illness and disease.

Most people relate to complex lives. Whether personal lives, at the job, or in leading levels of transformation. One essential need in these complex lives, is the ability to explore the simultaneous existence of many stories being true. It may play with our brains — after all, it is so nice to impose a simplicity — and create significant confusion and frustration. Yet, the essential capacity is more curiosity, not more certainty supported by blustering boldly. The disposition of being able to pause, to wonder — less blame and fix — is what will walk us more meaningfully and productively in today's plethora of complex environments.

Recently in speaking with an elder friend that I trust, when I asked how she was doing, she responded, "I don't take any of it too seriously any more." I know her well enough to know that she takes many things seriously. It isn't apathy that she was describing. I believe it was the kind of wisdom that comes with experience, and perhaps age, to not get hooked into impositions of truth. I believe it was the kind of tempering that comes with experience to begin to recognize that story, is so often our choice.

Thick Description **

Thumbnail

If (any of these)
- your understanding of others seems incomplete or confusing,
- you need to convey details as well as essence of a context, or
- if what you see seems strange and alien;

then (all of these)
- experience as well as observe what you do not understand,
- recognize the familiar in the strange, and
- communicate with a thick description.

Context

Whenever you are required to change contexts or communicate across contexts.

Forces

Meaning and understanding are dependent on context as much as explicit words and language.

It is difficult, perhaps impossible, to convey a context in its entirety.

Perceptions of new contexts are dominated by an awareness of that which is unfamiliar, strange, or alien.

Problem

You need to communicate in depth understanding among a variety of individuals, each of whom is embedded in a specific context.

Therefore,

Solution

Provide a 'thick description' as used in cultural anthropology to maximize transmission of context and to increase understanding across contexts by "making the familiar strange and the strange familiar.

Resulting context

You possess a complete, to the greatest degree possible, body of knowledge and experience of the problem domain and all of the forces working within it.

Paradoxically, a thick description presents you with expanded challenges deriving from ambiguity, metaphoric relationships, and conflicting contexts.

You must balance the perspective that comes from your own knowledge and experience and the perspective presented and described by the thick description. Doing so will allow you to see things that those embedded in the context might not without making the mistake of projecting, and therefore misinterpreting, the true nature of that which is being thickly described.

270

Pattern Description

The pattern suggests that an anthropological concept, thick description, is the appropriate vehicle for communicating in-depth understanding across contexts, across cultures.

Discussion

Thick description is a term coined by Clifford Geertz in discussions about the limits of cultural understanding. Geertz believed that it was impossible to precisely describe all of the rules, relationships, and parts of a complex system like a culture. Following the lead of Gilbert Ryle, the philosopher, and using one of Ryle's examples, Geertz pointed out how difficult it is to understand even simple behaviors, like a wink. Is a wink, the contraction of the eyelid, a simple physiological response, or intentional? If intentional, what meaning does it convey? Or, might it be a parody, a wink in a context that implies the opposite of how the wink would normally be interpreted — a kind of meta-wink?

Although difficult, it is expected that cultural anthropologists come to understand a culture and offer an ethnography of that culture to the world, enabling others to gain an understanding and appreciation of cultures other than their own.

The anthropologist comes to his understanding as a result of extensive, one or more years, participant observation — living with a people, working in the fields, dancing in ritual performances, preparing and consuming food, every aspect of life. The amount of data collected, not to mention the observations, the stories, the knowledge — both explicit and tacit — and interpretations is massive. The anthropologist cannot transmit all of this, so he does the best possible by writing a thick description — what could be observed interspersed with annotations, explanations, variations, and illustrative anecdotes.

Designer's confront a situation analogous to that of the anthropologist whenever they engage with a client in a new domain. Members of a design team, de facto, live in different cultures and yet must communicate across those cultures, communication that is possible only with an in-depth understanding of their own culture as well as the cultures of others.

Exacerbating the problem is the fact that when you first confront a culture it seems alien, strange. You notice all

271

the differences and fail to see the similarities. You may also miss the similarities because you are not, usually, consciously aware of your own culture. A thick description attempts to "make the strange familiar" by connecting it to similarities shared across cultures; and seeks to "make the familiar strange" by describing aspects of your culture in the same 'objective' language used when describing the 'other'. The effect is to expose presuppositions and assumptions that inhibit understanding.

Designers do not write ethnographies of their clients, nor do members of design teams write ethnographies of each other's culture. What is done, and should be done, is to create an environment replete with cultural information, where story telling is common, where reminders of stories told populate the space occupied by the team. The environment becomes a thick description of the cultures of all of those working in that space.

Related patterns

Thick Description supports **Glossolalia** by contextualizing and thereby enhancing understanding of language. **Story Telling** has a reciprocal relationship with **Thick Description**, each supporting the objectives of the other. **Participant Observation** is the practice supporting the collection of information conveyed by **Thick Description**.

Suggesting that the environment of a 'multicultural team', **It Takes a Village**, should be a de facto thick description of those cultures is possible only when the team has **A Room of One's Own**. It is usually the case that more than one individual shares all or part of any of the cultures of the team, creating a connection to **Tribes**.

Story

Standing at the bus stop I happened to notice a beautiful woman standing nearby but with several other people between us. I could not help my self, and gazed longingly at her beauty. Oh, she noticed me. And she winked at me!

Or ... maybe not. The wind did pick up just then and perhaps a bit of dust caused her eyelid to spasm. After all why would such a beautiful person even acknowledge someone like me?

There! She did it again, only slower this time, making sure I saw her. She's inviting me over, to talk, perhaps to fall in love, and live together happily ever after.

Wait silly! She's making fun of me. Somehow she sensed how much I want to be near her, to kiss her, and hold her close to me. Her wink is really a parody, like an actor on the stage and the wink means the exact opposite of what I want it to mean.

She smiled as she winked, but how do I know what that means. Is the smile an invitation also, emphasizing the wink; or is it amusement at the idea that someone like here would even acknowledge someone like me?

How do I decide? What should I do? Why are such simple symbols tangled in a web of complex interpretations?

Oh no! Too late. She is getting on the bus and I will never see her again. Wait, she is frowning slightly. Is that disappointment that I did not accept her invitation, or annoyance that I was looking at her and she is telling me to stop it?

(With apologies to Gilbert Ryle and Clifford Geertz.)

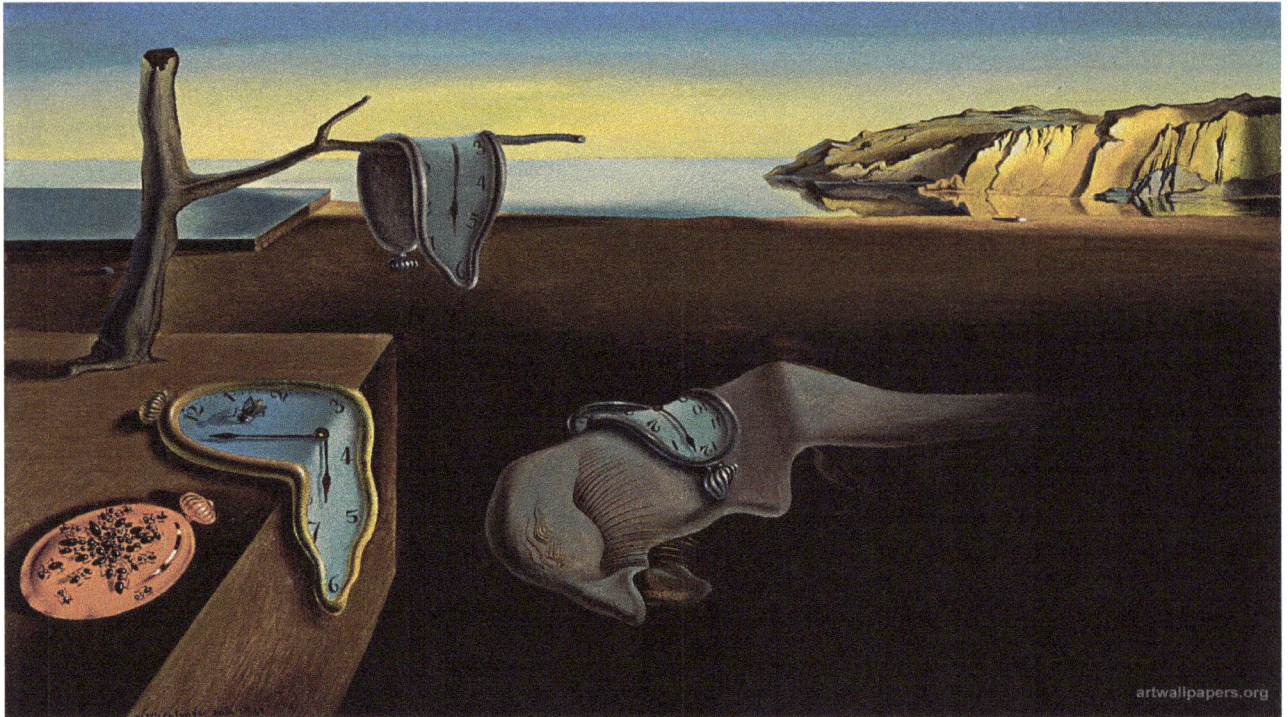

artwallpapers.org

It's About Time **

Thumbnail

If (any of these)
- your vocabulary includes words like 'before' and 'after',
- you can conjugate the verb 'to be', or
- your work will be done in the future;

then (all of these)
- recognize the power of time,
- recognize that time is a reflection of your mind, and
- leverage the illusion of time.

274

Context

Anytime. Every time.

Forces

Everything has a temporal aspect or is dependent
on time in some manner.

Our understanding of time is limited, restricted to linear
interpretations.

Time is so ubiquitous that we tend to overlook it and
its consequences.

Time is an illusion.

Problem

You cannot understand a dynamic system independent
of temporal considerations.

Therefore,

Solution

Sensitize yourself to, and understand, the various manifestations and consequences of time and how they affect your designs.

Resulting context

You will enjoy a more complete understanding of the temporal relationships among objects. Simultaneously you will understand the arbitrariness of time and how it is a projection of our minds, not something that exists outside of ourselves. This provides opportunities to play with time and order in order to make our designs more powerful.

Pattern Description

Time is intrinsic to and essential for our understanding

of the world and this patterns points out that while Sad-
vocating developing sensitivity to and an understanding
of temporal issues.

Discussion

Time and temporal considerations are essential to our
understanding of the world around us. Even though time,
metaphysically does not exist, our interpretation of the
world is impossible without it.

Time is assumed to be intrinsic to individual things.
The simplest example is a thing coming into existence
at one point of time and leaving existence at another.
Of course it might change its nature, exhibit a kind of
lifecycle, in between those two points in time. Slightly
more complicated is the notion of sequence, giving attention to discrete intermediary points between origin and
departure. A lifecycle is a sequence marked by points
where the nature of something changes, at least according to our perception of it. A commonplace example is
human aging, each year being somehow significant, some
more than others, e.g. the birthday that marks one's age
of majority.

We, in the industrialized world, tend to see time in terms
of a linear sequence of moments in time, a sequence that
flows from the past to the future with right now exempli-
fying a 'moment'. A moment in time is like a point on a
line. It has no dimension. It exists as a concept only.
A Buddhist, however, has a very different conception of
time as a single space where all things are, simultaneously. No past, no future, only Now. This would be an interesting curiosity except for the fact that theorists as diverse as Rupert Sheldrake and Richard Feynman suggest
that the Buddhist sense of time is more 'real' than our
customary linear understanding.

Rhythm is another important perspective grounded
in time. Rhythm is closely associated with pace and frequency. Christopher Alexander states that "Alternating
Repetition" is one of the fifteen fundamental properties
of nature and, although he discusses it in terms of space,
it is more appropriately applied to time. All living things
have natural rhythms, awake and active followed by rest
and quiescence. These rhythms occur at different scales,
e.g. hourly, daily, monthly, annually and are readily recognized. Examples of how rhythm is oft overlooked:
a business projecting sales without accounting for sea-
sonal, holiday, variations; or a payroll system that fails
to provide for quarterly and annual reports.

Pace is an important extension of rhythm. Pace maps two independent rhythms to each other. A runner, for example, attemps to map the rhythm of his exertions, the timing and duration of exertion, to the demands of the race. More frequent exertions, more exertions per unit of time, for a sprint, and less frequent for a marathon. A direct analogy in the world of work, the mental and physical exertion required to accomplish a task should, but often does not, map to the work schedule. When this does not happen, employees find themselves trapped in a "death march", the acceleration of pace beyond what is feasible in order to meet an arbitrary deadline.

As much as we think in terms of time, we simultaneous, somewhat paradoxically believe some things to be outside or independent of time. For example, I really believe that I am the same person that I was fifty years ago, that somehow all the observable changes do not reflect the "real me". Christopher Alexander titled the companion book to *A Pattern Language*, "*The Timeless Way of Building*". In this book, when speaking of essence, of Form, we both imply and explicitly state that essence is eternal, only expression or shape changes.

It is easy to overlook time in other, more critical ways as well. Consider how a word, a company name, or a logotype, all of which the coiner of the word or the designer intend to be timeless, may in fact be marked by time. It is possible for me to reveal my age, not by saying I am x years old, but simply by using a word that was common forty years ago but is seldom used today. A company naming itself might expose both the time and context of its origin; e.g. the abundance of high tech companies naming themselves with nonsense words or non sequiturs, after the success of Google, or how typefaces wax and wan in popularity, thereby revealing when the logotype was most likely created.

Time is reflected in our value systems and vary across cultures. Is a seventy-year old a superfluous nuisance or wise and venerable? Is a need for 'instant gratification' a character flaw? Note that your answer to that question might also reveal a time dimension, those born decades ago are more likely to say yes, than those in their teens and twenties.

Time is pervasive, and often subtle, but failing to take it into account assures misunderstanding and may lead to peril.

Playing with time can also be seen when inverting grammar as does Yoda, the teacher in the Star Wars movies:

e.g. "Truly wonderful the mind of a child is," or "Difficult to see, always in motion the future is." The examples given invert English grammar, but not German where the verb traditionally comes at the end of the sentence. This is an example of how time and expected sequence are idiosyncratic to culture. Another interesting example is how the language and cognitive reality of the Aymaran speaking peoples puts the future 'behind them' and the past 'in front of them'. (For Aymaran speakers, the future is unseen, like that which is behind you, only the past is visible and knowable.)

Awareness of time can therefore present opportunities to play but also demands to understand cultural context so that play does not lapse into nonsense.

Related patterns

It's About Time is connected to all of the other patterns in the sense that those patterns cannot be understood independent of a sense of time and how time is used in the various contexts of those patterns. The connection to three of the essence patterns is worth noting: **Form** is held to be beyond time, or at least eternal in time; the apparent sequence in **Unfolding** comes from our perspective as observers and is not intrinsic to the process itself; and, **Zen Mind** assumes an awareness that transcends time.

Story

It had been some time since Jack had seen the old man, his former neighbour. College, girls, career, and life itself got in the way. In fact, Jack moved clear across the country in pursuit of his dreams. There, in the rush of his busy life, Jack had little time to think about the past and often no time to spend with his wife and son. He was working on his future, and nothing could stop him.

Over the phone, his mother told him, 'Mr Belser died last night. The funeral is Wednesday.' Memories flashed through his mind like an old newsreel as he sat quietly remembering his childhood days.

'Jack, did you hear me?'

'Oh sorry, Mom. Yes, I heard you. It's been so long since I thought of him. I'm sorry, but I honestly thought he died years ago,' Jack said. 'Well, he didn't forget you.

Every time I saw him he'd ask how you were doing. He'd reminisce about the many days you spent over 'his side of the fence' as he put it,' Mom told him.

'I loved that old house he lived in,' Jack said.

'You know, Jack, after your father died, Mr. Belser stepped in to make sure you had a man's influence in your life,' she said.

'He's the one who taught me carpentry,' he said. 'I wouldn't be in this business if it weren't for him. He spent a lot of time teaching me things he thought were important ... Mom, I'll be there for the funeral,' Jack said.

As busy as he was, he kept his word. Jack caught the next flight to his hometown. Mr. Belser's funeral was small and uneventful. He had no children of his own, and most of his relatives had passed away.

The night before he had to return home, Jack and his Mom stopped by to see the old house next door one more time.

Standing in the doorway, Jack paused for a moment. It was like crossing over into another dimension, a leap through space and time.

The house was exactly as he remembered. Every step held memories. Every picture, every piece of furniture ... Jack stopped suddenly.

'What's wrong, Jack?' his Mom asked. 'The box is gone,' he said. 'What box?' Mom asked.

'There was a small gold box that he kept locked on top of his desk. I must have asked him a thousand times what was inside. All he'd ever tell me was 'the thing I value most,' Jack said.

It was gone. Everything about the house was exactly how Jack remembered it, except for the box. He figured some- one from the Belser family had taken it.

'Now I'll never know what was so valuable to him,' Jack said. 'I better get some sleep. I have an early flight home, Mom.'

It had been about two weeks since Mr. Belser died. Returning home from work one day

Jack discovered a note in his mailbox. 'Signature required on a package. No one at home. Please stop by the main post office within the next three days,' the note read.

Early the next day Jack retrieved the package. The small box was old and looked like it had been mailed a hundred years ago. The handwriting was difficult to read, but the return address caught his attention.

'Mr. Harold Belser' it read. Jack took the box out to his car and ripped open the package. There inside was the gold box and an envelope. Jack's hands shook as he read the note inside.

'Upon my death, please forward this box and its contents to Jack Bennett. It's the thing I valued most in my life.'

A small key was taped to the letter. His heart racing, as tears filling his eyes, Jack carefully unlocked the box. There inside he found a beautiful gold pocket watch. Running his fingers slowly over the finely etched casing, he unlatched the cover. Inside he found these words engraved: *'Jack, Thanks for your time! — Harold Belser.'*

'The thing he valued most ... was ... my time.' Jack held the watch for a few minutes, then called his office and cleared his appointments for the next two days.
'Why?' Janet, his assistant asked. 'I need some time to spend with my son,' he said. 'Oh, by the way, Janet ... thanks for your time!'

Life is not measured by the number of breaths we take, but by the moments that take our breath away.
Thanks for your time!

Room of One´s Own **

If (any of these)
- you are distracted by your surroundings,
- your thoughts are ill-shaped, or
- your ideas are as inflexible as the walls around you;

then (all of these)
- make your environment relevant,
- become one with your space, and
- be creative.

Context

You have a team and it needs a space in which to work.

Forces

What you need to remember exceeds the space available in your mind.

You cannot work amidst irrelevant distractions.

Environment shapes thought.

Flexible thinking requires flexible spaces.

The space must belong to the team and the team must belong to the space.

Problem

The people around you as well as yourself are stuck and are not as creative as possible.

Therefore,

Solution

Provide the team with an inspirational and "living" space that supports design thinking.

Resulting context

A place of joy and an efflorescence of ideas and solutions. Designers, like programmers, often need both quiet, reflective, introverted environments, with public and communication dense environments. The ideal space will provide a multiplicity of spaces and allow the free and easy movement among them so everyone can be in the space that provides the most appropriate context for their current effort.

Pattern Description

The pattern describes the intimate relationship between a space and what people can accomplish in that space. A relationship that must be nurtured.

The dSchool (d stands for design) works in conjunction

284

with the Hasno-Plattner Institute in Potsdam, Germany, was the first academic program focused on teaching design thinking to non-designers. 'Make Space', by Doorley and Witthoft is the first book, of which we are aware, that addresses the kind of thing taught at the dSchool.

Discussion

"We make space and space makes us," said Scott Doorley and Scott Witthoft, exposing the intimate relationship between thinking and the environment in which the thinking takes place. Their book, *Make Space*, is concerned with understanding the spaces that support design activities and design thinking and how to create them, how to make them.

There is an extensive literature on the relationship between thinking, working, and learning and the environments where those activities take place. Jean Lave and Etienne Wenger show how our ability to apply what we learned in on place, the classroom, is diminished when we leave that space. For example, you can learn how to solve story problems about rations in the classroom, and ace the test, the fail to solve the problem of which size bottle of juice offers the better price per ounce while standing in the supermarket.

Pelle Ehn and the Scandinavian School of Design showed the relationship between workspaces and the ability of workers to perform tasks. Reinhard Keil-Slawik demonstrates how the artifacts created by software developers, diagrams on whiteboards, code samples on desks, etc., are actually forms of external memory. Alistair Cockburn and others in the Agile realm talk about 'information radia-tors' when talking about those same artifacts and make the argument that the software developer functions more effectively and efficiently when their workspace contains these artifacts.

Steelcase, a manufacturer of office furniture, has spent decades researching the effect of office space and the contents of that space and how they enhanced or inhibited the ability of workers. There is also the issue of morale, whether or not you simply feel good about being at work because it is or is not a pleasant environment.

Morale also affects your ability to perform.

Despite all this evidence, one of the hardest tasks faced by software teams adopting Agile approaches was

285

convincing management to let them escape the 'cubicle farm'.

Design teams, and teams that wish to think like designers, need a supportive space. It must be open with all work in the 'public' eye. It should be filled with artifacts and the malleable components that can be rapidly configured into prototypes. The team should be responsible for designing their own space and their own tools, as this is the mark of true artisan. And the space must be filled with white space upon which anyone can write or draw. And there must be a mix of common and semi-private spaces.

West, Gabriel, et. al., defined an ideal work and learning space based on the botegga where Leonardo da Vinci apprenticed — a space full of activity, of examples of finished work, a multitude of prototypes and works in progress, a place of conversation, or music, with shared meals, and lots of masters, in various disciplines, and a host of apprentices.

Doorley and Witthoft have synthesized their understanding of what must be done to establish a space supporting and nurturing creativity. Some of their observations:

Design for primates. We're smart apes. Deal with it. Design ways to keep our bodies moving.
Seek inspiration from unexpected locations. Inspiration is everywhere; keep your eyes open all the time.
Leave room to evolve. As a new space gets used, new needs emerge.
Leave room to adapt. Allow the space and the people to continue to adapt and grow.
Build in little rituals. Deliberately incorporating a ritual into a routine can transform the mundane into a minor magic moment.
Make technology radically accessible, but don't use it often. Keep the latest technology around and available, but learn when to use it and when not to.
Build empathy by exploring all angles.
When re-designing a space, take the time to investigate different paths for different angles of view. The physical experience of 'walking the lot' is critical in identifying the details that will make a difference.
Keep supplies and tools visible for inspiration and instruction. People get inspired by what's around them. Surround them with inspiration. "Out of sight, out of mind."
Make thinking tangible. More and more, ideas are coming from the bottom up. All-inclusive expertise and spaces that solidify hierarchies are no longer apt fits

for many dynamic domains. Tangible thinking spaces support: quick visualisation; behavior modeling; making, sharing and feedback; closeness, safety and human understanding.

Beware of whizbang. The simple solution lasts longer, is always easier to build and iterate, and is usually less esoteric and more adaptable.

Powers of ten. When observing and designing a space, consider it in multiple scales,from the level of the individuals' hands to the scope of an entire neighborhood.

Patina gives permission. When designing a creative environment, default to "studio" or "workshop", not "office". The best creative spaces are highly resolved (thoughtful), but not highly refined (precious). Amid the chaos, creative spaces are carefully considered and often well organized.

Use limits to inspire creativity. More flexible spaces require more limits.

Platform vs. application. Think of space as a platform for creative collaboration. Insted of designing for users, think also of design ing for designers.

Flooring shapes creative activities. Whatever the characteristics, the space must belong to the team and the team must belong to the space. The only way that the latter is possible is if the team configures and reconfigures its own space to suit its needs.

Related patterns

A Room of One's Own is where **Unfolding** occurs, where **Form** has the greatest possibility of expressing itself fully. The environment provided by **A Room of One's Own** is full of **Story Telling** and various artifacts that capture elements of the story or one's understanding of the story, enriching the environment and providing the common **Logos** while enhancing the power of **Glossolalia**.

Illustration
taken from the work of Belle Beth Cooper

Constraints can seem like the last thing you'd want for a creative project, but they're actually beneficial when it comes to doing good work. If you've ever faced the common writer's hurdle of the blank page, you'll know what it's like to be paralyzed by innumerable opportunities. What restrictions do is take away some of the choices available to us, and with them, the paralysis of choice that stops us from getting started. Check out a few examples of the amazing work that can come from creative constraints.

The short story that will bring a tear to your eye

This is one of those stories that's so old, no one can really prove who was part of it or how it went down. But even without certainty of the facts, it's worth retelling.

Supposedly Ernest Hemingway was the story author, who bet some friends that he could write an entire story in just six words. Of course, it seems an impossible feat: how do you introduce characters, explain their relationships and tell a tale about them in just six words? Here's how Hemingway did it:

For sale: baby shoes, never worn.

Powerful stuff, right? Like I said, it's a story worth telling, even if we'll never know the exact details. It certainly provides a lesson about working with constraints. With such an extreme brevity limitation, not only did Hemingway have to choose his words carefully, but he also had to craft them in a way that imbued the silence around those words with the rest of his story, since he'd run out of words to tell it.

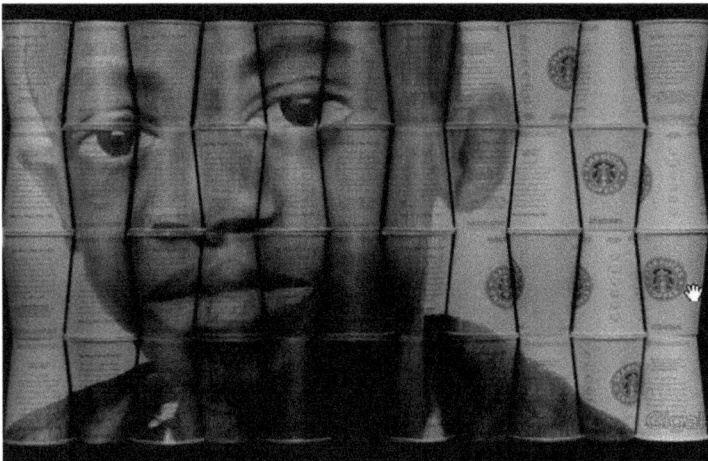

A career-ending injury that became a blessing

Phil Hansen's story is nothing short of inspiring. As an art student, Phil relied on a specific pointillist style he'd developed. He was understandably distraught when an injury from creating art this way meant he couldn't do it anymore. After walking away from the art world completely for three years, Phil returned and started using constraints to his advantage.

His shaky hand, a result of his art injury, led him to a new style incorporating the shaky lines he couldn't help making.

Eventually Phil realised how powerful constraints could be and started creating his own: from drawing on coffee cups to painting with karate moves to creating temporary art.

288

Physical limitations that lead to unique art projects

The last time I explored the use of constraints in creativity I came across this artist who creates amazing work within physical and spacial constraints. Michael Johansson takes used objects and repurposes them into artistic projects. I'm tempted to call them sculptures but it doesn't seem to fit with the almost 2D look of his work.

What's so impressive about Michael's work is that he seeks out frames to work within — physical spaces to use as constraints — and makes his used objects fit together inside those areas. Michael describes his work as being almost a game: like real-life Tetris.

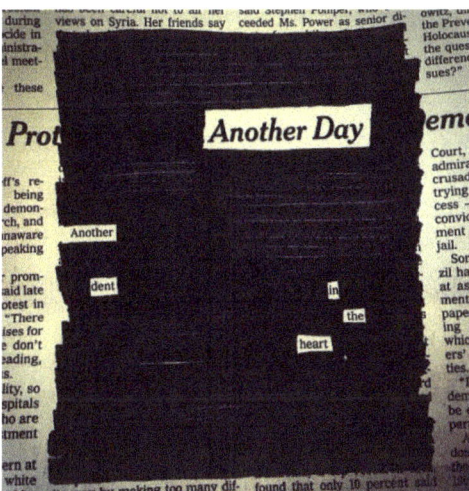

Using copyright restrictions as inspiration

Austin Kleon provides an excellent example of working within constraints. Though he's known for several things, perhaps what first made a name for Austin were his newspaper blackout poems.

Working from the constraints of the words already presents in a newspaper article or column, Austin uses a marker to black out words, subtracting from the original content until only his own message is left.

Even more than that, Austin has copyright restrictions to think about, since he's using someone else's work. In a New York Times piece, Austin explained how the various areas of copyright law provide inspiration for his work, as they give him constraints to work within.

For instance, he needs to ensure that the final message in each of his blackout poems, if not completely different to that of the original, reverses or parodies it. He also notes that the fewer words he uses from the original and the more space between them, the less likely he'll be to face a copyright suit.

289

Tribes **

Thumbnail

If (any of these)
- individuals must work collaboratively and cooperatively,
- each person believes their expertise is the most important, or
- independent work must be coordinated and integrated;

then (all of these)
- do what the natives do,
- make leadership ephemeral and situational, and
- someone must be the shaman.

Context

You have assembled your team and are ready to work.

Forces

Professionals know how to do their jobs.

Professionals work best with general direction.

People like to be 'in charge'.

Absolute power corrupts absolutely.

Problem

Cooperative and collaborative work is difficult because the default mode of organization conflates leadership with power, and assumes the need for hierarchical structure. It is not clear how peers with diverse skills and backgrounds can be organized for cooperative work.

Therefore,

Solution

Adopt and adapt a form of peer organization exhibited in nomadic tribes.

Resulting context

A self organized team expressing their creativity. Although self-organization and situational leadership was dominant and successful for 23,000 of the 25,000 years humans have had social organizations, some would argue that it is no longer feasible nor desirable.

Design teams and designful organizations must evaluate, and perhaps find pattern variations, that take into account the challenges presented by large scale teams and corporate organizational structures. (More on this issue in discussion section.).

Pattern Description

The pattern advocates the kind of social organization seen in tribal cultures, with leadership established on

292

the basis of situational need coupled with individual expertise and a special role, the shaman, who acts as a buffer and channel of communication with the world outside of the group.

Discussion

Tribal members are peers. Decisions regarding the tribe are made by consensus. Tribes may have 'Chiefs', individuals selected to make 'operational' decisions about day to day, normal, activities. The tribe has already established, by consensus, the parameters within which the Chief is allowed to make decisions, so this does not conflict with the peer structure of the tribe.

Although they are peers, individual differences and special talents are acknowledged and respected. In extraordinary situations, like a war party on the horizon, the individual whose skills best match the demands of the situation assumes leadership and everyone follows his lead. Once the situation is resolved, the tribe will evaluate the performance of the 'leader' and re-evaluate them vis-a-vis everyone else so they know who should assume the role next time that role is needed.

The only enduring, from investiture until death, role is that of the Shaman, the intermediary between the tribe and the supernatural world. The Shaman intercedes with the supernatural on behalf of the team and conveys guidance from that world to the team.

Design teams can readily adopt and adapt this form of organization simply by recognizing that, in the highly dynamic design process. Every moment is potentially an 'extraordinary situation', a point where attention is focused on one particular aspect of the design or one particular design activity. The member of the team with the skills that best match that situation assumes the lead. Lead, as in guide, or in military terms, point. Lead is not an authoritarian position, leads offer suggestions and guidance. Teams need an enduring role analogous to the shaman, a coach, an intermediary between the team and the managerial world. The Coach intercedes with management on behalf of the team and conveys guidance from management to the team.

Management theory as taught in business schools suggests that tribal organization is no longer feasible, nor desirable. It is argued that only hierarchical organizations and dedicated communication channels can support the information consolidation and filtering necessary to present decision makers, those at the top, to do their jobs. Similarly, decisions, it is claimed, must be translated from strategic, to tactical, to operational terms and then executed as stated.

These ideas are so pervasive and accepted so blindly that efforts, like "extreme programming" or "employee empowerment" seemingly are doomed to failure.

Empirical measures and an-ecdotal observations suggest that the prevailing wisdom is wrong. Self organizing teams, well coached, are more than adequate to meet the challenges of large scale organization without the need to impose superficially reinvented organizational structures.

Further, there is a lot of evidence that humans will organize themselves, unofficially and apparent only to an outside observer like an anthropologist, as tribes despite communication channels, procedures, and job descriptions.

Related patterns

Tribes is directly related to only one other, **It Takes a Village**, and suggests the way that the village is organized and how it manages itself.

Story

Brave Cowardly Chief

When young Nerino was made chief of the tribe, everyone expected that — as was the custom on the island — he would direct his attention to fighting the great fiery-eyed beast; a horrible creature that had terrorised the tribes-people for centuries. Nerino had promised to slay the beast and, though he was a good fighter, he seemed no better than the others who had previously perished in the attempt. The tribe reckoned that, as chief, he wouldn't last much more than a year. This was about the amount of time needed to train and prepare a band of warriors, prior to ascending to the volcano's summit, where their horrendous enemy lived. And once they got there, no matter how strong or brave they were, all the warriors would be annihilated within a couple of hours.

However, nothing was done. Nerino didn't train any fighters, nothing out of the ordinary was done, no new assault tactics were devised. When summer came — the time the monster attacked most frequently, engulfing all in flames from his fiery eye — all the tribe did was move their village.

Everyone looked worryingly and insistently at Nerino. They demanded that he fight, that he do something, that he should be brave and fulfill the destiny of a chief. But Nerino simply said: *"I shall defeat the beast, but now is not the time."*

And so the years passed by, and Nerino became an old man. And though they respected him as their chief, and his strategy of moving their village around the island had saved many lives, all the people believed he was a coward.

Yet, just when no-one expected it, Nerino finally assembled a squad of fighters. He announced this suddenly, without warning, on a cold winter night. Snow was rare on the island, but now it blanketed the ground, and the band of warriors had to march out barefoot, with frozen feet. They hurriedly ascended the volcano and, at the summit, they approached the monster's cave. Nerino confidently entered, while his companions performed the usual death preparation rituals, ready to leave this life ...

When they were all inside they cave they saw old Nerino standing over the beast. The monster was lying, curled up, on the ground, trembling and groaning, close to death. Nerino and his warriors easily took the creature prisoner.

On arriving back at the village, everyone wanted to hear about Nerino's fight with the monster. Not even the tiniest baby was absent when Nerino began telling his story: — *I never intended to fight against something so terrifying, and nor did I do so today,* he said, filling all with surprise and expectation. He continued.

— *Did none of you notice that the beast would never attack during the worst days of winter? Or that, after an especially cold spell, his fire was never very strong, nor his attacks very damaging? For many years I was waiting for a snow as heavy as this one. All along, we didn't need fighters; we needed the cold. When we got to the volcano, the monster was so weak he couldn't fight. Finally we have put an end to fighting and death. Now we have the beast, and his fiery eye, at our service.*

Everyone congratulated the chief for his wisdom, particularly those who had most criticised him for supposed cowardice.

And so it was that even the most impatient among the tribe learned that, sometimes, patience can be much more useful than action, even if it means you require the bravery to accept people treating you like a coward.

Practices

Practice patterns focus on actions, things a designer might do, or artifacts they might use, while engaged in designing, thinking about design, and communicating design ideas. They capture the general characteristics of an action. Simultaneously they provide specific examples of applying those general characteristics. We make this point to reinforce the notion that a pattern is not an answer, not a solution. Instead, even when as specific as an action step, a pattern captures a bit of thought, a bit of knowledge that facilitates thinking. In the case of practice patterns: facilitates doing.

Communication remains key when dealing with practice patterns, focusing here on inter-personal communication. How members of the team communicate with each other and how the team communicates with users and clients.

There are patterns that support communication of the ineffable. We considered several; like 'Just Do It' focusing on the role of experience as it supports **Form** and **Logos**. Central is the idea that you understand only through experience, you understand design only by designing. We have not polished these patterns and have not included them in this book, but they will be among the first posted to our companion website, *designthinking. systems*

A concern accompanies Practice patterns. Because they are specific and seem to provide concrete instruction, the fact that these patterns, like all others, are not answers, not prescriptions, but things to think about and with. Each designer and each design team will select, adapt, configure and combine the practice patterns in unique ways suitable to unique situations and challenges.

We present our patterns in the rough order in which they are used in a typical development cycle. For example, **Participant Observation**, **Design Brief** and **Prometheus Bound** most likely appear at the beginning of a design effort. All three focus on the communication necessary capture and communicate what is to be designed and any limitations that must be observed while doing so.

Story Telling and **System Metaphor** share a reciprocal relationship. The team might tell stories in order to discover an appropriate metaphor, but then retell or tell additional stories premised upon that metaphor. **Story Telling** continues throughout the design effort.

Show Me provide insights into how tangible intermediary results help focus and direct the design effort. They too are seen at any phase of the design effort.

Practice patterns define things that must be done, by the client, by users, or by the design team and therefore will incur costs, time and almost certainly money. It is not unreasonable to have some kind of assurance that those costs will result in offsetting benefits. To address this matter we have included an additional section, following Discussion, titled 'Business Value' to each of the practice patterns.

Participant Observation ***

Thumbnail

If (any of these)
- you must interpret the requirements given to you,
- you feel like you are conversing with the village idiot, or
- the trees give you no clue about the forest;

then (all of these)
- immerse yourself in context,
- do the work, and
- share the understanding.

Context

You are gathering information and developing insights about your client, the domain in which the client operates, and the context that defines issues that your design effort is expected to resolve.

Forces

Everything you need to know is embedded in a context.

Facts do not capture meaning when isolated from context.

People within a context, a culture, are unaware of how that culture affects their perceptions and colors their assertions.

The client cannot clearly, concisely, and unambiguously state requirements.

Full understanding comes only from experience.

Problem

People do not understand that which they do not do, and this applies to designers as well. You cannot understand what you need to design without experiencing the context and conditions to be resolved by that design.

Therefore,

Solution

Gain a full understanding of what is needed by immersing yourself in context and sharing the experiences of people in that context.

Resulting context

Only a participant-observer is likely to obtain the comprehensive understanding of the whole, the parts and relationships among them all, to produce the kind of thick description that assures congruence between the design and the context in which it is deployed.

Four concerns must be addressed: 1) the participant observer must constantly balance his outside perspective with his experiential understanding; 2) simultaneously avoid projecting his "objective" understanding onto those being observed and "going native" — adopting the purely local and culturally idiosyncratic perspective of those being observed; 3) significant time is required to acquire immersive understanding, time that management might not be willing to provide; and 4) you must be sensitive to ways in which your presence and participation alters what it is that you are observing.

Pattern Description

The pattern limns a practice that will lead to a more comprehensive understanding of what the outcomes of your design effort are to be.

Discussion

"The map is not the territory" stated Alfred Korzibski, the founder of General Semantics. Similar sentiments have been stated by military theorists, who insist on the need to experience the battleground as a prelude to devising strategy. Maps are an abstraction and are necessarily incomplete. Maps contain only that which was of interest or importance to the cartographer, not what is essential for you and your understanding. The same thing that is true of maps is true of the traditional way, a 'requirements document', in which a business expresses its needs to a software developer, for example. Design briefs, requests for proposal, and other ways of conveying business need are also 'maps' and are also deficient.

The first anthropologists were known as 'armchair anthropologists' who performed their analyses based on traveler's reports and stories without any actual contact with the cultures or peoples they were analyzing. This practice rapidly became seen as ludicrous, as the practitioners had no real understanding, and the results were worthless at best and misleading and harmful at worst. Software developers have long recognized the need for extensive and deep communication between developers and stakeholders, but have just as long ignored this need. It cost to much, was seen as a waste of time, and even unnecessary. One of the 'revolutionary' aspects of Agile development was re-asserting this need and incorporating it as overt practices. The Toyota Way expressly incorporates the need for designers — industrial, process, and product designers — to "go where the work is," or Gemba, in order to gain the understanding essential for their work. Gemba was rapidly adopted by Lean and Agile developers as a standard and essential activity.

These examples are but part of the vast literature that explains why you cannot understand something that you do not experience and do not experience in context. Our minds are capable of acquiring and integrating massive amounts of information and using that information to guide our actions and our thinking. When we limit those minds to a single channel — words on paper — we are effectively starving the mind and making it impossible to do what it needs to do. Outcomes from starved minds weak and sickly.

Participant observation carries with it a risk, but one that can be ameliorated if you are aware of it. The risk is the influence that the observer has on what is being observed. Physics tells us that the observer influences the outcome of experiments, especially those involving quanta. Anthropologists have long recognized that the presence of a field worker, a participant observer, may alter the behavior of those she is observing. Even a parent knows that his children behave differently when he is in the room. This effect diminishes to the degree that the observer becomes an actual participant — doing the same work, eating the same food, sleeping on the same straw mats, as everyone else. We assert, in this pattern, that there is a real need for the designer, or the software developer, to experience, fully, that which they are designing for.

Another caution for the participant observer, a lesson learned by cultural anthropologists. When you first come to a village the people see you as strange and an outsider. They are very reluctant to talk to you or interact with you. The one exception is the 'village idiot' — a person that the villagers already perceive as strange and somewhat useless. The villagers do not interact with this person and they are desperate for human contact, so they immediately attach themselves to the anthropologist, and provide the most distorted information and sense of what the village is all about. Take caution, lest your client or business manager restricts your interaction to the person in the organization that they feel has the least value.

___

Related patterns

Participant Observation manifests the principles presented in **Gestalt** and **Thick Description** assuring the likelihood of comprehending the whole and advocating a richer description of your understanding than is possible in mere requirements.

Design Brief, **Prometheus Bound** and even **System Metaphor** are based, in part, on the results obtained from **Participant Observation**.

Story Telling is integral to **Participant Observation**. Much of the knowledge of the client and users will be conveyed to the designer in the form of stories and the designer will use stories to familiarize the client with what they are doing as designers while confirming that the designer has understood what was said to him.

Business Value

When business engages software developers it incurs significant cost and faces substantial risk. Business value is obtained if a marginal increase in cost will result in dramatic reduction of risk. We have decades of statistics that show the risk is very high, that the likelihood that most or all of the expenditures on software will be lost, be waste. The primary cause, incomplete, erroneous, or ambiguous information. The traditional means of providing information to software teams is sterile specification. Replacing that means with Participant Observation will increase the costs of 'requirements gathering' but will offset that cost by reducing risk, usually by more than half, and assuring the desired return on investment in the software.

Businesses engaging the services of designers will see the same benefits, in amounts proportional to the money at risk.

Design Brief**

Thumbnail

If (any of these)
- your team needs direction on how to proceed,
- you have a general idea of where to go, or
- exploration is required;

then (all of these)
- use a design brief to outline your journey,
- balance precision and ambiguity, and
- establish harmony between freedom and boundaries.

Context

Engagement with your client has resulted in an understanding of **Form**, have chosen a fruitful **System Metaphor**, and have a holistic understanding of the problem space, a **Gestalt**. Your understanding includes boundaries, **Prometheus Bound.** You are ready to assemble a team and provide them with the direction required to work creatively and cooperatively to find an outcome that will **Fit**.

Forces

Five forces are at play: ambiguity, precision, frame, information balance, and unknowns.

Ambiguity is necessary so that the designer has latitude to explore possibilities but if everything is vague you have no clue as to what to do. Facts, when included, are best stated with precision. Some things, like known constraints, must be clear because they establish boundaries (frames) that need to be respected.

Enough information must be present in the brief to limn the space where a designer will most likely find a design and information fuels the imagination. Too much information, however, inhibits the designer, both by creating a smaller space to be explored and increasing the risk of wasting time on considerations that will prove to be irrelevant.

Unknowns, which are often un-knowable, must be acknowledged because they draw the attention of the designer to difficult, but often critical, aspects of the design. Too many unknowns, like too much ambiguity, leaves the designer in a vacuum.

Problem

You have obtained information, from multiple sources and perspectives, about the problem space, the client, and have a general idea of what needs to be achieved. The information is necessarily incomplete, often vague or ambiguous, with some constraints and facts.

The team needs directions that will allow them begin exploration of potential solutions and generate tentative results. The team needs criteria for determining if their efforts are on track.

Therefore,

Solution

Write a Design Brief — a narrative that incorporates essential qualities expected to be present in the solution along with parameters that bound scope. The design brief is a starting point for iterative and incremental exploration activities. It is like the most primitive of maps, giving only general information about the journey to come.

Resulting context

The team is engaged in productive activities. Each member of the team knows what to do and how to do it and they might follow multiple paths to reach a common destination, a destination (solution) that capture the qualities and parameters in the design brief. The emergent outcome is enhanced by the richness that comes from multiple journeys and insights gained along the way.

308

It must always be remembered that, "the map is not the territory" and that there must be a feedback cycle whereby your increasing understanding of the territory — the context and the design problem — must update the "map" — the guidelines and constraints.

Pattern Description

A design brief is not a standalone document. It is understood in the context of both the **System Metaphor** and the various stories expressing conceptions of self, situation, and goals; told by the client and stakeholders*.

The design brief itself synthesizes metaphor and story and expresses them as a guide for the design teams. The design brief serves as a kind of reference, a touchstone, that designers can use to assure themselves that they are on track.

Stakeholders must be recognized and used comprehensively — including boards, regulators, social context, suppliers, managers, employees, customer, and users.

Discussion

The team using the design brief will include business professionals and software developers as well as designers. Although designers are accustomed to working with this kind of document, the others will need to learn how and why it is preferred to the customer requirements or specification documents that have traditionally driven their projects.

The design brief empowers the team in the way that the other documents do not. It makes the explicit assumption that the members of the team are professionals and know what to do and how to do it. Working without a net, without the security of detailed micromanagement, might be scary at first, but leads to confidence and ennoblement.

Related patterns

The design brief expresses the qualities of the **Form** that must be respected in the solution, shape, that result from the process of **Unfolding**. Appropriate terms and vocabulary, **Logos**, is rooted in the design brief. **System**

Metaphor, **Story Telling**, and **Gestalt** are complementary to **Design Brief**, with the latter synthesizing much of the former.

It Takes a Village. The design brief will inspire the formation of a team whose skills and aptitudes are complementary to the qualities expressed in the brief. Each member of the team is expected to define and follow his or her individual direction from a shared understanding of the design brief.

Reading a design brief will spark creative activity in the minds of the team, many of those activities are discussed in evaluation patterns like **Fit** and **Attractiveness.**

Business Value

Stating and documenting objectives and providing directions is a necessary cost of business, internally or when working with designers. 'Heavyweight' approaches, e.g. a massive requirements document, increases costs and actually inhibits effective outcomes. 'Lightweight' approaches, e.g. user stories or design briefs, lower the costs of produc-ing the documentation and set in place a process that has far greater likelihood of producing appropriate and profitable results.

The beautiful fables of the Greeks, being proper creations of the imagination and not of the fancy, are universal verities. What a range of meanings and what perpetual pertinence has the story of Prometheus! — Ralph Waldo Emerson

Prometheus Bound ***

Thumbnail

If (any of these)
- you are being told what to do,
- things are "a little bit tight in the shoulders", or
- the only explanation is, "that's the way we do things";

then (all of these)
- expose both explicit and tacit constraints,
- resolve constraints as you would any other force, and
- respect honest constraints.

312

Context

Initially at the beginning of a design effort where prob-able constraints are identified, but also in conjunction with most design activities when you are evaluating the validity and application of the constraints.

Forces

Your work requires resources that are usually limited.

The client may have preconceived notions of what is possible or desirable and sets them as constraints.

It is not clear how many resources, in what quantity, are required or if you have them available to you.

Constraints may be more apparent than real.

Unforeseen circumstances may eliminate constraints or impose new ones.

Problem

You need to respect the constraints you are given while leaving them open to consideration, modification, elim-ination or replacement.

Therefore,

"I suppose I'll be the one to mention the elephant in the room."

Solution

Expose, analyze and leverage all the constraints that affect a design project.

Resulting context

A design that respects real constraints while resolving, in the design, all constraints than can be transcended. Often, very real constraints, like budget or client preferences, will be exposed as purely arbitrary and even "wrong." A designer in this situation needs to find and present to the client solution options that subtly challenge these constraints in such a way that the client can recognize and resolve potentially undesirable consequences arising from given constraints.

Pattern Description

Identification, evaluation, and accommodation of constraints is the point of this pattern.

314

Discussion

Clients tend to be as eager to tell you what not to do, or what you cannot do, as they are in telling you what they want or expect. This is their way of protecting themselves from the unknown, from risk, by establishing boundaries that they believe will control risk.

Unfortunately, most of those boundaries, those constraints, are more apparent than real, just as requirements are guesses about an outcome, so are constraints. Nevertheless the designer must respect them while discovering which ones truly limit the design outcome and which ones might be resolved, just as any other force, in the design.

No designer has absolute freedom. Some designs cannot be implemented due to technological or scientific limitations. Others are bound by the amount of money or time available from the client. Still others may falter because available skills are insufficient or mismatched. But the designer likely has more freedom than they realize because even the hardest or most absolute constraints are just forces. Forces that might be countered or resolved given sufficient insight and creativity.

Constraints that are given to the designer, by the client or others in the client's organization, must be acknowledged. At the same time it is essential to recognize that some of those constraints have more validity than others. Some boundaries should be observed and others challenged.

Boundaries can limit but they can also liberate. Boundaries allow the designer to focus, to make their work more productive by limiting the space in which an optimal design might be found. A corollary, somewhat paradoxical, is the fact that absolute freedom is really a constraint. A blank page is freedom, but facing a blank page can inhibit the designer that is not prepared to fill it.

It is easy to see overt boundaries, like the client setting an 'absolute' budget. The most important constraints, the ones that your design must accommodate and resolve are tacit. Some examples: the skills and abilities of your users is a constraint; organizational culture is a boundary; when applicable, a regulatory environment is a constraint; relationships between your client and other organizations with which they do business can impose boundaries; and the community and environment in which your client operates delineate constraints.

It is important to identify all applicable constraints, but then treat them as if they were just forces, issues, that need to be addressed and resolved by your design. Take no constraint as absolute — Prometheus was bound but had ways of escaping those bounds if he chose to use them.

Related patterns

Participant Observation and **Story Telling** relate to **Prometheus Bound** by proving important tools for discovering and exposing tacit constraints. Design Brief assumes the inclusion of some explicit, usually client originated, boundaries that need to be considered within **Prometheus Bound**.

Business Value

It is very easy for a business to become bound in a web of constraints that may have been but are no longer limitations. Most of the time the organization has lost its awareness of these boundaries or why they were put in place. They simply assume, "this is the way we are and how we do business". A designer provides an 'outsider's perspective' and helps to make tacit constraints explicit, exposing them to evaluation. Once exposed the designer and design team can treat them as forces and have the freedom to seek a design that best and most appropriately addresses and resolves those forces. Sometimes the best resolution is to acknowledge a force as a constraint and respect it.

The return on investment in this process is a leaner, more focused, organization that saves money by optimizing and reallocating budget, reducing operating costs and maximizing opportunities for profit.

System Metaphor*

Thumbnail

If (any of these)
- cacophony prevails,
- everyone wants to know where and how they contribute, or
- you have no clear and simple way to proceed;

then (all of these)
- let metaphor be your guide,
- use the elephant to make sense of the 'wall', 'rope', 'snake', and 'tree', and
- achieve harmony and joy.

318

Context

The team has a design brief and is ready to begin working. There are a number of people working on the project, each with their own expertise, perspective, and expectations.

Forces

A design must speak with one voice.

Multiple perspectives exist among members of a design team.

Each member of the team needs to determine where and how they might make a fitting contribution.

Cacophony is the default effect of multiple perspectives expressing themselves at the same time.

Harmony requires a common reference point.

Problem

You need to maintain a common understanding over time and among a diverse group of individuals or teams without limiting their creative thought.

Therefore,

Solution

Find a metaphor that suggests fruitful avenues of exploration, preserving wholeness and integrity throughout the project.

Resulting context

A joyful work environment where everyone sees how their work complements the work of others and contributes to the whole.

A metaphors have a lifecycle. In the beginning they can enhance understanding the unknown via comparison to the known and the suggestion of referents, aspects of the known, that can be observed, or not, to increase our knowledge of the unknown. However, if the referents are not confirmed then the metaphor should be replaced.

Pattern Description

This pattern asserts the value and the utility of having a single unifying concept, a metaphor, that coordinates both work and thought among a diverse team.

320

Discussion

Teams are formed to accomplish tasks beyond the abilities of an individual. Members of teams are motivated to contribute, to help, to assure collectively, they accomplish those tasks. There are many tools that will help a group of motivated individuals form a team, a collective unity. A totem, for example, might supply a unifying team identity.

System Metaphor is a fantastic tool, providing a common reference point and a warp that supports the integration of the threads of individual efforts and ideas (woof) in order to form a tapestry that is the whole of the design.

Metaphor increases in power and utility when it suggests secondary and tertiary metaphors that can be used to understand aspects of the original metaphor or details of the system behind it. For example, Kent Beck suggested the use a single metaphor to capture the whole of a system, to serve as a global reference point. That metaphor then suggested others with the power to expose the nature of components in that system, and eventually, as a guide for deciding upon the names of program elements like variable and function names.

Metaphors have a lifecycle, beginning with a poetic correlation between a familiar thing and an unfamiliar thing. Our knowledge of the familiar thing suggests referents, e.g. if X is like Y and Y has this property, then we should see an analogous property in X. The more referents it suggests, the more powerful the metaphor. When referents are confirmed the metaphor evolves towards, and eventually becomes a lexical term. If they are refuted the metaphor is weakened, is less helpful or our understanding, and it is abandoned.

If a System Metaphor is fruitful, suggesting lots of referents to be explored with most of those explorations resulting in either secondary metaphors or confirmation it helps the design team. If however, the referents are not confirmed or are otherwise sterile, the System Metaphor should be discarded and a new one found.

It is not unusual that a team, or a designer, becomes overly attached to a metaphor. It continues to be used even when most of the referents it suggested were refuted. For example, many still insist that the brain is a computer or that a computer thinks, long after the metaphor was proven sterile. This kind of thing happens when metaphor is no longer used to inspire and coordinate creative thought, but is instead used as an argument for a particular point of view.

Coordinating communication and assuring the fidelity of understanding across individual minds is another essential function for System Metaphor. The metaphor provides a common context, a common reference point as we communicate with each other, just as language does. This is important because team members spend much of their time conversing with one or two team members and not the whole team at once. Without the common reference provided by a System Metaphor, these conversations can come to resemble the outcome of the "gossip game". In that game, one person whispers a phrase into her neighbor's ear, who whispers it to his neighbor and so forth around the circle. What the final person repeats to the originator is seldom recognizable.

Related patterns

Form should be reflected in **System Metaphor** and **Unfolding** parallels, in important regards, the evolution of metaphor. **Design Brief** should inspire and inform the selection of a **System Metaphor**. Implicit in **System Metaphor** is a bit of the **Magical Liminal**, the metaphor suggestive of all kinds of possibilities. As a metaphor, **System Metaphor** plays on the power or archetypes, i.e. **Forever Jung**. Metaphor is a linguistic device and therefore connects **System Metaphor** to **Logos**. **System Metaphor** should limn a **Gestalt**. **Everything An Object** is an example of the use of **System Metaphor**.

Business Value

The primary value is a reduction in the time and effort required to reach a satisfactory outcome. This is easily seen simply by thinking of all the meetings that occur in a projects lifetime and how many of them were directed at resolving misunderstandings and miscommunications among team members.

Significant benefit comes from selecting a metaphor that is appropriate for the problem, and hence for the solution. For example a logistics problem, like picking up logs from various cutting sites in a forest. You might use the metaphor of a bus system with fixed routes, fixed pick-up and drop-off locations, and no way of predicting how many fares are located at each stop. This metaphor leads to static solutions that can easily

become inconsistent if demand is dynamic and variable. If, instead, a taxicab system provided the metaphor guiding the solution, flexibility and adjustment are 'built in' and the overall logistics problem is easier solved.

Studies have shown that a happy workforce is more productive and System Metaphor contributes to happiness, to joy.

323

It takes a Village ***

If (any of these)
- you are facing a large complex problem,
- you need to call in a specialist, or
- you need a mother;

then (all of these)
- assemble a multi-speciality team,
- ensure team members have breadth as well as depth of knowledge, and
- establish a collective worldview with which to resolve your problems.

Context

The challenge, the problem you face, is large scale, complicated, perhaps complex, and beyond the ability of one person to resolve. The problem has many facets, each of which may require the use of a specialized area of knowledge, experience, or practice.

Forces

People seek recognition.

People are different in terms of their world view, understanding, knowledge, experience, skill, and language. There are limits on what we can hold in our minds at any one time.

Unshared language limits communication.

Knowledge from many disciplines is required to solve complex problems.

Problem

The breadth of knowledge required to resolve complex problems exceeds that possessed by a single individual, discipline, or specialty.

Therefore,

Solution

Assemble a team of contributors with multiple viewpoints and areas of expertise, who also have sufficient breadth of knowledge that they can effectively communicate.

Resulting context

Multidisciplinary teams, organized in accordance with Tribes, are able to produce great designs that transcend individual abilities. Producing great designs transforms participating individuals as they see themselves part of something larger than themselves while being aware of and feeling happy with their contribution to the greater whole.

However, successful assembly of the 'village' necessary to design a solution to today's problem does not mean that the 'village' is suitable and appropriate for all design challenges. 'Villages' can become inbred and will almost certainly become conservative in terms of values and outlooks. Care must be taken to assure that your 'village' is a living adaptive entity.

Pattern Description

This pattern suggests the need for a team with multiple perspectives. The members of the team have sufficient breadth of knowledge that cross-specialty communication is possible. Together this makes it possible to resolve the most difficult problems.

Discussion

We begin our discussion with a bit of an aside. We think it is important that this pattern applies to more contexts than the one that introduced the pattern. The name of the pattern implies one such context. "It takes a village to raise a child," is the quote from which we took the name of the pattern. The context is the nurture, enculturation, and education of a child and all the roles and specialized knowledge required to accomplish that. A bit more orthogonal, the quality, the liveness, of a city is enhanced when the inhabitants of that city contribute diverse viewpoints, understandings and experiences creating a rich, shared, environment.

The pattern context is the need to resolve large-scale complex problems and the fact that this cannot be done by individuals working alone. A team is required and that team must collectively possess the breadth of knowledge, experience and skills required.

The need is for 'collective' knowledge, but, because of specialization, knowledge tends to be isolated in the minds of individual specialists. We have previously discussed the fact that specializations, academic disciplines, and organizations develop and use their own language to identify themselves, differentiate themselves from others, and enhance their ability to communicate among themselves.

A collection of specialists, each exclusively speaking his or her language, is not useful. Tools, like translation, do not solve the inter-communication problem of the team and may make things worse. The optimal solution is for each member of the team to possess sufficient breadth of knowledge that they can form communicational bridges that cross specializations. The degree of breadth should be sufficient that any one individual has sufficient general knowledge of multiple specialities and therefore be able to form multiple bridges. The more this is true the more each bridge becomes a community of shared understanding. This also increases the likelihood that the entire team will share one collective

327

understanding grounded in the multiple threads of individual, deep specialized, knowledge.

Effective teams rely on skills other than those derived from a body of knowledge and an individual's experiences applying that knowledge. Leadership, for example, is a skill that may be developed in parallel to mastering any speciality and individuals will have differing aptitudes for mastering that skill. Skills of this sort are often associated with roles: e.g. Project Manager, Business Analyst, Designer, Coach, Lead Programmer, etc.

We recognize and understand the range of roles and associated skills in familiar domains, like business and software, but easily overlook the existence of and need for other roles that are just as essential. Adele Goldberg and Kenneth S. Rubin suggested that teams engaged in object oriented software development needed unfamiliar roles like prototyper, implementor, and object coach.

Tom Kelly, a designer, has identified a set of roles that he believes are essential for design teams. A sampling:

Anthropologist — someone skilled in participant observation that can elicit all of the tacit forces at play in a domain and a problem.

Experimenter — someone who tinkers with potential solutions.

Cross-Pollinator — some with a breadth of knowledge that can bring ideas from diverse fields to bear on the problem, someone who can suggest fruit- ful metaphors.

Experience Architect — someone who can see how all the pieces of a solution fit together to create the 'world' in which the customer will live and work.

Storyteller — someone who can take the most complicated conversation and reduce it to a simple, repeatable, and recallable story; who can recall and relate the most appropriate story for any given moment.

These roles, and the skills associated with them, may be associated with one or more individuals, or a single individual might play different roles at different times. The key is to have overlap in skills sets among team members, just as you want overlap in general knowledge. The greater the overlap the stronger the integration of the team, bot in terms of what they know and what they can do.

328

Early morning meeting, tribal Orissa, India.

Related patterns

It Takes a Village, concerned with the team, is related to **A Room Of One's Own**, the space a team will occupy and 'think with' and **Tribes**, the way the team is organized. The detail of a large problem can disguise the underlying **Form**, but the multiple perspectives provided by **It Takes a Village** can help reveal essence as each perspective identifies what the **Form** is not.

It Takes a Village relies upon insights captured by **Logos** and **Glossolalia** to address communication problems arising from teams of diverse specialists. Practices like **Story Telling**, **System Metaphor**, and **Show Me** infuse the activities of the team in **It Takes a Village**.

Business Value

High-performance teams are more productive and high-performance multidisciplinary teams are capable of effectively resolving the increasing complex problems faced by business. Additional value is found if the solution resolves the whole problem, something possible only when multiple perspectives are applied to understanding that problem. Also, there will be improved integration of a solution into its context, the business.

329

Nutrition Facts
Serving Size 1 avocado (201 g)

Amount Per Serving	
Calories 322	Calories from Fat 247

	% Daily Value*
Total Fat 29g	45%
Saturated Fat 4g	21%
Trans Fat	
Cholesterol 0mg	0%
Sodium 41mg	1%
Total Carbohydrate 17mg	6%
Dietary Fiber 13g	54%
Sugar 1g	
Protein 4g	

Vitamin A	6%	•	Vitamin C	33%
Calcium	2%	•	Iron	6%

*Percent Daily Values are based on a 2,000 calorie diet.
Your daily values may be higher or lower depending on
your calorie needs.

Story Telling ***

Thumbnail

If (any of these)
- you need to convey meaning,
- the facts fail to speak for themselves, or
- you want to mesmerize your audience;

then (all of these)
- eschew sterile formality,
- listen to stories told, and
- tell a memorable story.

Context

The most powerful and effective form of communication is the simple story. Stories are ubiquitous at every stage of any design effort.

Forces

Meaning is dependent on context.

The human mind is limited in its ability to hold discrete, unrelated, bits of information.

There is a lot of information, a lot of meaning, to be conveyed.

Context is dynamic and therefore meaning is dynamic.

Problem

You need to share large amounts of information and ensure that the meaning of that information is understood by all.

Therefore,

Solution

Exploit the power of story telling.

Resulting context

Everyone shares a common understanding and has the tools at hand to reinforce that understanding as necessary.

Stories are the most powerful means of communicating understanding, meaning, knowledge and wisdom available to human beings. There are situations when stories are not the answer. Computers, for example, are incapable of understanding story (to much ambiguity and context determined variability) so an alternative must be found. Similarly, designs that lead to or incorporate engineered elements cannot rely on story to provide necessary formal specificity. The trick is to use stories as long, and to as detailed a level, as possible and only then decide how to convert the story into procedural narrative for the computer or blueprints and specifications for the engineer.

Pattern Description

This pattern addresses why and how stories can be used to facilitate the sharing of information and understanding.

Discussion

Storytelling has been essential to human communication since the invention of language. The story is a universal mechanism for sharing our collective understanding of the world and our place in it. Teaching and the communication of knowledge is dramatically enhanced when embodied in story. Stories are the backbone of human cognition. Stories allow us to coalesce a complex set of facts or intuitions into a coherent whole. Stories are effective, powerful, easily remembered, high bandwidth tools of problem solving, entertainment, and information transfer.

A story is any narrative depiction of the interactions among a group of characters and their environment as the collective moves from one state of affairs to another. Stories can be told at many levels and from various viewpoints. Stories can be nested, intertwined, and set in opposition. Stories are shaped by their context and provide a context that shapes other stories. Stories are evocative and even the simplest story, operating like a vacation snapshot, will bring to mind a dense association of other stories, circumstances, and knowledge. That is why we like them, tell them, and remember them. Stories have a huge advantage over representational forms of communication, e.g. blueprints or UML diagrams, because of the added ability of a story to evoke, recall to mind, all the information that was necessarily omitted from representational models.

Design is about turning ideas into expressions, and this requires an understanding of a broad range of information about the world and how potential designs will work in that world — a theory, if you will. In this regard, software development parallels design. Peter Naur said that software development is theory construction. A theory was an understanding of "an affair of the world and how the software would handle and support it." The construction of a theory is an iterative process of story telling, prototyping, and assessment. Although the Theory exists only in the heads (minds) of those who participated in its development, stories can be told, written down, and shared and then used to 'recall to mind' any aspect of the Theory as needed.

333

The world is dynamic so too are contexts and meanings. A representational model is static, and therefore breaks any time that which it represents changes. Stories, however, are as dynamic as the world they capture. You can change the characters, the setting, and even actions in a story and it will retain the same meaning and relevance. It might be Ahab obsessed with the White Whale or Picard obsessed with the Borg, but it is the same story. Stories are also dynamic in that they are polyvocal, you can alter a story to fit the context of its telling, simply with inflection of voice or emphasis on different phrases. The essence of the story does not change, only its shape in the retelling.

Stories support and are infused throughout a dynamic cycle: think about the problem; articulate a proposed solution; express the solution; use feedback to evaluate the solution; and repeat. The cycle ends when everyone, the client, users, and design team, agree that the solution is optimal.

Related patterns

Story Telling derives its relevance from principles like **Gestalt** and **Thick Description**. The power and effectiveness of **Story Telling** is best seen when narrative reflects **Unfolding**. **Design Brief** shares a reliance on informal and aformal means of knowledge capture with **Story Telling**. **Participant Observation** relies upon **Story Telling**. **Story Telling** is done with words and therefore shares an intimate relationship with **Logos**. If you want to learn another language and be fluent in that language you must be able to understand the literature, the **Story Telling**, in that language and this provides a key for achieving the intent of **Glossolalia**. One aspect of **Show Me** is the tangible expressing of **Story Telling**. **System Metaphor** inspires **Story Telling**. Stories and **Story Telling**, rely upon archetypes, symbolism and myth, and are closely connected to **Forever Jung**.

Business Value

Huge savings in cost and in time are achieved when you recognize and rely upon the power of story. The savings are realized by eliminating the expensive and time consuming step, in essentially every business and software project, of converting the stories about what you want and need into formal models: e.g. business

334

plans, requirement documents, specifications, or UML diagrams. The formal models have no value, so any expenditures arising from their production is pure waste. John Seeley Brown provides a powerful example supporting these assertions. Xerox repairmen had an informal means of sharing their knowledge about diagnosing and repairing photocopiers — the morning 'bull session', swapping stories about their exploits over coffee. This was deemed too informal for management and an effort was made to create a formal model of copier diagnosis and repair knowledge — an investment of hundreds of thousands of dollars. This formal model was then implemented as a computer program, a knowledge-base, at a cost of many millions of dollars. The net result, less shared knowledge and decreased productivity.

Designers have long recognized the power of the informal, or perhaps aformal, and rely on the general directives of a design brief and a rich environment of shared story telling to do their work. Business and software should emulate this approach, rely on stories, and save a ton of money while increasing effectiveness of designed outcomes.

Show Me ***

If (any of these)
- you forgot the solution that was so clear in your mind yesterday,
- you can't imagine how those two pieces fit together, or
- you think that extra ounce doesn't matter;

then (all of these)
- mock it up and experience it,
- let your senses, all of them, be your guide, and
- make corrections when they are easiest and least costly.

336

Context

You are designing, solving problems, and generating tentative designs.

Forces

You do not understand what you do not experience.

Models are abstractions and do not include the whole.

Problem

Knowledge and understanding are acquired in increments and you must assimilate the current increment before you can proceed to the next.

Therefore,

Solution

Create an expression of your concept, the solution in your mind, that is accessible to your senses.

Resulting context

You have a rich new source of information and feedback. Your design made manifest can now participate in its own design. At minimum your prototypes provide invaluable feedback as to the feasibility and desirability of your design solution. Expressing your design in tangible form also suggests new lines of investigations, unexpected insights into relationships or potential new objects — the designed becomes a co-designer. However, this means the designer must stop seeing the prototype, and even the design, as an object upon which his will is imposed and, instead, see the design as an active collaborator.

Discussion

Human beings learned how to integrate sensory data to gain an understanding of their world long before they invented language and conceptual thinking. We recognized and responded to patterned aggregates of sensory input and paint the shape of them on cave walls before we invented names for them. Our 'right brain' developed and utilized before the left.

As much as we would like to pretend we are thinking beings, our thoughts are but a veneer on our senses and our integration of those senses without words. If we want a full and complete understanding of something we must integrate the mind with the senses.

Creating a prototype, a sketch or even a few marks in the sand, takes something out of our minds and puts it in front of our senses. Prototypes, even the simplest are essential to all thought. Leonardo da Vinci's sketchbooks are exemplars of externalized thoughts, capturing on paper bits of understanding. In addition to being a more dependable form of memory, the notebook sketches provided feedback that could be used to extend understanding. Often you can trace the evolution of the development of Leonardo's ideas in a succession of sketches.

The importance of prototyping is the creation of a feedback loop, the mind expresses itself, the senses perceive that expression, and the mind integrates the sensory data with what is already in the mind.

Prototypes also provide a way for the design to participate in the designing. When the designer looks at a prototype, even a sketch, a void in the imagination (the ability to extract meaning from words alone) is filled. The prototype 'speaks' to the designer and things are seen that would otherwise be missed.

We have more than one sense and our designs may be directed to stimulating many of them. The 'look' of something and the 'feel' of something. The five senses — sight, touch, taste, smell, and hearing — are not the only forms of 'sensory' input. We sense inertia and motion, for example, as a kind of kinesthetic sense. We sense, usually we say feel, emotions. We sense gravity and spatial orientation.

Depending on what it is that we are designing, our work can be enhanced by some or all of these various 'senses'. A graphical designer is not usually concerned with 'heft' but an industrial or product designer is more likely to take it into consideration.

Prototypes should stimulate all of the senses relevant to the design issue at hand. A black and white, 2-dimensional sketch might suffice in one case while a full scale mockup with simulated functionality might be required in others.

We should also be aware that prototyping is not always done 'in-line', i.e. somewhere between the beginning and end of a project. An artists sketchbook is an example of prototyping, often simply of isolated ideas, that may be produced at any time and, perhaps, later used within the confines of a project.

It is also useful to note that sometimes a design seems to spring immediately from mind, it is correct and true and appropriate the first time it is tangibly expressed. However, the designer does not know and cannot know that it is done, let alone that it is correct until it is expressed and sensory feedback confirms what is believed, but not yet known.

Related patterns

Show Me should reflect **Unfolding**, each prototype representing an expression of **Form** in a context, the context being the the understanding of the designer at a moment in time. **Seed Recognizes Flower** provides an evaluation perspective, does the **Show Me** prototype preserve essence? You can also relate **Seed Recognizes Flower** and **Show Me** in terms of the feedback loop, does what the senses report to the mind conform to what the mind believed it was expressing. Some claim that **A Room of One's Own** is enhanced when it contains a multitude of **Show Me** prototypes from sketches on whiteboards to foam-core models, whether directly relevant to the project at hand or not. **Story Telling** might be enhanced by **Show Me** illustrations — but not always, as the imagination often paints a fuller, more detailed, and 'truer' vision than possible with an artifact.

Business Value

The business value is obvious and very well known. It is always cheaper and more effective to alter a prototype than it is to correct a finished result when the production line is in place. As we write these words we recognize and appreciate how much easier it is to correct a typo in the last line of a page with a word processor than a manual typewriter.

What is not as recognized is that prototyping, in large scale projects, should be frequent and continuous. One precept of the Toyota Way is, "defer critical decisions to the last responsible moment". Implicit in this precept is the use of increasingly sophisticated and realistic prototypes, used to generate the information necessary to make that critical decision.

Evaluation

What criteria do you use to decide if a design is finished? Is it the best it can be in the circumstances? Is it consistent with the principles of design thinking? Is it the best possible expression of **Form** in context?

There are different ways to answer these questions. One approach is to define a comprehensive set of criteria and use it as a checklist, as did Alexander with his 253 Patterns in *A Pattern Language*. Or you could spend decades, as did Alexander, seeking the characteristics common to those things perceived to have QWAN, or Life. Alexander's search led to fifteen "properties" enumerated and discussed in his four volume *Nature of Order*.

We chose to introduce a small set of evaluation patterns: two grounded in and derived from our Essence patterns; and two inspired by successful designs. The latter two are also common to other work on design and design evaluation.

Fit and **Seed Recognizes Flower** flow directly from the principles and our definition of design: informed decisions that assist a **Form** to **Unfolding** a series of essence preserving transformations until it expresses itself as best it can in a given circumstance.

Invisibility and **Attractiveness** reflect the integration of design in context and how well integrated design is perceived by clients and users of the design.

A fifth pattern reflects our conviction, our personal philosophy that design must make the world a better place. If our design is humane, if it enhances our humanity as well as our world, we will experience Joy.

Ultimately, each designer, each design team, each client must define their own set of evaluation criteria. It is essential that these be communicated to the design team, probably in the context of Design Brief and Prometheus Bound, to guide the designer's thinking.

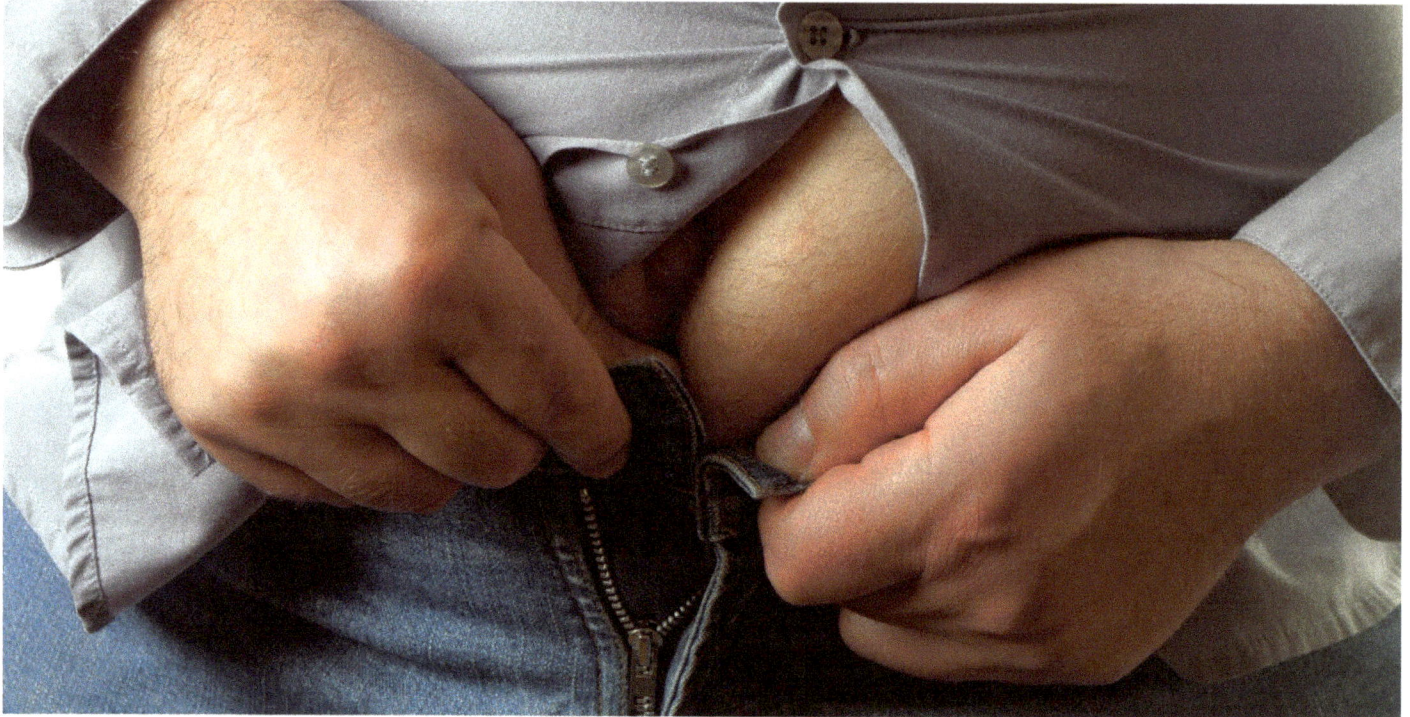

![paw print icon] **Fit** ***

Thumbnail

If (any of these)
- there are gaps between form and context,
- you need to tweak something, or
- you have an idea of something to be changed;

then (all of these)
- reduce and eliminate gaps,
- tweak the right thing, and
- recognize fit.

344

Context

Multiple points in the design process where you wish
to determine if your design is evolving as you wish,
and especially at any point you believe your design
to be 'finished'.

Forces

Form is expressing itself.

Your understanding of form and of context
is incomplete but evolving, growing.

There are no 'correct' answers.

Problem

You need to know if your design is an appropriate
response to the problem at hand.

Therefore,

Solution

Check to see if it 'fits', if the solution is congruent with the problem.

Resulting context

A 'natural' design that pleases its context and the people inhabiting it. This is not, however, the end. Every design, by definition, changes the context in which it is deployed. It is possible that the contextual change requires definition of the problem the design was supposed to address — invalidating the design. When this happens you are dealing with a "wicked problem" and design iteration is the only way out.

Your design can be a 'static' element in an otherwise dynamic system. As your context changes and evolves new sources of misfit present themselves. It is quite possible for your designed solution to morph into a problem. This is actually quite common when a computer system ceases to be an enhancement of a business system and instead becomes a hindrance.

346

Pattern Description

This pattern suggests one aspect of a design, fit, that the designer needs to think about in order to determine if a design exhibits QWAN and is the best possible outcome.

Discussion

Our concept of Fit has roots in Christopher Alexander's first book, *Notes on the Synthesis of Form* (Notes). Alexander's intent with that book was to define a 'science' or a 'mathematics' of design — he wanted to make design 'scientific'. Alexander argued that a design solution should reflect the problem that is was solving. A simple example of this kind of congruence is seen in the grinding of a mirror for a telescope. You have a template block with a convex shape, and a glass blank with a flat surface. You use the template, along with some emery powder, to grind the blank until it has a concave shape that exactly matches the convex shape of the template. If you consider the template as the 'problem' then the 'solution' is the blank when its shape is exactly the same as the template, but in reverse direction.

Most design problems are not as simple as a telescope mirror, there are more than one element, what Alexander called a force, that needs to be addressed. The principle remains the same, identify all the forces and use them to define a 'shape' and craft your solution until its shape is identically but obverse. Another simplified example. David has on his desk a toy that consists of a set of small steel rods in a frame. The rods are closely arranged to form a flat surface. The pins are moveable in one direction only such that if you put an object on the pins they will move away from that object. Remove the object and the impression that was made remains. If you think of a set of discrete forces as the set of pins whose degree of depression is determined by the 'problem' you can look at them and immediately see the shape of the solution — whatever object would have made that impression if the toy was used normally.

Alexander failed in defining a science or mathematics of design because the world is not as simple as the toy on David's desk. It can be impossible to determine the full set of forces at play, know with any kind of certainty what their values might be, or account for the fact that the values are dynamic and, in fact, the solution itself might have an affect on those values.

Designers can still use this idea of fit to guide their thinking about their solution. Think of the context as a set of forces that constrain an expression and Form as a set of forces expressing themselves. The design solution should reflect and satisfy that set of forces, it should be an expression that fits form to context.

Related patterns

Fit is to be used in conjunction with and as a complement to, **Seed Recognizes Flower**, **Invisibility**, **Attractiveness**, and **Joy**. **Fit** evaluates the success of **Form** expressing itself most appropriately to a context.

Story

Goldilocks and the Three Bears

Once upon a time, there was a little girl named Goldilocks. She went for a walk in the forest. Pretty soon, she came upon a house. She knocked and, when no one answered, she walked right in. At the table in the kitchen, there were three bowls of porridge. Goldilocks was hungry. She tasted the porridge from the first bowl. "This porridge is too hot!" she exclaimed. So, she tasted the porridge from the second bowl. "This por-ridge is too cold," she said. So, she tasted the last bowl of porridge. "Ahhh, this porridge is just right," she said happily and she ate it all up.

After she'd eaten the three bears' breakfasts, she decided she was feeling a little tired. So, she walked into the living room where she saw three chairs.

348

Goldilocks sat in the first chair to rest her feet. "This chair is too big!" she exclaimed. So she sat in the second chair. "This chair is too big, too!", she whined. So she tried the last and smallest chair. "Ahhh, this chair is just right," she sighed. But just as she settled down into the chair to rest, it broke into pieces!

Goldilocks was very tired by this time, so she went upstairs to the bedroom. She lay down in the first bed, but it was too hard. Then she lay in the second bed, but it was too soft. Then she lay down in the third bed and it was just right. Goldilocks fell asleep. As she was sleeping, the three bears came home.

"Someone's been eating my porridge," growled the Papa bear. "Someone's been eating my porridge," said the Mama bear. "Someone's been eating my porridge and they ate it all up!" cried the Baby bear.

"Someone's been sitting in my chair," growled the Papa bear. "Someone's been sitting in my chair," said the Mama bear. "Someone's been sitting in my chair and they've broken it all to pieces," cried the Baby bear.

They decided to look around some more and when they got upstairs to the bedroom, Papa bear growled, "Someone's been sleeping in my bed." "Someone's been sleeping in my bed, too", said the Mama bear. "Someone's been sleeping in my bed and she's still there!" exclaimed Baby bear.

Just then, Goldilocks woke up and saw the three bears. She screamed, "Help!" And she jumped up and ran out of the room. Goldilocks ran down the stairs, opened the door, and ran away into the forest. She never returned to the home of the three bears.

349

Where is Waldo?

Invisibility***

Thumbnail

If (any of these)
- your user have to think about what they are doing,
- your design clashes with its environment, or
- design and purpose of design conflict;

then (all of these)
- find simplicity,
- understand your design as a extension of the user, and
- make your design obvious.

350

Context

Multiple points in the design process where you wish to determine if your design is evolving as you wish, and especially at any point you believe your design to be 'finished'.

Forces

Form is expressing itself.

Your understanding of form and of context is incomplete but evolving, growing.

There are no 'correct' answers.

Users avoid what they do not understand.

Problem

You need to know if your design is both appropriate and usable.

Therefore,

Solution

Check to see if your design melts in.

Resulting context

A design so intuitive that everyone immediately understands it without instruction or explanation. This pattern like the one before it must be sensitive the the ways in which design alters context, and so the same cautions enumerated there apply here.

An interesting consequence of achieving design invisibility is the fact that it usually results in designer invisibility. We all seek recognition for our work and our ego is stroked when others see ourselves in our designs. Designers, again like programmers, are seldom recognized as individuals. When a design, or design style, is recognized the identity attached is usually a corporate one. Apple has immediately recognizable designs and design elements but, excepting the corporate face provided by Jon Ivey, individual designers are completely invisible.

352

When designs, design elements, or design languages become readily recognizable and are identified with an organization, they become 'assets' that must be protected with patents, copyrights, and legal defenses. The resulting context increases business value.

Pattern Description

This pattern suggests one aspect of a design, invisibility, hat the designer needs to think about in order to determine if a design exhibits QWAN and is the best possible outcome.

Discussion

A design exhibits invisibility when it is obvious how and where it fits into our normal surroundings; when it is obvious what the design 'does' or how it contributes to our lives; and when it is obvious how we make use of it. Mobile phones can be used to illustrate these three aspects and the degree of invisibility of a design.

Where a mobile phone would fit into our normal surroundings evolved over time, making them more invisible when they would fit into a shirt pocket or a purse instead of requiring a special purpose accessory.

When they were first introduced, the purpose of mobile phones was just as obvious as the old land-line phones: you used them to make and receive phone calls. As features, e.g. to do lists and calendars, were added to the phone its purpose was muddied. Is it a phone or an organizer?

The advent of powerful smart phones increased the confusion. Is that device a phone, a media delivery platform, or a computer?

The third aspect of invisibility, how obvious is the use of the design, is also illustrated with a mobile phone. When they were introduced, mobile phones deliberately mimicked the old land-lines. To use it you simply picked it up and put it to your ear; or you picked it up and punched a few buttons to initiate a call. Flip-phones moved a small degree away from invisibility by imposing a new action, unfolding the phone, prior to making normal use of it. Smart phones made this problem worse as well. While receiving phone calls was relatively straightforward and obvious, making a call requires opening an 'app' and making decisions: do I need the keypad? or a contact list? Depending on the size of the phone and its physical or virtual keypad, it could take a lot of concentration to make sure you hit the desired button and not two or three at once.

When the keypad became a keyboard to enable texting, or computerlike use, the problem was worsened as the keys shrunk in size.

We mentioned the need to concentrate, to focus and apply more of your attention resource, in order to use the keypad on a mobile phone. Concentration is but one type of cognitive function that determines whether or not a design is invisible. The more we have to think about how to use something, the less invisible it is. How much we have to think is often called 'cognitive burden'. Cognitive burden increases whenever the amount of concentration increases, when we have to make decisions about what we are doing, or when we have to reorient our mind to accommodate an entirely new set of circumstantial factors before we take an action or make a decision.

A mobile phone, not smart phone, will likely have an 'answer' button. But the label on that button might not be "answer". The same button might also be used, if you have a call waiting feature, to switch between phone calls. All of this increases the cognitive burden for using that button's design. Texting requires significant cognitive burden, including the fact that your eyes must be on the phone to confirm the actions of your fingers — hence the undesirability of texting while driving, another activity that imposes a significant cognitive burden. The more sophisticated the phone's capabilities, the more cognitive burden required to find what you want to do and to do it.

Invisibility decreases in inverse proportion the amount of cognitive burden imposed by the design.

Related patterns

Invisibility is to be used in conjunction with and as a complement to, **Seed Recognizes Flower**, **Fit**, **Attractiveness**, and **Joy**. **Invisibility** is an outcome from a well chosen **System Metaphor**. A design will have **Invisibility** if it expresses itself with **Personae**.

354

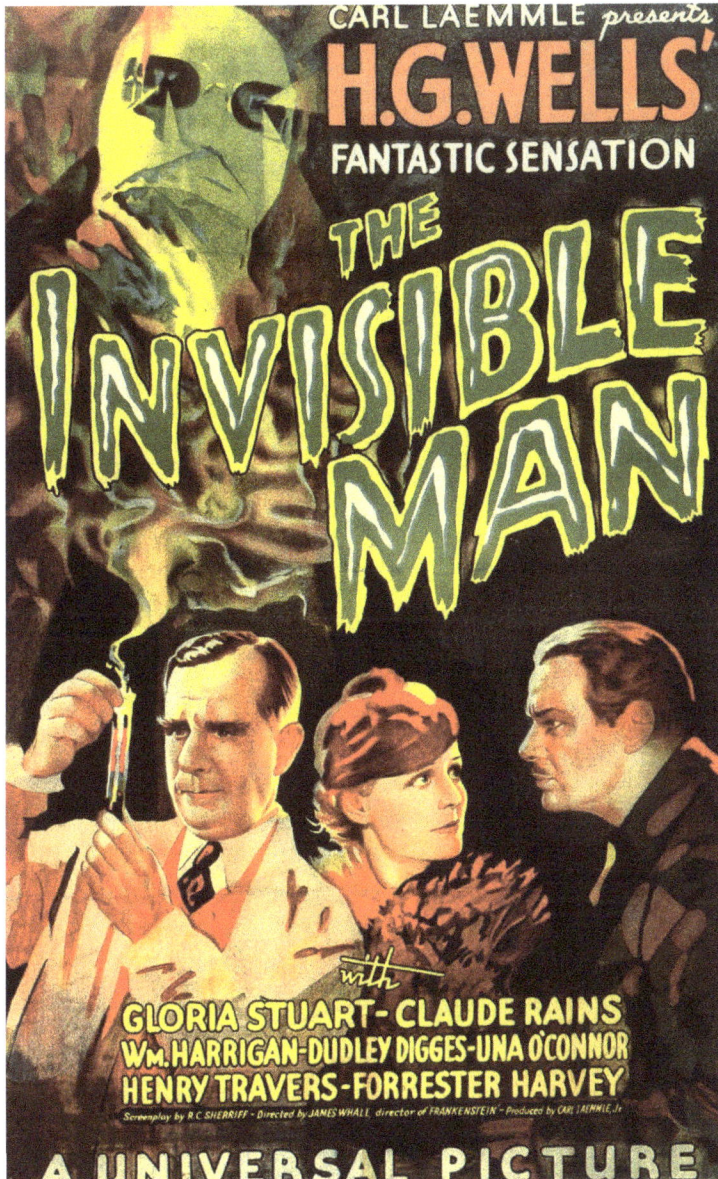

Illustration

The invisible Man

An interesting man arrives in the small town of Ippling fully covered; only a pink nose shows through his scarf. Many people wonder where he comes from and what his business is there, but they soon find that they wish they never saw him ...

This is a classic science-fiction book with over 100 pages of pure excitement and wonder. The Invisible Man may start out slowly, but once you pay close attention, the book becomes a spine-tingling thriller that will leave you breathless. It all starts when a mysterious stranger comes into the town of Iping, all wrapped up in bandages. He never takes off his glasses, bandages, or coat, and brings all sorts of strange chemicals in little bottles with him. He sits in his hotel room all day, working with the chemicals. No one knows what he's doing, but eventually, people get suspicious. Who is this disguised man? Is he a criminal in hiding? Or maybe he's horribly disfigured! All the same, they want to get a glimpse of this strange man's face.

Just imagine their surprise when they find out that this man is invisible!

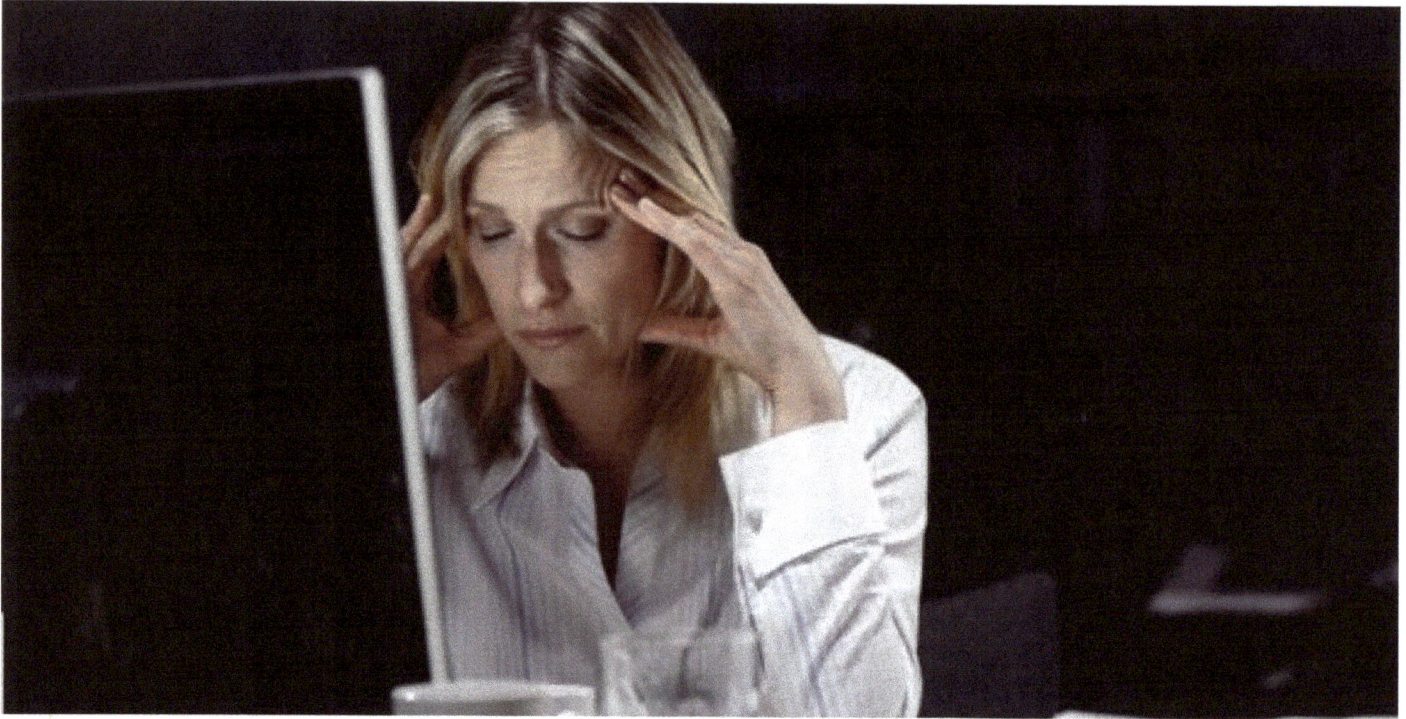

Seed Recognizes Flower***

If (any of these)
- results are not as expected,
- you just broke it, or
- essence is unhappy;

then (all of these)
- re-seek essence,
- confirm the way forward, and
- express again, with confidence.

Context

Multiple points in the design process where you wish
to determine if your design is evolving as you wish,
and especially at any point you believe your design
to be 'finished'.

Forces

Form is expressing itself.

Your understanding of form and of context is incomplete
but evolving, growing.

It is not obvious which of the multitude of potential
outcomes is optimal.

Problem

You need to know if your design is essence preserving.

Therefore,

Solution

Check to see if essence has been preserved.

Resulting context

A design that obviously expresses Form optimally for the context at hand, and this Fit is evident to all. Saying this implies that the process, the sequence of design activities followed, conformed to the demands of Unfolding — essence preserving transformations. Design almost always involved multiple iterations, multiple process sequences, not all of which are identical.

Valuable knowledge that will enhance our abilities as individuals and teams can be found by examining process and reflecting on activities and sequences. Part of the resulting context is increasing awareness of process and its effect on outcome.

Great care must be taken that reflection on process does not result in egocentric method!

358

Pattern Description

This pattern suggests how to confirm that transformations are essence preserving.

Discussion

The concept of unfolding is inspired by nature. Christopher Alexander used the example of a seed becoming a flower. Others have seen unfolding in the actions of a cell and the lifecycle of a human individual. In all cases there is some kind of essence. The most fundamental, at least in biology, being a string of DNA. The essence expresses itself, e.g. segments of the DNA strin prompt the formation of proteins. Through repeated expressions an aggregate whole emerges, a whole consistent with, and an expression of, the original essence.

Expression is both prompted by and constrained by context. Different segments of the DNA string might be cued to express themselves or have their expression suppressed by some environmental factor: the presence or absence of a chemical in the cell that contains the DNA, for example.

Alexander used his understanding of the biological to create an abstract principle of unfolding, one that could be applied to any instance of an essence being expressed as a form. Examples, for Alexander, would include the construction of a building or the evolution of a town. He believed that behind every built thing there was an essence, a form, and that form exhibited the fifteen properties that assured 'liveness' — another biology based metaphor. The architect's role was to assure that every building act was done in accordance with the essential form.

Expression of essence seldom occurs in a single step. The seed becomes a seedling, an immature plant, a mature plant, and a bud before the flower emerges. Ideally, seldom a condition in the real world, each of these steps would occur without interference and the flower would be true to the seed. In this ideal case, each expression and re expression — each transformation — would preserve the original essence. Unfolding is then defined as a sequence of essence preserving transformations.

This sense of unfolding is fundamental to our conception of design and this is reflected in the fact that Unfolding is one of our essential patterns. We have also suggested that the role of the designer is facilitating unfolding. She does this in two ways: one is ameliorating the bounda-

359

ries of context by altering the context. somewhat analogous to weeding a garden; and second, by proposing expressions, somewhat like forming an espalier to train climbing roses. When taking either of these actions the expression that comes to be must be evaluated, must be checked to see if the designer facilitated the expression of essence or interfered.

It must be noted that the active roles of the designer are subsumed in a third role — that of medium, or means, by which the essence expresses itself.

Related patterns

Seed Recognizes Flower is to be used in conjunction with and as a complement to, **Invisibility**, **Fit**, **Attractiveness**, and **Joy**. **Unfolding** relies upon a series of essence preserving transformations each of which is validated with **Seed Recognizes Flower**.

Story

There was a business executive who was deep in debt and could see no way out.

Creditors were closing in on him. Suppliers were demanding payment. He sat on the park bench, head in hands, wondering if anything could save his company from bankruptcy.

Suddenly an old man appeared before him. *"I can see that something is troubling you,"* he said.

After listening to the executive's woes, the old man said, *"I believe I can help you."*

He asked the man his name, wrote out a check, and pushed it into his hand saying, *"Take this money. Meet me here exactly one year from today, and you can pay me back at that time."*

Then he turned and disappeared as quickly as he had come. The business executive saw in his hand a check for $500,000, signed by John D. Rockefeller, then one of the richest men in the world!

"I can erase my money worries in an instant!" he realized. But instead, the executive decided to put the uncashed check in his safe. Just knowing it was there might give him the strength to work out a way to save his business, he thought.

With renewed optimism, he negotiated better deals and extended terms of payment. He closed several big sales. Within a few months, he was out of debt and making money once again.

Exactly one year later, he returned to the park with the uncashed check. At the agreed-upon time, the old man appeared. But just as the executive was about to hand back the check and share his success story, a nurse came running up and grabbed the old man.

"I'm so glad I caught him!" she cried. *"I hope he hasn't been bothering you. He's always escaping from the rest home and telling people he's John D. Rockefeller."*

And she led the old man away by the arm.

The astonished executive just stood there, stunned. All year long he'd been wheeling and dealing, buying and selling, convinced he had half a million dollars behind him.

Suddenly, he realized that it wasn't the money, real or imagined, that had turned his life around. It was his newfound self-confidence that gave him the power to achieve anything he went after.

⟳ **Attractiveness** **

Thumbnail

If (any of these)
- your work must be appealing,
- you must internationalize your design, or
- your work is judged by conflicting values;

then (all of these)
- acknowledge the power of perception,
- separate superficial from essential, and
- leverage the superficial.

Context

Multiple points in the design process where you wish
to determine if your design is evolving as you wish, and
especially at any point you believe your design to be
'finished'.

Forces

Form is expressing itself.

Your understanding of form and of context is incomplete
but evolving, growing.

There are no 'correct' answers.

Satisfaction drives acceptance.

Problem

Perception trumps and image is everything.

Therefore,

Solution

Leverage aspects of shape.

Resulting context

An attractive design will attract people. Attractive products gain more market share. Attractiveness begets attention. Attractiveness increases perceived value.

To the extent that the attractiveness of your design is valued by those using it, you become constrained by their perceptions. Once attracted, people tend to become fixated on that which attracted them and will resist future changes. This resistance can create profound constraints for future design work. An example: David lives near Santa Fe, New Mexico, an historic city known for the attractiveness of its architectural style. So committed are the citizens of Santa Fe to preservation of its attractiveness that a legal body has been established to enforce the minimization of architectural change — down to details like the exact shade of blue paint (oil based, not latex) that can be used for trim.

Pattern Description

This pattern suggests one aspect of a design, attractiveness, that the designer needs to think about in order to maximize the likelihood that the outcome will be perceived as acceptable.

Discussion

Beauty is only skin deep … but often, it matters.

Design is concerned with the faithful expression of essence as fully as as possible in a given context. Designed expressions will have what Alexander called QWAN (Quality Without A Name) or, in later works, 'liveness'. QWAN or liveness will be recognizable to anyone and will be appreciated by anyone. It is, however, not a synonym for beauty or attractiveness. Alexander found QWAN in the slum cities of Rio de Janeiro even though most people looking at those slums see ugliness.

How can it be that an expression, a design outcome, can be as full an expression of essence as possible in a context and not be attractive? And, if this is the case, what should the designer do about it?

QWAN does not assure attractiveness for the simple reason that QWAN focuses on the intrinsic essence and how it is expressed. Attractiveness comes from the "eye of the beholder". Attractiveness is therefore idiosyncratic, subjective, and a matter of perception not essence.

But perceptions are part of the context, are they not? Yes. And that is why the designer is not done, a design is not finished, until and unless attractiveness factors are addressed. What is different is how they are addressed, how those contextual factors are satisfied.

That which makes something attractive is ephemeral. It varies from one time to another; it is idiosyncratic, varying from individual to individual; and it is cultural. Because of all this variability and subjectiveness, attractiveness forces should be the last to be resolved and they should be resolved in such a way that they can easily be altered, without affecting the fit between essence and context, customized to whoever's perception must be satisfied at this moment.

Related patterns

Attractiveness is to be used in conjunction with and as a complement to, **Seed Recognizes Flower**, **Invisibility**, **Fit**, and **Joy**. **Attractiveness** embellishes **Form** in order to assure acceptance in context.

Story

The Ugly Duckling

Once upon a time down on an old farm, lived a duck family, and Mother Duck had been sitting on a clutch of new eggs. One nice morning, the eggs hatched and out popped six chirpy ducklings. But one egg was bigger than the rest, and it didn't hatch. Mother Duck couldn't recall laying that seventh egg. How did it get there? TOCK! TOCK! The little prisoner was pecking inside his shell.

"Did I count the eggs wrongly?" Mother Duck wondered. But before she had time to think about it, the last egg finally hatched. A strange looking duckling with gray feathers that should have been yellow gazed at a worried mother. The ducklings grew quickly, but Mother Duck had a secret worry.

"I can't understand how this ugly duckling can be one of mine!" she said to herself, shaking her head as she looked at her last born. Well, the gray duckling certainly wasn't pretty, and since he ate far more than his brothers, he was outgrowing them. As the days went by, the poor ugly duckling became more and more unhappy. His brothers didn't want to play with him, he was so clumsy, and all the farmyard folks simply laughed at him. He felt sad and lonely, while Mother Duck did her best to console him.

"Poor little ugly duckling!" she would say. *"Why are you so different from the others?"* And the ugly duckling felt worse than ever. He secretly wept at night. He felt nobody wanted him. *"Nobody loves me, they all tease me! Why am I different from my brothers?"*

Then one day, at sunrise, he ran away from the farmyard. He stopped at a pond and began to question all the other birds. *"Do you know of any ducklings with gray feathers like mine?"* But everyone shook their heads in scorn.

"We don't know anyone as ugly as you." The ugly duckling did not lose heart, however, and kept on making inquiries. He went to another pond, where a pair of large geese gave

him the same answer to his question. What's more, they warned him: *"Don't stay here! Go away! It's dangerous. There are men with guns around here!"* The duckling was sorry he had ever left the farmyard.

Then one day, his travels took him near an old country-woman's cottage. Thinking he was a stray goose, she caught him.

"I'll put this in a hutch. I hope it's a female and lays plenty of eggs!" said the old woman, whose eyesight was poor. But the ugly duckling laid not a single egg. The hen kept frightening him.

"Just wait! If you don't lay eggs, the old woman will wring your neck and pop you into the pot!" And the cat chipped in: *"Hee! Hee! I hope the woman cooks you, then I can gnaw at your bones!"* The poor ugly duckling was so scared that he lost his appetite, though the old woman kept stuffing him with food and grumbling: *"If you won't lay eggs, at least hurry up and get plump!"*

"Oh, dear me!" moaned the now terrified duckling. *"I'll die of fright first! And I did so hope someone would love me!"*

Then one night, finding the hutch door ajar, he escaped. Once again he was all alone. He fled as far away as he could, and at dawn, he found himself in a thick bed of reeds. *"If nobody wants me, I'll hid here forever."* There was plenty a food, and the duckling began to feel a little happier, though he was lonely. One day at sunrise, he saw a flight of beautiful birds wing overhead. White, with long slender necks, yellow beaks and large wings, they were migrating south.

"If only I could look like them, just for a day!" said the duckling, admiringly. Winter came and the water in the reed bed froze. The poor duckling left home to seek food in the snow. He dropped exhausted to the ground, but a farmer found him and put him in his big jacket pocket.

"I'll take him home to my children. They'll look after him. Poor thing, he's frozen!" The duckling was showered with kindly care at the farmer's house. In this way, the ugly duckling was able to survive the bitterly cold winter.

However, by springtime, he had grown so big that the farmer decided: *"I'll set him free by the pond!"* That was when the duckling saw himself mirrored in the water.

"Goodness! How I've changed! I hardly recognize myself!" The flight of swans winged north again and glided on to the pond. When the duckling saw them, he realized he was one of their kind, and soon made friends.

"We're swans like you!" they said, warmly. "Where have you been hiding?"

"It's a long story," replied the young swan, still astounded. Now, he swam majestically with his fellow swans. One day, he heard children on the river bank exclaim: "Look at that young swan! He's the finest of them all!"

And he almost burst with happiness.

368

🙂 Joy**

Thumbnail

> *If (any of these)*
> - you would rather go to the beach than go to work,
> - people sigh when they encounter your design, or
> - your work diminishes you;
>
> *then (all of these)*
> - nurture consideration for others,
> - atone for your sins of omission, and
> - be exuberant in your work.

Context

Multiple points in the design process where you wish to determine if your design is evolving as you wish, and especially at any point you believe your design to be 'finished'.

Forces

Form is expressing itself.

Your understanding of form and of context is incomplete but evolving, growing.

There are no 'correct' answers.

Design is subject to moral imperative.

Problem

You want to take pride in our work.

Therefore,

Solution

Design joyfully.

Resulting context

A better world.
A humane world.
Exhilaration!

Pattern Description

A moral imperative, to make the world a better place,
is asserted by this pattern.

Discussion

Designers care about people. Design is intended to evoke
reactions both emotional and intellectual. Designers
attempt to create environments that are habitable, that
make people feel a sense of belonging, a sense of fulfill-
ment from experiencing the designs.

It is essential that these values follow design thinking into the realms of business and software development. Business professionals are not known for creating pleasant and fulfilling places to work and, as a result, few people enjoy going to work. Software developers are responsible, more than any other influence, for how people accomplish their work. Here too, few people feel that the work tools they use are enriching. Too often they make work harder rather than easier, and most of the time they remove anything human from the work.

There is a moral imperative at work in the culture of design: "Make the world a better place." At present, business and software development professionals are not subject to this imperative. But they should be. Together they, quite literally, create the Reality where all of us live, work, play, and think. Should they not be accountable for doing that work such that our humanity is affirmed, our human abilities enhanced?

And it is not so hard. The way ensure joy in the world that others inhabit is to first make your world, your world of work, joyful. The products of work reflect the nature of those doing the work. If the team is joyful, then joy is infused in the outcomes of their work. If joy is in the work, then those interacting with that work bring joy into their lives.

Related patterns

Joy is to be used in conjunction with and as a complement to, **Seed Recognizes Flower**, **Invisibility**, **Attractiveness**, and **Fit**. Fully realized **Form** should evoke **Joy**.

Story

It started innocently.

Many years ago, I worked in an office with large windows that looked out over a busy overpass. I stood by one of those windows one day, when a woman in a passing car looked up and made eye contact with me — naturally, I waved.

A chuckle escaped my lips as she turned and tried to identify me. It was the beginning of a year of window antics. When things were slow, I stood in the window and waved at the passengers who looked up. Their strange looks made me laugh, and the stress of work was washed away.

My co-workers took an interest. They stood back out of view and watched the reactions I received with amusement.

Late afternoon was the best time. Rush-hour traffic filled the overpass with cars and transit buses, and provided a wealth of waving opportunities for my end-of-day routine. It didn't take long to attract a following—a group of commuters who passed by the window every day and looked up at the strange waving man. There was a man with a construction truck who would turn on his flashing yellow lights and return my wave. There was the carpool crowd and the business lady with her children fresh from day care.

My favorite was the transit bus from the docks that passed my window at 4:40PM. It carried the same group every day. They were my biggest fans.

Waving grew boring, so I devised ways to enhance my act. I made signs: *"Hi!"*, *"Hello!"*, *"Be Happy!"*. I posted them in the window and waved. I stood on the window ledge in various poses; created hats from paper and file-folders, made faces, played peek-a-boo by bouncing up from below the window ledge, stuck out my tongue, tossed paper planes in the air, and once went into the walkway over the street and danced while co-workers pointed to let my fans know I was there.

Christmas approached, and job cuts were announced. Several co-workers would lose their jobs. Everyone was depressed. Stress reached a high point. We needed a miracle to break the tension.

While working a night shift, a red lab jacket attracted my attention. I picked it up and turned it in my hands. In a back corner, where packing material was kept, I used my imagination and cut thin, white sheets of cloth like foam into strips and taped them around the cuffs and collar, down the front, and around the hem of the lab jacket. A box of foam packing and strips of tape became Santa's beard. I folded a red file folder into a hat and taped the beard to it. The whole thing slipped over my head in one piece.

The next day I hid from my co-workers and slipped into the costume. I walked bravely to my desk, sat down, held my belly, and mocked Santa's chuckle. They gathered around me and laughed for the first time in weeks.

A few minutes later, my supervisor walked through the door. He took three steps, and then looked up and saw me. Pausing, he shook his head, turned, and left. I feared trouble. The phone on the desk rang. It was my boss, and he grumbled, *"Mike, come to my office!"* I shuffled down the hall. The foam beard swished across my chest with each step.

"Come in!" the muffled voice replied to my knock. I entered and sat down. The foam on my beard creaked. He looked away from me. A bead of sweat rolled down my forehead. The only sound in the room was the hammering of my heart. *"Mike ..."* That was all he managed to say. He lost his composure, leaned back in his chair, and bellowed with laughter as he held his stomach. Tears formed in his eyes, while I sat silent and confused. When he regained control, he said, *"Thanks, Mike! With the job cuts, it's been hard to enjoy the Christmas season. Thanks for the laugh, I needed it."*

That evening, and every evening of that Christmas season, I stood proudly in the window and waved to my fans. The bus crowd waved wildly, and the little children smiled at the strange Santa. My heart filled with joy.

For a few minutes each day, we could forget the job losses.

I didn't know it then, but a bond was forming between my fans and I. The next spring, I discovered just how close we had become.

My wife and I were expecting our first child. I wanted the world to know. Less than a month before the birth, I posted a sign in the window, *"25 DAYS UNTIL 'B' DAY."* My fans passed and shrugged their shoulders. The next day the sign read, *"24 DAYS UNTIL 'B' DAY."* Each day the number dropped, and the passing people grew more confused.

One day a sign appeared in the bus, *"What is 'B' DAY?"*
I just waved and smiled.

Ten days before the expected date, the sign in the window read, *"10 DAYS UNTIL BA-- DAY"* Still the people wondered. The next day it read, *"9 DAYS UNTIL BAB- DAY"* then *"8 DAYS UNTIL BABY DAY"*. My fans finally knew what was happening.

By then, my following had grown to include twenty or thirty different busses and cars. Every night, they watched to see if my wife had given birth. The number decreased and excitement grew. My fans were disappointed when the count reached "zero" without an announcement. The next day the sign read, *"BABY DAY 1 DAY LATE"*. I pretended to pull out my hair.

Each day the number changed and the interest from passing traffic grew. My wife was fourteen days overdue before she finally went into labor. Our daughter was born the next morning. I left the hospital at 5:30 AM, screamed my joy into the morning air, and drove home to sleep. I got up at noon, bought cigars, and appeared at my window in time for my fans. My co-workers were ready with a banner posted in the window:

"IT'S A GIRL!"

I didn't stand alone that evening. My co-workers joined me in celebration. We stood and waved our cigars in the air, as every vehicle that passed acknowledged the birth of my daughter. Finally, the bus from the docks made its turn onto the overpass and began to climb the hill. When it drew close, I climbed onto the window ledge and clasped my hands over my head in a victory pose. The bus was directly in front of me when it stopped in heavy traffic, and every person on board stood with their hands in the air. I was choked with emotion as I watched them celebrate my new daughter.

Then it happened—a sign popped up. It filled the windows and stretched half the length of the bus. *"CONGRATULATIONS!"* it read.

Tears formed in the corners of my eyes as the bus slowly resumed its journey. I stood in silence as it pulled away from view. More fans passed. They tooted their horns and flashed their lights to congratulate me. I hardly noticed them, as I pondered what had just happened.

My daughter had been born fourteen days late. Those people must have carried that sign for weeks. Each day they must have unrolled it and then rolled it back up. The thought of them going through so much just to celebrate my new baby made me cry.

I made a fool of myself in that window for eight months. I made those people smile after a long day at work. They must have enjoyed it, because on the happiest day of my life they showed their appreciation. That day, more than twenty years ago, changed me. I just wanted to make my day better. I didn't realize how it affected others.

Ever since then, I try to put a smile on someone's face every day. I compliment strangers on their clothing. I start conversations in elevators. I even make jokes in crowded New York City subways. Some may think I am stupid, but I know there is a chance that I'm making someone's day — someone who may one day hold up a sign that says *"Congratulations!"*.

by Michael T. Smith

Conclusion

The interest in "design" and "design thinking" shown by professionals in business and information technology among other, has increased dramatically the past decade.

Our bibliography consists of more than 150 books, most of which address non-designers, is partial witness to this interest. An intense focus in the business press — notably *Fast Company*, *Bloomberg Business Week*, *Fortune*, and the *Harvard Business Review*; added websites like *fastcodesign.com*, *engadget.com*, *NYTimes.com*, and *Forbes.com* provide additional evidence of deep interest in the subject.

Our intention for this book is to provide clarity, a foundation for understanding, and a perspective from which non-design professionals can evaluate and make effective use of what has been, and will be, written about design and design thinking.

First, we want the reader to understand a pragmatic definition of design as a decision making process.

Second, that design is focused on enhancing composite systems in a way that increases our shared humanity.

Third, that design thinking is grounded in a set of concepts, principles, and practices that have been developed in, and substantially comprise, the professional design culture.

And fourth, that design thinking is far more than a formulaic method. Successful adoption and adaption of design thinking in the context of business and the enterprise requires understanding, and applying the concepts, principles, and practices we develop and discuss as "patterns of design thinking."

Defining Design

With few exceptions, design and the role of design in business has been misunderstood. Design was art. Design was mere embellishment. Design was done by 'artists' and was of little or no interest to managers.

Even those whose work explicitly incorporated 'design' activity, e.g. engineers and software developers, labored under misconceptions of what they were doing and how their 'design' activities differed from, or were the same as, the activities of graphic, interior, and industrial design professionals.

We introduced a pragmatic and concrete definition of design as the **intentional** and **informed** alteration of a system — by adding, deleting, or modifying an element or relationship comprising that system — so as to **enhance** the system itself and the **humanity** of individuals within or using that system.

This definition is pragmatic in that it is predicated upon nothing more than making decisions and taking action, both of which we do all the time. It is concrete in that each decision, each action, is discrete and explicable.

376

We suggest, with the word 'intentional', a need to be sensitive to and aware of actions we take, too often without thought or intent, that alter the systems within which we take those actions and which lead to outcomes that are undesirable and counter-productive.

The word 'informed' implies deep and comprehensive information: of the system being modified and the multi-disciplinary knowledge that must be possessed by the designer to effectively make decisions and take actions. Required knowledge includes an understanding of concepts, principles, and practices developed within the professional design community that complement and extend the thinking tools developed by engineers and scientists.

Enhancing a system implies putting the system in a more desirable state. This suggests we know, or believe we know, what is more or less "desirable." This in turn suggests a need to be aware of questions like, "more desirable for whom?" Also of critical importance, given that we are dealing with highly dynamic and complex systems; is the new state of the system stable and sustainable?

The final phrase of our definition with its emphasis on humanity is an unabashed moral imperative. We sincerely believe that design and design thinking must lead to systems that increase our humanity, enhance our innate human abilities, and are more humane and nurturing of the human beings that are, inevitably, among the components of any designed system.

Composite Systems

The idea of a system as a collection of interacting components seems to date, at least, to the invention of writing.

Astronomy, probably the first 'science', was intensely concerned with understanding a system consisting of the Earth, the Sun, the Moon, stars, comets, and "wanderers" (planets).

In the 1900s an academic discipline, General Systems Science, attempted to document, codify, and extend our understanding of how systems as diverse as the cosmos, transportation networks, cities, plants, animals, and ecologies could be understood, modeled, and interpreted. Of particular interest was how that which was understood about one system could inform our understanding of other, qualitatively different, systems.

In the 1970's our understanding of systems expanded to include Complex Adaptive Systems with properties such as 'emergence' and 'self-organization'. "Composite systems" — composed of both human and computer-based parts — received a bit of fleeting attention circa 1990 and within the AI community.

Our categorization of systems in a space defined by two axes — natural-to-artificial and deterministic-to-complex — is based upon the preceding discussions about systems. The definition of systems that we employ in this book is directly taken from General Systems Theory: "a system is a set of elements and the relationships among them." And, our definition of 'composite system' merely extends the one proposed in the AI community to accommodate systems that are comprised of a mixture of natural and artificial, deterministic and complex elements.

Two defining characteristics of composite systems: 1) they are always 'artificial' in that they are defined and come into existence via human action; and 2), they are, as a whole system, always complex, i.e., they exhibit properties like self-organization, emergence, and unpredictability.

Examples of composite systems range from human culture to a simple business procedure. The enterprise — a business, a government or an organization — is a composite system.

All composite systems are 'designed' because they are established and altered as a result of human action. A culture can be altered with the introduction and adoption of a new technology; like clay pots to store food and water. A business is altered when desktop computers running basic spreadsheets are introduced. Economic systems are changed with the acceptance of Bitcoins as a medium of exchange.

Whether or not the alteration of a system via human action satisfies our definition of design — especially the dual requirements of "intentional" and "informed" — is dependent on the degree to which those actions are grounded in "design thinking."

Science and Art

Early in the book, we noted that the term, 'design', is difficult to nail down to a single, clear and defined meaning. Much of the writing about design and design thinking is inhibited by this lack of clarity and precision.

The focus on systems and design as the intentional and informed alteration of a system in our pragmatic definition is the first step towards a useable concept of design. Remaining to be resolved: two widespread uses of the notion of design that transcend mere definition of a single term or concept. We refer to two separate 'traditions' or 'cultures' of design; one of which can be characterized as "engineering" design, the other as "artistic" design. The divergence of the two cultures can, in the Western world, be traced to the Roman, Vitruvius, considered to be the first professional "architect."

Most 'design' before Vitruvius might have been intentional, but it was informed primarily by trial and error experimentation, the results of which became embodied in myth, ritual, habit, and culture. With Vitruvius, we see a subtle, but powerful, shift in focus toward the concrete and quantifiable elements of systems. When Leonardo da Vinci immortalized some of the ideas of Vitruvius in his drawing, the Vitruvian Man, we see the attention being paid to those elements of a human that are measurable and quantifiable — as if these were the most important, if not the only, aspects of a person that merited attention.

This is not to say that architecture, in Vitruvius' time or now, is devoid of 'Art'. Clearly this is not the case. However, there is a qualitative difference in how design is perceived when the architect is focused on structural integrity and when she is concerned with aesthetic proportion.

The rise of Science reinforced and shaped how most people came to use the term, "design", just as Science was defining and shaping Western culture in general. When Herbert Simon wrote in the twentieth century about "The Sciences of the Artificial" he was codifying this scientific, really engineering, perspective of what, exactly, design was. Design, from this perspective remained the intentional and informed alteration of a system; however, with a major assumption about the nature of the systems being designed.

Systems in the engineering design culture were always deterministic, essentially mechanical, in nature.

Every element, every relationship among elements, and every property of every element or relationship is, in principle, both knowable and precisely quantifiable. It is therefore possible, given this assumption, to develop a "science of design" that includes 'formulaic' "laws" and principles, all of which yielded predictable outcomes, that could "inform" design action.

The culture of 'artistic design' lagged, historically, behind engineering design. With the exception of architecture, professions that focused on 'artistic design' (e.g. graphic, interior, and industrial, design) did not become part of the academic world — too often considered the hallmark of being a "profession" — until the 19th and 20th centuries. When they entered the university, the were grouped with the Fine Arts and not with the sciences and this, in turn, tended to marginalize the role of 'artistic design' as embellishment of 'engineered' systems.

The systems addressed by architecture (at its core) and the applied arts — the culture of artistic design — intrinsically and intimately involve human beings, and therefore are composite systems. In addition to human beings, these systems include complex elements like politics, social relations, culture, aesthetics, and ethics, making them composite systems as we have defined them.

Unlike deterministic systems, composite systems include elements that are not precisely defined, are not quantifiable, and that are, in principle as well as in fact, unknowable. Designers of these systems must, necessarily, be able to deal with ambiguity, unknowns, and unpredictability. 'Artistic' design professionals, like Pelle Ehn, Horst Rittel, and Christopher Alexander recognized, and we discussed, that "design" could not be reduced to a formulaic science.

'Artistic designers' have, in fact, developed a large body of knowledge, not of "formulas" and "laws" but of heuristics and stories and principles that allow them to be successful in their design endeavors.

This body of knowledge comprises "design thinking." It is important to note that incorporated, and integrated, within this body of knowledge are the principles, practices, and even formulas of engineering design. Composite systems contain both complex and deterministic parts. A design thinker must be equally adept at applying "artistic design thinking" to complex elements as he is applying "engineering design thinking" to deterministic elements.

The value of design thinking becomes increasing apparent as we advance our understanding of composite systems and realize how many of the systems around us — our businesses, our schools, our governments, our societies, our cities, our economy, etc. — are intrinsically composite and holistically complex.

Business professionals started to change their perception of the enterprise from "well oiled machine" to complex adaptive system as early as the 1970s and 1980s; Tom Peter's Thriving on Chaos being a notable harbinger. It is no surprise, therefore, that it is the community of business professionals that have led the move towards understanding and applying design thinking to the enterprise.

Patterns of Design Thinking

Design thinking is a body of knowledge and a set of practices grounded in that knowledge that, together, facilitate our understanding of and ability to modify and enhance composite systems.

Design thinking complements and extends the 'scientific' and 'engineering' thinking common to industrial cultures. Design thinking mandates respect for, and humane treatment of, all people affected by or involved in the systems being designed.

The professional design community developed texts, curricula, and experiences to convey design knowledge to novices; and, like all professions, those texts are articulated in the vernacular and specialized vocabulary of the domain and culture; in this case the design culture. This can make it difficult for those in other disciplines and other communities to fully understand and apply that knowledge.

Our task, with this book, is to find a way to communicate across disciplines, from professional design as understood by architects and applied artists to business and computer/information technology professionals. The first half of the book laid a foundation by putting forth ideas about design thinking, tracing the historical development of essential concepts, and limning a general outline of the body of knowledge that underpins design thinking.

The second section of the book presents discrete portions of the design culture's body of knowledge as: a concept, a principle, a practice, or a perspective for evaluation. Each is presented in the form of a "pattern." The reasons for choosing this format are provided in the introduction to the patterns themselves. By way of concluding the book, we wish to extend what has been said before about patterns with some ideas for how the reader might think of them and begin to apply them.

We stressed, in our introduction to the patterns, that a pattern is neither "a solution" nor a "template for crafting a solution." Instead we argued that patterns are encapsulated knowledge and a means of knowledge transmission akin to a story.

Here, we wish to metaphorically relate patterns to a 'seed'. In doing so, we are simply elaborating our assertion that patterns are best understood as stories.

A seed has a nucleus, an essence, which will unfold into a specific instance of a particular plant. Surrounding the nucleus is a body of 'nutrient material' — sustenance required as the nucleus begins the process of unfolding and to be used until development advances sufficiently that the embryonic plant is able to find what it needs in the soil, or natural environment.

Surrounding both nucleus and nutrients is a semi-permeable membrane or shell. This membrane contains and protects the seed during initial development, but it does allow some essential substances, e.g. water, to pass through and trigger development. In some cases the membrane itself can be a source of nutrients for the developing plant as it emerges from the confines of the shell.

Each of our patterns encapsulates an essence. The "if-then" statement at the beginning of the pattern; the core of the "problem" and "solution" segments of the pattern; and the name and illustrating picture all point to this essence.

The essence of each pattern is "information dense" and transcends being a mere prescriptive 'law' or 'truth'. An essence is a rich idea, often the distillation of multiple related ideas, and experiences accumulated and inter-related over time from within multiple contexts, polished by various perspectives.

Most of the pattern text is "nutrient material," provided to assist the reader in "unpacking" the essence of the pattern. Within the 'problem' and 'solution' segments of the pattern, the reader can find clues about 'germination triggers', conditions that must be satisfied if the pattern is to expeditiously unfold. These segments also provide information about the kind of contexts in which the pattern essence can best express itself.

Each pattern is an encapsulated unit that can, initially, be understood apart from any or all of the other patterns. But like the seed membrane, the artificial isolation of patterns as individual entities is not absolute. Complete understanding of each and any pattern comes from connection to other patterns. The "related patterns" segment provides some relationships with other patterns, but are not intended to be complete. It is quite possible for patterns to be strongly and overtly connected in one context or domain and subtle and tacit in others. The reader will find connections, not seen by the authors, based on the reader's individual and contextualized knowledge and experience.

Our seed metaphor is consistent with the assertion that patterns are best understood as stories made earlier. A great story also has an essence, a "point" or a "moral," some discrete idea that the author is trying to communicate. That central idea is also information dense and most of the story prose provides the means for explaining and enriching the point of the story. Simultaneously the story helps the reader make connections between things depicted in the story to their own experience. In this way the reader experiences insights and obtains new knowledge that can be used for change and enhancement.

Christopher Alexander and the patterns community in general, speak of "pattern languages" in which individual patterns provide a 'vocabulary' and connections among patterns provide an incipient 'grammar' with which it is possible to generate new design insights or express designs in novel contexts.

We prefer to think of our patterns as a cosmology, a body of work that, collectively, captures and expresses a deep understanding of the world we inhabit. Individual patterns express specific ideas about what is true, what is valuable, or what is important. Our ability to combine these individual insights to create innovative and illustrative new 'stories' that, in turn, explain the unknown and enhance the depth of our understanding of the known is critical. We believe that combining patterns to generate new stories satisfies and exceeds Alexander's hopes for "pattern languages."

Our purpose in writing this book, especially in presenting our selection of patterns, was not to provide a language or a method of design thinking. Neither design nor design thinking are 'decided' or reducible to rote memory, method, or practice.

Our intent is to sow ideas, to scatter seeds, which will find refuge in the fertile minds of our readers; resulting in "letting a hundred flowers bloom and a hundred schools of thought contend."

Bibliography

Alexander, C. *The Production of Houses*. Center for Environmental Structure Series, Oxford University Press, USA, 1985. ISBN 195032233

Alexander, C. *Notes on the Synthesis of Form*. Harvard Paperbacks. 1964.

Alexander, C. *A Pattern Language*. Oxford University Press. 1977.

Alexander, C. *The Timeless Way of Building*. Oxford University Press. 1979.

Alexander, C. *Nature of Order, Book 1: The Phenomenon of Life*. Center for Environmental Structure. 2002.

Alexander, C. *Nature of Order, Book 2: An Essay on the Art of Building and the Nature of the Universe*. Center for Environmental Structure. 2006.

Alexander, C. *Nature of Order, Book 3: A Vision of a Living World*. Center for Environmental Structure. 2004

Alexander, C. *Nature of Order, Book 4: The Luminous Ground*. Center for Environmental Structure. 2003.

Baldwin, C. Y. and Clark K. B. *Design Rules, Vol. 1: The Power of Modularity*. The MIT Press, 2000. ISBN 262024667

Ball, P. *Branches: Nature's Patterns: A Tapestry in Three Parts*. Oxford University Press, USA, 2009. ISBN 199237980

Ball, P. *Flow: Nature's Patterns: A Tapestry in Three Parts*. Oxford University Press, USA, 2009. ISBN 199237972

Ball, P. *Shapes: Nature's Patterns: A Tapestry in Three Parts*. Oxford University Press, USA, 2009. ISBN 199237964

Barnatt, C. *3D Printing: The Next Industrial Revolution*, CreateSpace. Independent Publishing Platform, 2013. ISBN 148418176X

Baskinger, M. and Bardel, W. *Drawing Ideas: A Hand-Drawn Approach for Better Design*. Watson-Guptill, 2013. ISBN 385344627

Bentley, P. J. *Evolutionary Design by Computers*. Morgan Kaufmann, 1999. ISBN 155860605X

Berger, W. *CAD Monkeys, Dinosaur Babies, and T-Shaped People: Inside the World of Design Thinking and How It Can Spark Creativity and Innovation*. Penguin Books, 2010. ISBN 143118021

Binder, T., De Michelis, G., Ehn, P., Jacucci, G., Linde P. and Wagner, I. *Design Things*. Design Thinking & Design Theory, The MIT Press, 2011. ISBN 262016273

Blanciak, F. *Siteless: 1001 Building Forms*. The MIT Press, 2008. ISBN 262026309

Bonner, J. T. *Randomness in Evolution*. Princeton University Press, 2013. ISBN 691157014

Boyd, R. *New Directions in Japanese Architecture*. George Braziller, 1980. ISBN 080760481X

Brand, S. *How Buildings Learn: What Happens After They're Built*. Penguin Books, 1995. ISBN 140139966

Broug, E. *Islamic Geometric Patterns*. Thames & Hudson, 2008. ISBN 050028721X

Brown, T. *Change by Design: How Design Thinking Transforms Organizations and Inspires Innovation*. HarperBusiness, 2009. ISBN 61766089

Brunetti, I. *Cartooning: Philosophy and Practice (reprint)*. Yale University Press, 2011. ISBN 300170998

Buxton, B. *Sketching User Experiences: Getting the Design Right and the Right Design*. Interactive Technologies, Morgan Kaufmann, 2007. ISBN

123740371
Cameron, J. *The Artist's Way Workbook*. Tarcher, 2006. ISBN 1585425338

Card,S. K., Mackinlay J., Shneiderman B. *Readings in Information Visualization: Using Vision to Think*. Interactive Technologies, Morgan Kaufmann, 1999. ISBN 1558605339

Christianson, S. *100 Diagrams That Changed the World: From the Earliest Cave Paintings to the Innovation of the iPod*. Plume, 2012. ISBN 452298776

Coyne, R. *Designing Information Technology in the Postmodern Age: From Method to Metaphor*. Leonardo Books, The MIT Press, 1995. ISBN 262032287

Critchlow, K. *The Hidden Geometry of Flowers: Living Rhythms, Form and Number*. Floris Books, 2011. ISBN 863158064

Cross, N. *Design Thinking: Understanding How Designers Think and Work*. Bloomsbury Academic, 2011. ISBN 1847886361

Cuffaro, D. and Zaksenberg, I. *The Industrial Design Reference & Specification Book: Everything Industrial Designers Need to Know Every Day*. Rockport Publishers, 2013. ISBN 1592538479

Curedale, R. A. *Design Methods 2: 200 more ways to apply Design Thinking (Volume 2)*. Design Community College Inc., 2013. ISBN 988236214

Curedale, R. A. *Design Thinking Pocket Guide*. Design Community College Inc., 2013. ISBN 098924685X

Curedale, R. A. *Design Thinking: process and methods manual*. Design Community College Inc., 2013. ISBN 988236249

Demaine, E. D. and O'Rourke J. *Geometric Folding Algorithms: Linkages, Origami, Polyhedra*. Cambridge University Press, 2007. ISBN 521857570

Doorley, S., Witthoft S. and The Hasso Plattner Institute of Design at Stanford University *Make Space: How to Set the Stage for Creative Collaboration*. Wiley, 2012. ISBN

1118143728
Drucker, J. *Graphesis: Visual Forms of Knowledge Production*. MetaLAB projects, Harvard University Press, 2014. ISBN 674724933

Edson, J. *Design Like Apple: Seven Principles For Creating Insanely Great Products, Services, and Experiences*. Wiley, 2012. ISBN 1118290313

Edwards, B. *Drawing on the Right Side of the Brain: The Definitive (4th Edition)*. Tarcher, 2012. ISBN 1585429201

Edwards, D. *Artscience: Creativity in the Post-Google Generation*. Harvard University Press, 2012. ISBN 674034643

Ehn, P. *Work-Oriented Design of Computer Artifacts*. Lawrence Erlbaum Assoc., 1988. ISBN 9186158457

Elam, K. *Geometry of Design: Studies in Proportion and Composition*. Princeton Architectural Press, 2001. ISBN 1568982496

Emoto, M. *The Hidden Messages in Water*. Beyond Words Pub Co, 2004. ISBN 1582701148

Erwin, K. *Communicating The New: Methods to Shape and Accelerate Innovation*. Wiley, 2013. ISBN 1118394178

Esslinger, H. *A Fine Line: How Design Strategies Are Shaping the Future of Business*. Jossey-Bass, 2009.

Few, S. *Information Dashboard Design: The Effective Visual Communication of Data*. O'Reilly Media, 2006. ISBN 596100167

Florida, R. *Cities and the Creative Class*. Routledge, 2004. ISBN 415948878

Folkmann, M. N. *The Aesthetics of Imagination in Design*. Design Thinking & Design Theory, The MIT Press,2013. ISBN 026201906X

Fox, G. *The Essential Guide to Making Handmade Books*. North Light Books, 2000. ISBN 1581800193

Frederick, M. *101 Things I Learned in Architecture School (3rd Edition)*. The MIT Press, 2007. ISBN 262062666

French, K. L. *The Hidden Geometry*

of Life: The Science and Spirituality of Nature. Gateway Series, Watkins, 2012. ISBN 1780281080

Friedhoff, R. M. *Visualization: The Second Computer Revolution.* W H Freeman & Co (Sd), 1991. ISBN 716722313

Garfield, S. *Just My Type: A Book About Fonts.* Gotham, 2011. ISBN 1592406521

Gelb, M. J. *How to Think Like Leonardo da Vinci: Seven Steps to Genius Every Day (Reissue).* Dell, 2000. ISBN 440508274

Ghyka, M. *The Geometry of Art and Life.* Dover Publications, 1977. ISBN 486235424

Ginsberg, A. D., Calvert J., Schyfter P., Elfick A. and Endy D. *Synthetic Aesthetics: Investigating Synthetic Biology's Designs on Nature.* The MIT Press, 2014. ISBN 026201999X

Giudice, M. and Ireland, C. *Rise of the DEO: Leadership by Design.* Voices That Matter, New Riders, 2013. ISBN 321934393

Greenbaum, J. and Kyng, M. *Design at Work: Cooperative Design of Computer Systems.* CRC Press, 1991. ISBN 805806121

Greenberg, S. and Carpendale, S., Marquardt, N.,

Buxton, B. *Sketching User Experiences: The Workbook.* Morgan Kaufmann, 2011. ISBN 123819598

Greene, J. *Design Is How It Works: How the Smartest Companies Turn Products into Icons.* Portfolio Hardcover, 2010. ISBN 1591843227

Griffin, W. G. and Morrison D. *The Creative Process Illustrated: How Advertising's Big Ideas Are Born.* HOW Books, 2010. ISBN 1600619606

Guenther, M. *Intersection: How Enterprise Design Bridges the Gap between Business, Technology, and People.* Morgan Kaufmann, 2012. ISBN 123884357

Hanington, B. and Martin B. *Universal Methods of Design: 100 Ways to Research Complex Problems, Develop Innovative Ideas, and Design Effective*

Solutions. Rockport Publishers, 2012. ISBN 1592537561

Hanks, K. and Belliston L. *Rapid Viz: Techniques for the Rapid Visualization of Ideas.* Crisp Publications Inc., 1980. ISBN 913232769

Harris, R. L. *Information Graphics: A Comprehensive Illustrated Reference.* Oxford University Press, USA, 2000. ISBN 195135326

Hartwell, M. and Chen J. C. *Archetypes in Branding: A Toolkit for Creatives and Strategists.* HOW Books, 2012. ISBN 1440308187

Heller, S. *Halloween: Vintage Holiday Graphics.* Icons, Taschen, 2005. ISBN 382284585X

Heller, S. and Landers R. *Infographics Designers' Sketchbooks.* Princeton Architectural Press, 2014. ISBN 1616892862

Heskett, J. *Design: A Very Short Introduction.* OUP Oxford, 2005.

Holston, D. *The Strategic Designer: Tools & Techniques for Managing the Design Process.* HOW Books, 2011. ISBN 1600617999

IDEO, *Human-Centered Design Toolkit: An Open-Source Toolkit To Inspire New Solutions in the Developing World (2nd Edition).* IDEO, 2011. ISBN 984645705

Jackson, P. *Folding Techniques for Designers: From Sheet to Form.* Laurence King Publishers, 2011. ISBN 1856697215

Janosh, *Sacred Geometry.* Sounds True Inc., 2007.

Johnson, S. A. *Interface Culture.* Basic Books, 1999. ISBN 465036805

Justice, L. *China's Design Revolution.* Design Thinking & **Design Theory,** The MIT Press, 2012. ISBN 262017423

Katz, J. *Designing Information: Human Factors and Common Sense in Information Design.* Wiley, 2012. ISBN 111834197X

Kaye, D. *Red Thread Thinking: Weaving Together Connections for Brilliant Ideas and Profitable Innovation.* McGraw-Hill, 2013. ISBN 71808213

Kemp, M. *Seen / Unseen: Art, Sci-*

ence, and Intuition from Leonardo to the Hubble Telescope. Oxford University Press, USA, 2006. ISBN 199295727

Kentridge, W. *Six Drawing Lessons*. The Charles Eliot Norton Lectures, Harvard University Press, 2014. ISBN 674365801

Kneller, G. F. *The Art and Science of Creativity*. Holt, Rinehart & Winston, 1965.

Kolko, J. *Exposing the Magic of Design: A Practitioner's Guide to the Methods and Theory of Synthesis*. Oxford Series in Human-Technology Interaction, Oxford University Press, USA, 2011. ISBN 199744335

Koren, L. *Wabi-Sabi: for Artists, Designers, Poets & Philosophers*. Imperfect Publishing, 2008. ISBN 981484603

Krahula, B. *One Zentangle A Day: A 6-Week Course in Creative Drawing for Relaxation, Inspiration, and Fun*. One A Day, Quarry Books, 2012. ISBN 1592538118

Kumar, V. *101 Design Methods: A Structured Approach for Driving Innovation in Your Organization*. Wiley, 2012. ISBN 1118083466

Kyng, M. and Mathiassen L. *Computers and Design in Context*. The MIT Press, 1997. ISBN 026211223X

Lang, R. J. *Origami Design Secrets: Mathematical Methods for an Ancient Art (2nd Edition)*. A K Peters/CRC Press, 2011. ISBN 1568814364

Lawlor, R. *Sacred Geometry: Philosophy & Practice*. Art and Imagination, Thames & Hudson, 1982. ISBN 500810303

Lidwell, W., Holden, K., and Butler, J. *Universal Principles of Design, Revised and Updated: 125 Ways to Enhance Usability, Influence Perception, Increase Appeal, Make Better Design Decisions, and Teach through Design (2nd Edition)*. Rockport Publishers, 2010. ISBN 1592535879

Liedtka, J. and Ogilvie, T. *Designing for Growth: A Design Thinking Toolkit for Managers*. Columbia Business School Publishing, Columbia University Press, 2011. ISBN 231158386

Liedtka, J., King, A. and Bennett, K. *Solving Problems with Design Thinking: Ten Stories of What Works*. Columbia Business School Publishing, Columbia University Press, 2013. ISBN 231163568

Lim, S. C. *Realizing Empathy: An Inquiry Into the Meaning of Making*. 2013 ISBN 985884606

Lipson, H. and Kurman M. *Fabricated: The New World of 3D Printing*. Wiley, 2013. ISBN 1118350634

Little, S. *Isms: Understanding Art*. Universe, 2004. ISBN 789312093

Loori, J. D. *The Zen of Creativity: Cultivating Your Artistic Life*. Ballantine Books, 2005. ISBN 345466330

Lundy, M. *Sacred Number: The Secret Quality of Quantities*. Wooden Books, Walker & Company, 2005. ISBN 802714560

Lupton, E. *D.I.Y.: Design It Yourself*. Design Handbooks, Princeton Architectural Press, 2006. ISBN 1568985525

Lupton, E. and Lupton, J. *Design Your Life: The Pleasures and Perils of Everyday Things*. St. Martin's Griffin, 2009.

Lupton, E. and Phillips, J. C. *Graphic Design Thinking*. Design Briefs, Princeton Architectural Press, 2011. ISBN 1568989792

Lupton, E. *Indie Publishing: How to Design and Publish Your Own Book*. Princeton Architectural Press, 2008. ISBN 1568987609

Lupton, E. *Thinking with Type, 2nd revised and expanded edition: A Critical Guide for Designers, Writers, Editors, & Students (2nd Review)*. Princeton Architectural Press, 2010. ISBN 1568989695

Macnab, M. *Decoding Design: Understanding and Using Symbols in Visual Communication*. HOW Books, 2008. ISBN 1581809697

Maeda, J. *Creative Code: Aesthetics + Computation*. Thames & Hudson, 2004. ISBN 500285179

Maeda, J. *Design by Numbers (Reprint)*. The MIT Press, 2001. ISBN 262632446

Maeda, J. *The Laws of Simplicity*. The MIT Press, 2006.

Martin, R. and Christensen, K. *Rotman on Design: The Best on Design Thinking from Rotman Magazine*. University of Toronto Press, Scholarly Publishing, 2013. ISBN 1442616202

McAlhone, B. *A Smile in the Mind*. Phaidon Press, 1998. ISBN 714838128

Mikami, T. *T. Mikami's Sumi-e Digest*. Hozansha Pub., 1965.

Moggridge, B. *Designing Interactions*. The MIT Press, 2007. ISBN 262134748

Mootee, I. *Design Thinking for Strategic Innovation: What They Can't Teach You at Business or Design School*. Wiley, 2013. ISBN 1118620127

Nelson, H. G. and Stolterman, E. *The Design Way: Intentional Change in an Unpredictable World (2nd Edition)*. The MIT Press, 2012. ISBN 262018179

Neumeier, M. *The Designful Company: How to build a culture of nonstop innovation*. New Riders, 2008. ISBN 321580060

Neutra, R. J. *Survival Through Design*. Oxford University Press, USA, 1969. ISBN 195007905

Norman, D. A. *The Design of Everyday Things*. Basic Books, 2002. ISBN 978046506710

Norman, D. A. *Emotional Design: Why We Love (Or Hate) Everyday Things*. Basic Books, 2004. ISBN 965810305

Patt, D. *How to Architect*. The MIT Press, 2012. ISBN 262516993

Payne, M. *How to Kill a Unicorn: How the World's Hottest Innovation Factory Builds Bold Ideas That Make It to Market*. Crown Business, 2014. ISBN 804138737

Pearson, M. *Generative Art*. Manning Publications, 2011. ISBN 1935182625

Peterson, B. *Understanding Exposure, 3rd Edition: How to Shoot Great Photographs with Any Camera (3rd Edition)*. Amphoto Books, 2010. ISBN 817439390

Protzen, J.-P. and Harris, D. J. *The Universe of Design: Horst Rittel's Theories of Design and Planning*. Routledge, 2010. ISBN 415779898

Quillien, J. *Clever Digs: How Workspaces Can Enable Thought*. lulu.com, 2011. ISBN 110539185X

Roam, D. *The Back of the Napkin: Solving Problems and Selling Ideas with Pictures*. Portfolio Hardcover, 2008. ISBN 1591841992

Roam, D. *Blah Blah Blah: What To Do When Words Don't Work*. Portfolio Hardcover, 2011. ISBN 1591844592

Rushkoff, D. *Get Back in the Box: Innovation from the Inside Out*. HarperBusiness, 2005. ISBN 60758694

Segall, K. *Insanely Simple: The Obsession That Drives Apple's Success*. Portfolio Hardcover, 2012. ISBN 1591844835

Segaran, T. and Hammerbacher, J. *Beautiful Data: The Stories Behind Elegant Data Solutions*. O'Reilly Media, 2009. ISBN 596157118

Sibbet, D. *Visual Meetings: How Graphics, Sticky Notes and Idea Mapping Can Transform Group Productivity*. Wiley, 2010. ISBN 470601787

Sibbet, D. *Visual Teams: Graphic Tools for Commitment, Innovation, and High Performance*. Wiley, 2011. ISBN 1118077431

Siegel, A. and Etzkorn, I. *Simple: Conquering the Crisis of Complexity*. Twelve, 2013. ISBN 1455509663

Silver, M. *Programming Cultures: Architecture, Art and Science in the Age of Software Development*. Architectural Design, Academy Press, 2006. ISBN 470025859

Stafford, B. M. *Echo Objects: The Cognitive Work of Images*. University Of Chicago Press, 2007. ISBN 226770516

Stafford, B. M. *Visual Analogy: Consciousness as the Art of Connecting*. The MIT Press, 2001. ISBN 262692678

Steffens, J. *Unpacking My Library: Architects and Their Books*. Unpacking My Library Series, Yale University

Press, 2009. ISBN

Stefik, M. *Internet Dreams: Archetypes, Myths, and Metaphors*. The MIT Press, 1996. ISBN 262193736

Sterling, B. *Shaping Things*. Mediaworks Pamphlets, The MIT Press, 2005 ISBN 262693267

Suri, J. F. and IDEO *Thoughtless Acts? Observations on Intuitive Design*. Chronicle Books, 2005. ISBN 811847756

Sutton, D. *Islamic Design: A Genius for Geometry*. Wooden Books, Walker & Company, 2007. ISBN 802716350

Todd, S. and Latham, W. *Evolutionary Art and Computers*. Academic Press, 1992. ISBN 012437185X

Tufte, E. R. *Beautiful Evidence*. Graphics Press, 2006. ISBN 961392177

Tufte, E. R. *Envisioning Information*. Graphics Press, 1990. ISBN 961392118

Tufte, E. R. *The Visual Display of Quantitative Information (2nd Edition)*. Graphics Press, 2001. ISBN 961392142

Tufte, E. R. *Visual Explanations: Images and Quantities, Evidence and Narrative*. Graphics Press, 1997. ISBN 961392126

Weinschenk, S. *100 Things Every Designer Needs to Know About People*. Voices That Matter, New Riders, 2011. ISBN 321767535

Wexler, B. E. *Brain and Culture: Neurobiology, Ideology, and Social Change (Reprint)*. A Bradford Book, 2008. ISBN 262731932

White, K. *101 Things to Learn in Art School*. The MIT Press, 2011. ISBN 262016214

Whitney, H. *Data Insights: New Ways to Visualize and Make Sense of Data*. Morgan Kaufmann, 2012. ISBN 123877938

Williams, C. *Origins of Form: The Shape of Natural and Man-made Things — Why They Came to Be the Way They Are and How They Change (Reprint)*. Taylor Trade Publishing, 2013. ISBN 1589798082

Williams, R. *The Non-Designer's Design and Type Books, Deluxe Edition*.

Peachpit Press, 2007. ISBN 321534050

Williams, R. *The Non-Designer's Design Book (2nd Edition)*. Peachpit Press, 2003. ISBN 321193857

Williams, R. and Tollett, J. *The Non-Designer's Illustrator Book*. Peachpit Press, 2011. ISBN 321772873

Williams, R. *The Non-Designer's InDesign Book*. Peachpit Press, 2011. ISBN 321772849

Williams, R. and Tollett, J. *The Non-Designer's Photoshop Book*. Peachpit Press, 2011. ISBN 321441761

Williams, R. and Tollett, J. *Robin Williams Design Workshop (2nd Edition)*. Peachpit Press, 2006. ISBN 321441761

Winograd, T. *Bringing Design to Software*. ACM Press, 1996. ISBN 201854910

Wong, W. *Principles of Form and Design*. Wiley, 1993. ISBN 471285528

Wood, A. *The Graphic Designer's Digital Toolkit: A Project-Based Introduction to Adobe Photoshop CS5, Illustrator CS5 & InDesign CS5 (5th Edition)*. Cengage Learning, 2010. ISBN 111113801X

van Wulfen, G. *The Innovation Expedition: A Visual Toolkit to Start Innovation*. BIS Publishers, 2013. ISBN 9063693133

Yau, N. *Visualize This: The FlowingData Guide to Design, Visualization, and Statistics*. Wiley, 2011. ISBN 470944889

Iconography

Page 51   *Author unknown.*
Page 52-53 *Big eye Trevally Jack, (Caranx sexfasciatus)*
                Forming a polarized school, bait ball or tornado.
                Cabo Pulmo National Park,
                Cousteau once named it The world's aquarium.
                Baja California Sur, Mexico
                By Leonardo Gonzalez
                Shutterstock - 169126637
Page 58   *Fred Brooks*
                Photo by Jerry Markatos
Page 61   *Madagascar day gecko on white background*
                By Robert Eastman
                Shutterstock - 115705162
Page 63   *Charlie Chaplin in Modern Times*
Page 64   *Risk confusion business concept as a businessman on*
                a high wire tight rope walking towards a tangled mess
                as a metaphor or symbol of overcoming adversity
                in strategy and finding leadership solutions.
                By Lightspring
                Shutterstock - 150831014
Page 66   *From Wikimedia Commons. European Space*
                Agency astronaut Frank De Winne, Expedition
                21 commander, exercises on the Combined Opera-
                tional Load Bearing External Resistance Treadmill
                (COLBERT) in the Harmony node of the International
                Space Station. 17 November 2009. NASA
Page 68-69 *Expressway in downtown at twilight, Bangkok, Thailand*
                Photo by Chalalai Atcha
                Shutterstock - 335727269
Page 71   *Illustration by Foster & Partners 1998*
Page 72   *youngarchitectureservices.com*
Page 73   *Drawing by product designer Tony Ton*
Page 74   *circos.ca/guide/visual/*
Page 77   *Main air routes in North America*
                By Antartis
                Depositphotos - 8933681
Page 80-81 *NASA Earth Observatory*
Page 84   *Goldfish jumping out of the water*
                By Mikael Damkier
                123rf.com - 3764064
Page 86   *Comic strip Dilbert by Scott Adams*
Page 87   *Cargo Cult. Author unknown*
Page 88   *beinghappiness.com/*
Page 88   *Author unknown.*
Page 90   *Vector dandelions on white*
                By Chrupka
                Shutterstock - 144600896
Page 91   *Blow Dandelion on white background*
                By Kolesov Sergei
                Shutterstock - 54094414
Page 94   *Illustration by Jeannel King*
Page 95   *Illustration by Rebecca Rikner*

About the authors

Rebecca is an award-winning designer, a bridge builder, an entrepreneur & business developer and has over 25 years of professional experience in qualified business-oriented communication and project management work from both small and large organizations, both from practical and strategic level, in industries like consumer goods, media, music, communication and IT.

She has assumed and successfully met the challenges and responsibilities associated with a variety of projects, including: driving the marketing activities for a health care products company present in eleven countries; leading a change project at Matsushita (Panasonic) in Osaka Japan; initiating and organizing international conferences in several cities in India; establishing communication channels, web presence, newsletter, and press releases for Sweden's most successful business incubator.

Rebecca holds bachelor degrees in communication design, web design and user interface design as well as in usability design. She holds also an Executive MBA from the Stockholm School of Economics with specialization 'Leading Innovation'.

David began his software career in 1968 as a computer programmer. His professional career included experience as a systems analyst, architect, designer, coach, and CIO. Simultaneously, he pursued an academic career as Professor of Computer Science and Software Engineering.

Combining is corporate training and academic careers, he has taught and mentored thousands of individuals, in more than 100 companies, and in 11 countries in every major aspect of software development, including: Structured development, Object development, Agile development, TQM, TDD, and, most recently, Micro-service architecture.

Steve Jobs attributed his success to "living at the intersection of art and science." Similarly David's unique approach to software development succeeds because it combines computer science, cultural anthropology, and Asian Philosophy, with extensive experience as a professional developer.

* 9 7 8 0 9 9 8 4 7 7 0 0 8 *